EVOLVE
Marketing (^as we know it)
is Doomed!

HESSIE JONES
DANIEL NEWMAN

EVOLVE
Marketing (^as we know it) is Doomed!

© 2015

By **Hessie Jones** and **Daniel Newman**

Cover art design by **Paul Ting**

ISBN: 978-0-578-15566-1

First Printing: 2015

Broadsuite
T: 817-480-3038
www.broadsuite.com

www.evolvebook.net

Advance Praise for Evolve

The entire business world is in the midst of a huge transition, and as marketers you can either be leaders of this revolution, or you can become irrelevant–it's your choice. Jones and Newman provide an outstanding guide for those who choose to lead this change, including insight from the top thinkers and practitioners in the field.

Jamie Notter, Partner, Culture That Works LLC and co-author of Humanize and When Millennials Take Over

It's hard to believe how fast the marketing landscape is changing. From content marketing to marketing automation, brands are almost at a sprint to keep up with the evolution while trying to also to provide more touch points between consumers and brands - more personal touch points that is. In this engaging book Daniel and Hessie have given clarity to the entire marketing landscape in a way that marketers can take meaningful action to get and stay ahead of the curve. If you are a marketer, I strongly recommend this book.

Steve Olenski, Forbes contributor & Sr. Content Strategist/Sr. Writer, Oracle Marketing Cloud

In a world where marketing is becoming more about being human and less about automating, there is an endless need for evolution. In this book Daniel and Hessie do a wonderful job of tying together tools and technology with the most important aspect of marketing...being human.

Bryan Kramer Author of Best Seller, Human to Human #H2H, TED speaker

As the Internet and technology have revolutionized how we live and interact with one another, so the ways in which companies market to and communicate with their customers have dramatically evolved. In this book Daniel Newman and Hessie Jones provide a wake-up-call to marketing professionals by demonstrating how a rapidly changing world demands new, sophisticated and clever methods of presenting products and services to the buying public. You'll do well to heed the research and conclusions that come from this book!

Joel Comm, New York Times Best-Selling Author and New Media Marketing Strategist

With the rapid evolution of digital marketing and social media, brands are being put in a position to keep up with the changes or get left behind. However, keeping up isn't as simple as it once was. The science of marketing is more prevalent than ever with new channels popping up daily, the proliferation of data and the shifting buyer's journey. This book does a wonderful job of helping marketers understand how we arrived here and more importantly where we are going. I highly recommend this book for brand marketers and agencies seeking to stay on top of their game.

Kevin Green, Executive Director, Digital Marketing - Dell, Inc.

In the Social Age, customers not only have all the power, they have learned to tune out when being talked 'at' instead of 'to'. In EVOLVE, Jones and Newman have outlined exactly what it takes to unlearn traditional marketing and learn how to invest in community, social listening and brand ambassadorship. For any marketer, entrepreneur or socially-minded executive… EVOLVE is a must-read book.

Mark Babbitt, CEO and Founder of YouTern and co-author of A World Gone Social: How Companies Must Adapt to Survive

At Harvard Business School I was taught that sales fell under marketing. I protested. Marketing is, was, and always will be something that falls under selling, as the creation of a customer is the real desired outcome. As Newman and Jones illustrate with example after example, this digital age now requires marketers to put the customer at the very center of everything they do. They quickly and irrevocably dismantle the vanity metrics of likes, retweets, and pluses, and show you that trust, the customer experience, and sales are what really matter. Follow their blueprint and evolve!

Anthony Iannarino, Speaker, Writer, Entrepreneur

If there was ever a time to think differently it's now. The travel industry has been one of the most vulnerable to the voice of the consumer. As a veteran Executive within the Airline and Travel industry, I know, all too well, relationships with customers have been a volatile love / hate ride. As customers become more knowledgeable and sophisticated, their expectations will continue to rise. Business must look to foster these customer relationships, to lead (and maybe even just to survive) in the future.

Hessie Jones and Daniel Newman understand the new landscape. Their book serves as a wake-up call for companies to be sensitized to the voice of the consumer, and to be relentless in not only understanding their needs, but establishing and encouraging an open line of communication. We can no longer expect the old ways of marketing to drive business today. EVOLVE delivers this message loud and clear.

Jim Young, CEO NewLeaf Corp, Former Senior Executive at Frontier Airlines and InterContinental Hotels Group

This book is the ultimate guide to helping a company define what they need to do to excel in this new era of marketing that so many companies struggle with. For a small investment you will get a massive return.

Ian Cleary, Founder Razorsocial.com

Watch out Marketers! The Future of Marketing is in the Midst of Revolution. Are You Ready?

It's clear that marketing has drastically changed in the last decade. The rise of digital accompanied by its ever-evolving technologies in mobile and advertising, will build a perpetual environment of test and learn. Continuous emergence of audience platforms will create a nomadic culture that follows the fickle consumer paths. Ultimately, this will dictate the sustainability of platforms.

No longer do we have only a few mediums for content consumption. In as little as two decades we've moved beyond TV, radio, print, billboards. We've also raced beyond the standard network channels, and the key national newspapers. We are now exposed to endless content, from our peer networks, our smart phones, and our inboxes. Consumers are overwhelmed and this fragmentation of channel and information continues.

As consumers, our attention has moved to sites that speak to our own areas of interest. They may not necessarily be popular or well known. Our peers greatly influence what we do and where we go. Our ever-trusted smart phones give us access to information about the things we want, when we want them and where we want them. At the other end of the spectrum, we, as consumers are more informed, and more wary of the digital footprint we're leaving behind. Perhaps, this has made us more fiercely protective of our privacy. Marketers must figure out how to maneuver the rugged terrain that lies ahead.

This always-on economy will never slow down. The growing consumer expectations will mandate companies to have greater visibility into where their customers are, what they're saying, their preferences, their preferred channels and modes of communication.

As Marketers, our roles have evolved. It hasn't been easy. Coupled with this consumer evolution we're witnessing, economic conditions have changed the way we operate. Marketing is no longer a cost center. We are now more accountable than ever. The old performance measures we were accustomed to have changed. We need to evolve beyond the mindset of traditional mediums, and embrace the inherent benefits of digital and where it's headed.

As two Marketers who have evolved within this volatile landscape, we have both succeeded and failed. Yet we've learned, and we've adapted…out of necessity.

This book provides you, the Marketer, with a view into how we've evolved. You'll be exposed to case examples that continue to shape the way we think the role of marketing needs to change. As digital becomes an increasingly important component of the marketing mix, data and analytics will be even more essential to help Marketers be accountable, and more importantly, more curious.

The future of marketing is riddled with new capabilities, which, in turn, creates new challenges. The answers however, are out there. This book doesn't only speculate on the change, it predicts, defines and clarifies what Marketers will need to do to excel at their trade and build brands that customers love.

We hope you enjoy it!

Table of Contents

Where We've Been and Why We've Been Fooling Ourselves

THE NEW RULES by Gini Dietrich

Nearly 20 years ago the Public Relations Society of America endorsed a new way of "measuring" marketing and communications efforts, particularly as they related to TV, print, and radio. Those metrics were advertising equivalencies (AVEs) and media Impressions. To determine your AVE, you would measure (with an actual ruler) the width and length of the article that had run about your organization. Then, using the media outlet's media kit, you'd figure out how much it would have cost you to run an ad of the very same size or length. If the story were the size of a quarter page ad or a 30 second TV spot, you'd have your advertising equivalency.

Media Impressions are just as silly. Suppose an article about your organization runs in the New York Times, which has a circulation of 2.2 million. According to the formula, there is a pass-along rate of two. This means we can feasibly assume someone will leave the paper on the train or in the doctor's office and at least two other people will pick it up and read it. That means we have an Impression value of nearly four and a half million people. Of course, there is no way of knowing the percentage of those four million people who actually read the article on page B10 about your organization, but Marketers convinced executives these metrics are reliable. Couple that with the introduction of social media, and we're suddenly obsessed with big numbers: How many Facebook Likes do you have? How many Twitter Followers do you have? How many LinkedIn connections do you have? How many LinkedIn groups do you belong to? One thing is missing, however: metrics that show a real dollar-for-dollar return-on-investment.

We call AVEs, media impressions and social media increases the vanity metrics. It sure does feel good to see those kinds of numbers, but they don't mean anything for your organization.

Enter The New Rules. It's time to educate executives on the metrics that really matter. They may still ask for the metrics of yesteryear because it's what they're accustomed to receiving; it feels good to go into board meetings and show big numbers, but the job of tomorrow's Marketer to change the conversation.

Tomorrow's Marketer is focused on the customer experience. Tomorrow's Marketer understands that it's less expensive to retain customers than acquire new ones. Tomorrow's Marketer is not complacent. Tomorrow's Marketer has a quest for knowledge. Tomorrow's Marketer knows which metrics really affect the growth of an organization and dismisses the 'feel good' metrics for what they are – meaningless nonsense.

> *Gini Dietrich is the founder and CEO of Arment Dietrich, a Chicago-based integrated marketing communications firm. She is the lead blogger here at Spin Sucks and is the founder of Spin Sucks Pro. She is the co-author of Marketing in the Round and co-host of Inside PR. Her second book, Spin Sucks, is available now.*

Gini Dietrich nailed it. This chapter is as much about questioning EVERYTHING we've ever known as it is an intervention for those who need a swift kick in the behind. My colleague, Amy Tobin, says she hates Marketers. Being a Marketer (something I reluctantly admit these days), my job was fairly easy until digital became dominant. And then it became hard. Really hard.

For those of you who need a dose of reality...

The Entitled Marketer:
The Fallacy and the Brutal Reality

I have heard this often from many of my peers:

> *Are you kidding? Do you know what I've accomplished in the last 5 years for this company? This organization is lucky to have me! I ran successful initiatives that helped grow the business 80% over that time period. With my experience, I will not accept less than a 20% increase from my current compensation*

This is from Marketers who have been in the industry for years but have remained stagnant. This is from Marketers who, at one point in time, were at the elite and could get any job they wanted. These same Marketers now find themselves looking for work and realizing that demand for what they do have "suddenly" changed... and not in their favor.

Sadly, they don't realize that the world has moved on without them. And even if they figure that out, they are challenged to understand, let alone keep up with, the "new" demands of the communication industry.

Here is a typical dossier of the Entitled Marketer:

Jan Doe has 15 years of solid experience in both Agency and Client side – particularly in QSR and Consumer Packaged Goods. Jan has a stellar resume, and has primarily worked in Fortune 500 companies, providing her with the luxury of large budgets to scale awareness through prominent mediums like television and billboard. Jan has a good understanding of consumer strategy and insight, and primarily relied on Neilson Reports and Ipsos Reid to make sense of audience receptiveness to the brand message. Usage and Attitude Surveys were executed annually, like clockwork, to validate audience needs and behaviors. Despite the high cost, Jan insisted on continuing Nielson and Ipsos studies as her go-to-references for consumer insights.

As digital media revealed another reference point to tap into consumer behavior, Jan also migrated spend across digital media and brought in experienced people who understood these channels. Then along came Social Media–yet another extension to continue to promote the company's message. It seemed easy enough: Jan would divert money from display advertising to purchase Facebook Likes and Promoted Tweets. After all, management was more than happy to see the growth of followers at a fraction of the price of traditional advertising. This new medium was clearly working for her.

Jan never abandoned the tried and true channels; television, as the main broadcast channel, continued to provide the strongest recall rate and continued to be an important metric in brand measurement. Digital and social media were great support channels for this main medium.

Jan was happy with her year-end performance goals. She was well compensated for the year over year jump in awareness levels. The strong digital performance on PPC and display ads, as well as the community volume growth on both Facebook and Twitter, was evidence that she was succeeding. Jan was sitting pretty... that is, until the day she was downsized, along with 20% of the staff.

THE FALLACY

I get my cues from the Millennial Think Tank sessions we conduct on a weekly basis at ArCompany. It has shifted our view on the notion of the "American Dream"- (the same myth we all grew up believing):

Get a good education and you'll be rewarded with a great job. Do well at your job and you'll climb the corporate ladder. With experience comes reward.

Maybe this was true when times were good – when there was a stable economy, and conditions were relatively unchanged decade to decade. We rested on our laurels and began to accept that there was a set formula for success. However, when a wrench was thrown into our Pollyannaish world, we were caught in a tailspin and had two choices: 1) recede into the comfort zone of what we knew, hoping that our old practice fixed this anomaly OR 2) figure out what this wrench really meant to the business. Most Marketers will fall into the first camp, hoping the tools that they were given can be the panacea to remedy this new sickness. After all, it worked in the past, right?

Here is my story: I was a traditional Marketer. I marched to the drum of those traditional KPIs — yes the ones we all bought into: Impressions, Click through rates, Open Rates. I had enormous budgets with which I could create cool campaigns to build awareness and audience. Hey, if it didn't meet my campaign goals, I'd develop a post-mortem deck to analyze what I could improve upon next time. The budget was never reduced. If overall company performance was good then hopefully my already enormous budget would increase next quarter. No harm. No foul. As a Marketer I was never really penalized for failure. After all, marketing has always been a cost center.

THE BRUTAL REALITY

One day, things changed radically, forced by an epic shift: the Financial Crisis of 2008. Anyone working at that time experienced these transformations within the company. At the time of the crash I was working for an ad agency, which allowed me to witness significant changes on client business:

- Budgets were squeezed while target objectives remained unchanged.
- Marketing now became a revenue center. New goals were established.
- Quarterly marketing performance dictated budget allocation for the succeeding quarter. Performance was paramount as strategy scrambled to define best way to optimize spend. ROI was the standard with which we were held. Traditional media budgets felt the strongest pinch as spend increasingly diverted to digital.

This soon led to an increasing demand for digital professionals in search, social, strategy, and development.

The recession fundamentally changed the way marketing operated within the organization. As traditional marketing increasingly took a back seat to digital media, traditional practitioners suddenly found themselves vulnerable in a way they had never imagined.

If your story reflects that of Jan Doe, the brutal reality is that you have continued to do the same things. You haven't evolved; you are now on the verge of obsolescence. It was important to me to change with the times. The skills that brought me success as a Marketer are now outdated…and irrelevant. To survive I needed to learn and embrace the new world order.

If you are a Marketer, here are the facts you must face:

> *"You are as good as your last project. Today's marketing discipline requires new skill sets. Your value has diminished if it doesn't match today's demands; don't expect to continue to see your paycheck increase. Your value is connected to your understanding of new and emerging media. Expect to keep learning. Expect to keep changing. Expect to keep moving to remain relevant."*

Yesteryear: Remember when Marketers Ruled?

It is clear that the Marketing discipline has evolved. For me, the choice to evolve was made partially out of necessity, but primarily out of excitement at all that this new media could do. When I talk about Traditional Marketing, I don't mean only TV, radio or mass channels — I am referring to the one-way push communication that businesses have used for the last century. It also includes the one way messaging, including an apparent arrogance about who would consume the product or service.

Remember the 4P's of Marketing: Product, Price, Placement and Promotion? Where was the customer in all this?

I, along with many of my colleagues, came from an era when the Marketer and business controlled everything:

- We built better mousetraps.
- We "assumed" we knew who bought our product.
- We catered the messaging to those we assumed would buy.
- We came to rely on pervasive channels to get our message heard.
- We relied on research that assumed "statistical significance and validity" and was, often, subject to "groupthink".

… all this to prove that we knew how to build markets for products…and not the other way around.

MODELS OF TARGETING WERE FLAWED

Think back. Marketers dictated acquisition-targeting parameters. Marketers conducted the consumer research – mainly expensive focus group testing with questions that largely served to benefit the "business." These focus groups were structured and moderated by the "business," and highly subject to groupthink. To top it off, this "focus" group would provide the basis of "representation" of the target customer, so the results of the research were leveraged to inform the targeting strategy.

My point is this: the research conducted was subject to false assumptions, questionable methodology and a strong reliance on the outcomes. Then these outcomes were used to provide the demographic profile of the target customer, which was fed to the media buy. User profiles dictated where, when and what type of offer or content was served. At that time there were mediocre optimization opportunities.

IMPRESSIONS? REALLY?

To add insult to injury, Marketers dreamed up this notion of reach, i.e. how many people were actually being impacted based on media? Impressions have been around a long time; it was the PR metric used to convince executives their message was seen by the masses. It was an imperfect KPI, but people bought into it because there was some correlation between household and audience reach.

Impressions emerged decades ago and arose out of a need to standardize broadcast media buys. It was impossible to know for certain who was watching a TV show or listening to the radio. Complex audience delivery formulas like Nielsen Ratings were based on data supporting actual audience size.

The number of Impressions equates to the "potential" reach for that particular medium. Yet "Impressions" is a misnomer: In order for Impressions to be "real" ALL subscribers or target households need to be able to consume that content when that content is available. This is highly unlikely.

So, here's the thing: Marketers and PR folks could NOT tell you how many people were reached as a result of the media reach. After all, Impressions don't buy → people do.

But somehow, regardless of the many flaws, Marketers convinced the C-suite that Impressions were important.

Fast forward to the late 90's: the more things change, the more they stay the same… then along came search:

Search and Quest to Rank Higher

In the late 90's the introduction of Google provided companies a way for people to find their websites. Early adopters cornered the market on search terms and capitalized on consumer traffic. I remember being able to own the term "credit card" and every variation therein for a few years, pulling in loads of traffic for people searching for credit cards … that is, until Google introduced the bidding system. Suddenly the playing field was leveled; Google and its search competitors opened up opportunities for many businesses to benefit from this new thing called Search Engine Marketing (SEM).

Consumers quickly came to understand the difference between organic search results and sponsored ones. As SEM began to ramp up as a viable business, Google also encouraged businesses to follow basic search principles to allow them to build integrity into their website to attract people with quality content. This opened up the market for black hat practices, link baiting and other questionable tactics as people tried to find shortcuts to achieve higher search rankings.

During this period, online media emerged as a mainstay vehicle, and the birth of the Internet Advertising Bureau (IAB) instigated the standardization of online media properties including core metrics. Google, for the first time, introduced the notion of 'click attribution,' i.e. the ability to track online behaviors to their end results. That's when CTR (click-through-rate) was born. This Click continued to follow the same path of the "Impression;" The biggest problem was that marketers became enamored by what could be most easily measured, but for most businesses there was no tie back to revenue or other meaningful business metrics. Measuring impressions was easy, but not meaningful. The scariest thing was that there was no real effort to measure the meaningful metrics.

Victims of Vanity: Why Marketers Buy Into Faulty Metrics

I sat there like a ghost in the meeting, told to be a fly on the wall by one of my clients as a marketing review meeting interrupted our planning session. I silently listened in on the call while one of the largest digital agencies in the world shared the outcome of their latest paid social media campaign. The agency stated that the goal of the campaign was to increase awareness of the brand's offerings to a specific vertical market.

In order to protect the innocent, and the guilty, I will share only what is pertinent.

I listened to this "Big Agency" run through the results of the campaign. Pulling up a cross matrix with the following on it:

- Name of the Article
- Number of Impressions
- Number of Clicks
- Clicks Per Thousand
- Cost Per Click

The results of the campaign were interesting, but probably not in the way the agency or the brand had hoped. Certain articles drove very low click through rates and extraordinarily high cost per click. It went further; the end result was 2 Million Impressions, 0.6% click-through rate and just over ten dollars per click. I did the quick math (no calculator required): I realized that this campaign generated 12 thousand clicks and cost the big brand over 120 thousand dollars for one article. In this case, they executed paid campaigns on 6 different articles. Now you do that math. Now ask yourself: what were they getting for this massive expenditure?

When the CMO of the global brand asked what exactly he should be looking at and what was the most important , the big agency account lead spouted out that the most important things to look at were Impressions and number of clicks.
WTF!!!

IT IS A HUGE LIE AND WE ARE ALL CO-CONSPIRATORS

As the call and the non-sense continued I couldn't help but feel for the client. They were spending a fortune on a campaign that was by all intents and purposes immeasurable.

But here is the kicker: it doesn't have to be that way.

Marketers have been lying to clients, and perhaps more problematically, to themselves for the past several years as they continue to sell the idea of vanity metrics like Impressions and clicks.

ENTER SOCIAL MEDIA: THIS NEW ORDER MUST DICTATE A NEW ACCOUNTABILITY

As social media started emerging as a strong vehicle about 5 years ago, I paid close attention to its lure. Here, these networks existed without the interruption of annoying advertising. It was not lost on me, because I was a regular source of that annoying advertising.

Slowly but surely, I was lured into this space where people could speak as people, uninterrupted. I engaged with esteemed bloggers and social media strategists who taught me the importance of active listening, transforming the marketing mindset, and leveraging relationships with the customer to succeed.

Even in MySpace days I spoke with people who were struggling to use the network to promote themselves. I knew a band that would develop new tracks every week so they could showcase it to their networks. They received accolades and validation–albeit from a tiny universe that admired and appreciated their efforts.

I became a purist–not overnight but soon after.

I became the anti-Marketer, espousing authenticity, transparency, and relationship-building. I would talk to anyone who would listen; I had experienced an epiphany.

When I started blogging 6 years ago it was merely an outlet for me to verbalize where this all would lead: social, emerging technology and why it would change the way companies operate. Along the way, it also provided others who stumbled upon my posts with an opportunity to learn. That was pretty cool… and it's what kept me going.

THE QUESTION:
DOES SOCIAL MEDIA DRIVES SALES?

While our media predecessors (traditional offline and online media) have built acceptable KPIs adopted by the industry, there continues to be a debate about the viability of social media.

The issue comes to the forefront because Marketing is now accountable for performance. Where, in a previous life, Marketing enjoyed the cozy position as a cost center, what became clear is the need for Marketing to drive sales, and deliver proof; that means that measurability has become more important than ever..

Unfortunately for social, Marketers continue to follow the existing path:

- The faulty baseline metrics spanned quickly beyond just Impressions into other metrics that had no clear business value.
- Likes on Facebook
- Followers on Twitters
- Pins on Pinterest

Heck, it's common for Marketers to ridicule Google Plus, but at least a +1 has intrinsic value in terms of driving improved search results.

Nevertheless, one Marketer after another promotes these self-serving statistics,[1] and the biggest concern may not be the fact that they are doing this, but the reason they continue…

Because it is easy.

Not only is it easy to compile these numbers, it is easy to report on these them. Sadly, to the busy Marketing Chief it is just as easy to pull the rug over their client's eyes by building campaigns chock full of great results across all metrics.

What marketing leader isn't going to like their expensive agency returning results like these:

- Campaign received "X" million Impressions
- Improved number of likes on your Facebook page by "Triple digit percent"
- Added "X" Thousand followers to your Twitter account
- But here is the problem: in all of the cases where I have seen these glorious improvements there are no answers to the following questions:
- "How many of those "Impressions" have moved to the next step in the buying cycle?"
- "Among those likes, did anyone buy anything?"
- "Which of these followers are real prospects?"

IT COULD ALL BE MEASURED, IF WE DID THE WORK

Let's reflect on the campaign discussion we started with: the big agency, the six pieces of content and the huge number of Impressions that meant nothing. When people clicked on the page what type of engagement opportunities existed? Was there an inbound form or some type of "Fill-the-funnel" method for capturing the interested visitor?

While we know there are certain risks in pop-ups, what about a less invasive signup or some type of premium content offer to capture the email or other pertinent information about the more than 10,000 "targeted" viewers that clicked on the content?

Although not a perfect science, this type of top of funnel activity could have provided much better insight into how many of the readers were really interested in the content, and potentially interested in moving to the next step of the sale.
I surmise that many Marketers don't want to put that type of capture on a campaign because, for highly profitable paid campaigns, they would find themselves showing

staggeringly low numbers of people engaged with the content. It wouldn't be as impressive to say "we garnered 32 email subscribers from the 2 million Impressions," but maybe it should be.

MEASURING WHAT MATTERS

The reason the 32 email subscribers wouldn't be impressive goes back to the practice of over-hyping of vanity metrics. How is a CMO or entrepreneur supposed to get excited about 32 subscribers when they are given impression numbers in the millions?

Those millions are a ruse - modern day smoke and mirrors. Where did the magician go? Yep, he disappeared.

The magic didn't disappear, because it was never there. It was all in your head and the magician (Marketer) put it there. Can it all be measured? Yes, but the agency partners you choose must think beyond the campaign and deliver results that really matter.

In the high tech and services space where I do most of my work, 32 genuine leads can be incredibly meaningful. If you were a technology company and you were able to convert just 1 or 2 of the 32 leads it could mean hundreds of thousands, even millions of dollars.

The only challenge is that it takes more time, more work and more willingness to see the whole picture to attain these more meaningful results.

Trust me when I say that I will focus there, where the results are, and let them, you know, those other guys, keep falling for the same old tricks of marketing yesteryear.

Even the "Madmen," with all of their sins, would be angry if they saw the crap some are pulling today. This says a lot about the changes that Marketers need to start making.

NEW METRICS AND NEW BASELINES

With all else being equal, Social becomes a unique beast that doesn't follow the same path as all other media. It's inherently different because major shifts have happened:

- Lack of corporate control over their messages
- New two-way interactions among consumers and brands that have the ability to shift consumer perception
- The emergence of engagement metrics that make it harder to correlate "user actions" to intent or purchase
- Media fragmentation that has made it more difficult to pin down customers to one medium at a time
- The steady performance decline of traditional online display advertising and sponsored search ads

We are in an era where consumers don't trust advertising. The average person is exposed to over 5,000 advertisements per day, and they don't trust most of them. Instead, the new consumer seeks to make purchase decisions through word of mouth and brand engagement via social platforms, native advertising and its close relative, content marketing.

WHAT SOCIAL BRINGS IS A
WHOLE NEW WAY OF DRIVING SALES

THE NEW RULES: RETURN ON TRUST

Imagine a world where you never have to sell anything…

Every day the ideal number of clients with perfectly aligned needs for your product would just walk through the door and shout out "I'll take it!"
Could business get any better?

What if I told you that this is already happening?[2] Albeit, it isn't quite so simple and the customers aren't simply arriving sight unseen ready to buy whatever it is you are selling. What is happening is that customers are showing up ready to purchase, leaving us all to ask, "How?"

Suppose it is January 2nd, 2015. Picture yourself waking up and deciding that it is time to buy a new car.

What is the first thing that you do? Do you hop in your old car and drive over to the local dealership? You pick up the newspaper and see what special savings are being offered? I suppose you could do either of these things, but if you were like the vast majority of people today you would do neither.

Instead you would take your iPad off the charger, head over to your sofa, put your feet up on the ottoman and start surfing.

You would find your way through the car review sites, and perhaps drop into the manufacturer sites to see if they have any special offers and incentives. Finally, you might pop over to Facebook to ask for your friends their opinions on the car(s) you should be short-listing.

Once you have your research done, you have determined the following

- Which car you want.
- What features you would like.
- How much your exact car should cost MSRP and Invoice.
- The target buy price from Edmunds.
- An exact estimate of what your trade-in should be worth via Kelly Blue Book.
- Your up-to-the-minute credit score from Experian
- The desired interest rate and term of loan based on your credit score.

Once you know all of this: You apply for a car loan on a competitive lending site and receive multiple offers.

Finally you walk, into the dealership with a printout in hand of the vehicle you want, the value of your trade, the price, interest rate and a pre-approved letter of credit and say to the salesman… "Bring my new car around"

Wow! What just happened? Essentially, you walked into the dealership and bought what they had to offer for the price that they wanted to sell it for and you are going home happy. Like magic, only it isn't.

What you experienced is the new way of doing business. [3] New rules, new engagement.

Only now these rules are impacting everything, not only how we as consumers buy things for personal use, but how businesses consume as well.

B2B, B2C, P2P, [4] it doesn't matter - we are all consumers looking to buy in a new economy, an informed economy, and it is scary, exciting and one heck of an opportunity for businesses to prosper.

Let's look at the numbers behind the change:

If I had you guess how many information sources, on average, a buyer engages with prior to making a purchase what would you guess? Would you say 2 or 3 or perhaps 4 or 5? What if I told you the number were 10.4?

In a study performed by Google (Zero Moment of Truth) [5], they found that buyers on average engage with more than 11 pieces of content prior to making a purchase decision, and according to a study by Forrester Research[6], that number has doubled year over year in 2012 and 2013.

In fact, 90% of consumers trust[7] a recommendation from their network and 81% of those go online [8] to get those recommendations. On the other hand, there isn't a single type of advertising that consumers trust at a rate greater than 50%, with many forms of advertising being trusted at rates in the 20-30% range.

Bottom line, not only is the way we are consuming changing, but our reference points are evolving rapidly, and trust is proving to be a precious commodity.

WHAT IS RETURN ON TRUST?
IS IT A REAL METRIC?

If I were a business and I knew that by gaining the support of a key group of in-fluencers we could achieve greater success in word-of-mouth marketing, would I make gaining their support a priority? You are darned right I would! As I mentioned above, 90% of buyers trust a network referral, leaving us as businesses to ask,

"Who represents the network and how do I gain the support of those influencers to evangelize my business?"

What is crazy is that even though 98% of business owners say that word of mouth is their lead driver of new business, only 3% of businesses have a strategy to capitalize on this. In short, what this means is that most businesses simply aren't pursuing the support of the brand influencer, begging the question "Why?"
Why go through the heavy lifting of building trust one by one when you can build a virtual army of ambassadors to support your brand? Is it too difficult? Perhaps you don't know where to start.

What if I told you that a group of loyal supporters is right there in front of you?

There are those already buying from you, and those that have worked with you in the past and had good experiences. While they may not be able to bring you all the business you can dream of, they can each bring one, or a few, and suddenly… you have arrived.

In the new economy this is all possible; to build a business where clients are banging on the door because they want to work with you. It may seem impossible, but it isn't. We are in a new economy with new rules that favor not those who have done it longer or spent more money, but those who know what their customers need and how to deliver it to their satisfaction.

WHERE GOOGLE IS RELEVANT

Google figured this all out and implemented it through Hummingbird. Facebook has taught Marketers to build a strong and engaged community through listening and relevant content, NOT promotion. Marketers who are used to having control are at a loss. They are now looking for quick fixes that allow them to engage, dialogue, and develop mechanisms that continue to foster this two-way interaction.

It's a brand new way of thinking. You can't fit everything you've learned and apply it to this new medium — it's akin to putting a round peg in a square hole. I know. I've tried. And I've had to learn.

Jon Loomer wrote:

 "Here's the brand's dilemma: Most Facebook users are on the network to engage with friends and family. People don't talk like this. Only brands do. And when brands do, these posts stick out unnaturally."

Adding value is unnatural for any brand. Let's face it, brands are in business to sell. How can Marketers truly care about listening to the customer and delivering engaging content if their prime directive is to move the product? THEY CAN'T!

While social has its challenges, the wealth of information it delivers has mitigated much of the guesswork. We have had to hone our skills over the years to become better at defining audience. The nonstop feedback loop directly from my customer gives me all the insight I need to make things better, to improve the service, develop a better product, and enrich the customer experience. We've never had the benefit of this channel before... and now we do.

I see a light at the end of the tunnel.

I have seen the smart Marketers... albeit they are few and far between. The smart Marketers do not live in a vacuum. They see the holistic view of the customer: the customer identity, needs (outside of the product), propensities, and their influences – in context with company specific transactions.

The smart Marketers see the inherent value in information and how it will morph the business plan for better results. The smart Marketers realize that the value of retaining amazing customers is far less costly than acquiring new ones.

The smart Marketers are not necessarily the disrupters. They see value in data and measurement. They see value in going out and finding the right customers as opposed to expecting that they will come willingly.

The smart Marketers choose not to remain complacent and accept the status quo. They are relentless in their pursuit to figure out this "new" customer and what turns their head. And they continue to remain plugged into the customer long after the first purchase. This is what they see as the new normal.

This new collaborative environment is about transparency and giving in to the loss of some control. More importantly, it's about managing the relationship with the customer for mutual benefit... and eventually strong business return. What many businesses have come to realize is that now they don't have to spend inordinate amount of dollars in trying to persuade and sell the customer. Determining what efforts will nurture the relationship with the customer to drive return is now our goal.

Are you ready for what is next?

These new rules of customer engagement represent a seismic shift that will turn everything we thought we knew about marketing on its head. We now live in a world where trust and customer experience come first. It is because of these new rules that marketers of all types need to Evolve, perhaps more than ever before.

REFERENCES:

1   http://millennialceo.com/social-media/b2b-marketing-measure-matters/
2   http://millennialceo.com/customer-service/customer-focus-information-inspiration/
3   http://millennialceo.com/leadership/death-sales-pro/
4   http://millennialceo.com/social-media/b2b-marketing-measure-matters/
5   https://www.thinkwithgoogle.com/collections/zero-moment-truth.html
6   http://blogs.forrester.com/lori_wizdo/12-10-04-buyer_behavior_helps_b2b_marketers_guide_the_buyers_journey
7   https://www.prophet.com/sites/transformation/infographic.html
8   http://www.digitalbuzzblog.com/infographic-the-social-consumer

How Direct Marketing Drives the Evolution of One to One Digital

THE POWERS OF DIRECT MARKETING
by Shelly Kramer

Direct Marketing isn't a new marketing tactic—it's been around a long time. Direct Marketing is personified by the ability for Marketers to connect directly with their customers through a variety of different channels, hence the catchy name! Many times when people think of Direct Marketing they think of catalogs or print pieces mailed to customers, but Direct Marketing actually includes many things beyond that. Today, Direct Marketing is an Omni-Channel discipline and can be done via tactics like text messaging, interactive websites or landing pages, social media advertising, mobile ads, telemarketing and, of course, via mailers and catalogs.

Keys to Success with Direct Marketing

Good, Reliable Data. The key to a successful Direct Marketing campaign is starting with good data. If you want to reach your customers and prospects, having a, clean database is an integral part of the equation. And today, the more personalized that data, the greater impact your campaign will have. Your database might include name, mailing address, email address, phone number as the basics, but it might also include information like age, purchase history, habits, preferences, and so on. The more data you have about your customers and prospects, the more you can deliver highly targeted direct messages to them and the greater your chances for success. Many times companies embark upon Direct Marketing initiatives without the benefit of a reliable database and that can most definitely have an impact on your overall chances for success.

Targeted Messaging. The beauty of Direct Marketing is that the better your data, the more personalized you can make your messages. And the more targeted you can make your messages, the greater chances of conversions. Here's an example that's applicable to many of us. I shop at Target all the time. Based on the data Target has on me and based on my purchase history, the retail giant knows that I have young daughters and that I like certain types of clothing and other items that girls like. As a result, Target can (and does) send me personalized messages via text or even special deals and coupons through its recently launched Cartwheel app, targeting the things they already know I like to purchase.

Personalized Messaging. There's all kinds of data out there that shows that the more personalized you can make your email marketing messages--another powerful direct mail tactic--the greater your chances of success. Experian's 2013 Email Marketing Study showed that personalized emails lifted transaction rates and revenue per email six times higher than non-personalized messages. Doesn't that only make sense? Here are some other compelling stats from the study:

- Want higher open rates? Personalized mailings result in a 29% higher open rate and 41% higher click through rates (CTRs) than non-personalized emails.
- Triggered mailings that are also personalized also have higher open rates and higher CTRs.
- Trigger campaigns (campaigns based on user behavior and intent) deliver double transaction rates over non-personalized email campaigns.

Clear Call to Action. This seems like a no-brainer, all too often there's not a clear call to action in Direct Marketing campaigns. When you're developing your campaigns, think about the benefit that whatever it is you're offering delivers to your prospective customers. Then, make sure you craft messaging that clearly articulates that benefit. Give them what they want, when they want it, and make it quick, painless and super easy for them to take the action you want them to take.

Think of it a bit like Amazon's Buy-With-One-Click button – you see it, you want it, you buy it. Done. Make your calls to action in your Direct Marketing campaigns just that easy and you'll be amazed by the results.

Design for Mobile First. It's tremendously important to optimize your direct marketing campaigns for cross channel effectiveness, and there's nothing more important than designing for mobile first.

For instance, if I get an old school print mailer in the mail with an offer that's attractive to me, chances are good that I'm going to investigate the offer using my omnipresent mobile device. Make sure that when I do that, it is not only a mobile optimized site that I see, but that it is easy for me to opt in, buy, or whatever it is you want me to do, from my mobile device.

These are some of the important elements to consider when you're developing your Direct Marketing campaigns. The beauty of Direct Marketing is that it's trackable, measurable, able to be highly customized and personalized and, of course, repeatable.

Direct Marketing as a marketing tactic has the ability to connect you intimately with your customers and prospects in a personal manner than can deliver powerful results. When you add in the fact that today you can use Direct Marketing in and across Omni-Channels, connect with your customers where they are in the manner in which they want to be reached, and you've got a powerful marketing tool.

Shelly Kramer is the Founder and CEO of V3 Integrated Marketing. A 20+ year marketing veteran, she's a brand strategist focused on delivering integrated marketing solutions and helping businesses leverage the web for growth and profitability. She's an expert at content strategy and execution and tying social media to business initiatives. Recognized by Forbes on a number of occasions, most recently as one of the Top 40 Social Selling Marketing Experts and Top 50 Social Media Influencers, she's half Marketer, half geek, with a propensity for numbers, producing results and a dash of quick repartee. http://V3im.com/blog has been recognized by Forbes as one of the Top 20 Best Marketing and Social Media Blogs and by PostRank as one of the Top 100 Most Engaging Social Media Blogs.

This chapter highlights the importance of Direct Marketing principles and why it's resurged as a key driver in understanding and communicating with customers in this emerging digital environment.

The Principles of Direct /Direct Response Marketing:

Shelly Kramer provided a clear journey that Direct Marketing has taken in the last 20 years. It's evident that this principle continues to be relevant today.

The concept of Direct Marketing evolved in the 1980's out of the need to have more targeted communications with customers and prospects. Conceptually Direct Marketing targets individuals or finite groups of customers with similar traits, with the objective of delivering customized messaging directly to that individual or group.

Over the years the medium has evolved from flyers, telemarketing, direct mail, direct response TV, response-driven print and outdoor ads to interactive websites, display ads, SEO, and SMS.

The characteristics of Direct Marketing focus on the following traits:

- A database of names (customers or prospects) is used to develop the target list: typically segmented by the following variables: geography, demographics, psychographic information, and behavioral history.
- Messages are directed to this list. This means being able to reach the target group via email, postal address, and web browser cookies or phone numbers.
- A call to action is the expected outcome or result of the communication e.g. "drive to website" or "call number."
- All Direct Marketing programs are trackable and measurable. The discipline can analyze beyond just response, and provide Lifetime Value (LTV) based

on the following variables: mode of communication, message, and target demographic.

Retention Programs were largely based on segmenting customers based on their value to the company. Customer value was typically based on an RFM Model:

- **Recency** – the last time a customer visited and purchased
- **Frequency** – how often a customer purchases
- **Monetization** – how much a customer spent

Marketers have often overlaid product purchase history into the RFM records of individual customers in order to develop predictive models for product recommendation propensities.

This has further evolved into development of complex cluster segmentation, which is the practice of grouping customers of similar traits (RFM behavior, demographics, etc.) into one cluster. In its simplest form, the premise of cluster segmentation assumes that tighter traits, which define a customer segment, allow for easier offer and message testing to a finite group.

DIRECT MARKETING EVOLVED

Back in the day, much of the heavy lifting came from database manipulation. While it always began with a prospect list, the data variables grew based on the increasing amounts of information we were able to glean about our customers and target groups. The more we knew about our customers, the more we were able to accurately predict what they were willing to buy and when.

One-to-one marketing has become much more sophisticated. Algorithms today have allowed Marketers access to mass customization within the digital space, as well as offline. What's more, the ability to take Direct Marketing principles and apply them across acquisition channels has become much more prevalent. Coupled with the rise of data capture from mobile, social media, and web browser cookies etc., the future of Direct Marketing has become even richer.

THE MORE SOPHISTICATED AD MODEL: BEHAVIOURAL TARGETING

I was fortunate enough to work for Hunter Madsen, the Yahoo! Data Marketing Guru who led the team that developed Behavioral Targeting back in early-to-mid 2005. Hunter explained the mechanics of targeting users within the network based on where they'd been, what content they consumed, what they searched for… also taking into consideration their geography, demographics and alignment with the target profile.

Aileen Hernandez Halpenny, a friend who heads up Rocket Fuel, reminded me of the "smart ads" — the dynamic ad units that would be served up to you based on geography, profile, search propensity etc. These were seemingly intuitive ads that understood the right offer for you at the right time. Simply put: "Optimize each ad for each user — right down to hyper-targeted local offers — so that you can drive your objectives, from awareness to conversion."

Combine that with ad retargeting that monitors user behavior on their site (cookies) and serves up a similar ad when they show up elsewhere in the network. Now we're talking relevance! No longer do we have to rely on latent conversion and assume that an ad viewed 10 days ago contributed to an online purchase of that same product. Retargeting takes out that guesswork.

HAVE DIGITAL DISPLAY AND PPC ADS HAD THEIR DAY?

Recently I have had several meetings with friends from traditional and emerging digital agencies. Digital ad models have evolved from banner to engagement ads, and targeting has becoming increasingly sophisticated. Paid search and SEO are getting less and less buzz; there is a fundamental shift happening that will turn the advertising space on its head.

The reality is that this new course of big data, gleaned from a wealth of unstructured information on the web and its users, is enough to make media people and publishing platforms rethink algorithms for maximizing performance.

Coming from the ad world, I have seen the banner ad rise and fall in a span of seven years. The value of Search Marketing (PPC) as we know it has had its heyday. I've seen content ad platforms emerge screaming about the need to create "value" to get user attention only to be met by a "meh" response from advertisers.

Real time bidding is the new buzzword for display advertising, where advertisers can now vie for a web user's attention, then overlay that with a complexity of user propensities. Display advertising is by no means dead or dying. It's still a thriving business but the algorithms and messaging/content on these mediums continue to change at a rapid pace.

Where SEO and Pay-Per-Click (PPC) have ruled for the last five years, some of the search pundits are realizing an eventual downturn. Consider this quote from *Adam Torkildson*, one of the top SEO Consultants in the country, in the Forbes article, "The Death Of SEO: The Rise of Social, PR, And Real Content" [1]

 Google is in the process of making the SEO industry obsolete, SEO will be dead in two years.

This statement is rooted in the fact that expectations of consumers have changed: in advertising, in content and in brand engagement. Social content is largely what makes up Google's search algorithm: relevance and recency. What does this entail? Shares, comments, tagging, organic search behavior and reviews.

Another factor will unseat Paid Search in providing a more relevant prospect framework: social data insights.

The advent of Social Media brought with it a host of variables and dynamics that were vastly different than what had existed in traditional media, display and search. As Social Media becomes mainstay, the quest to morph it into another paid media channel continues to be a learning environment for the largest social platforms.

The Merging of Pure Play Media and Social Media

During my first foray into social media some years back, I was faced with a channel that seemed so vastly different than what I'd come to know in my years as a digital Marketer. I became enthralled with the notion of relationships driving business; transparency and authenticity were integral to delivering value.

Willy Loman's character in Death of a Salesman[2] is the story of a man obsessed with the notion of his own greatness. Even in his later years he is convinced that success is directly attributed to "greatness, popularity and personal charisma."

However, many successful businesses have been built on something much less glamorous than the cult of popularity; many have been built with years of understanding customers and responding to their needs. This means building trusted relationships one by one over a long span of time. Customer relationships have been at the core of conversion. This is not new… but in the digital space, it is the absolute foundation of business sustainability.

And I have bought into that. While I understand that this continues to be a test and learn channel, I have not given up the principles that accompany the true merits of this channel: credibility, community, engagement and its undeniable result: sustainability.

NOWADAYS YOU CAN BUY SOCIAL... BUT THAT'S COUNTER-INTUITIVE TO WHY IT EXISTS

As a blogger, I have been coaxed by platforms into running media placements on my site. While that piqued my interest, it became apparent that "access" to niche bloggers, particularly ones with influence, actually meant buying ads on their sites. There was no real opportunity to engage with these influencers, nor develop a strong program to build brand engagement among their follower base. It was simply pure pay to play media. The argument from the media sales guy is always the same "...but it's still media, and it isn't free!"

THE QUEST TO MONETIZE SOCIAL NETWORKS

It is the enduring question: If these networks are to exist and be maintained, how are they going to make money? One of the reasons that Yahoo! reduced its investment in 360, Geocities, and Answers was that it struggled to merge online paid ads into a user-engagement environment; i.e., the two environments could not effectively co-exist. Ad performance was poor because users didn't want them there. There are some networks doing an ok job at monetizing the medium:
Google realized with the rise of engagement on video, users were willing to live with short banners or pre-video advertising before watching their favorite videos.

FACEBOOK AND MONETIZATION…
A FLAWED BUT PROFITABLE AD SYSTEM

Facebook, despite the criticism of its pundits, continues to invest heavily in its ad network as the key to monetization. 88% of all its revenues are derived from ads. However, in September of 2013, this ad platform became a center of attention.

According to Social Media Today[3], Facebook had to apologize for the dating ads that appeared on its service featuring Canadian teenager, Rehtaeh Parsons, who had taken her own life in April, 2013. The teenager had been the target of cyber-bullying because of online circulation of photos taken of her, after an alleged gang rape in 2011.

This was a clear incident of an advertiser scraping images from the site and using them without authorization. Facebook immediately banned the advertiser from submitting future ads. However, this does not negate the fact that if the ad had not been reported, Facebook would never have known about it. There was no mechanism in place to flag these types of violations. By the time the review process took place, the damage had already been done.

Twitter's ad model continues to prove itself. The promoted ads run within the user's timeline and targets based on profile, interest and geography. Twitter has said that they want to display Promoted Tweets in a way that's both useful and authentic to the Twitter experience. What's become clear over time is that the Promoted Tweets are highly correlated to an increased number of followers; however one could argue that the quality of those followers is questionable.

THE FUTURE AD MODEL: ENTER SOCIAL DATA

Now imagine if you had the best of both worlds: behavioral data and conversation data.

Case in point: Mary Johnson searches for information about a future trip to Taipei, Thailand. She also goes to travel sites, reads hotel reviews and has excitedly spoken to close friends on Twitter and Facebook about her plans and preparations. Don't forget, Google also scans Mary's email and captures the threaded discussion with her husband about the upcoming trip. (We'll address this in the Chapter on Privacy)

Now we have recent behavioral activity based on where Mary has been on the Internet and what she's communicated via email, but we are also aware of conversations that validate her behavior. It is safe to assume that Mary will "definitely" be going to Taipei.

Imagine what this information does for a travel company. They now have information on a user that will allow them to not only serve an ad, or respond to that user with relevant offers, but to do so with a certain degree of confidence that Mary will, at the very least, click on the ad.

What excites me about social data is that it does the job of the Marketer, for the Marketer. No longer do we have to guess "who" is right for our product. The conversation data alone is enough to verify the right target audience. Coupled with recent/past web behavior, the two variables will increase response lift significantly.

Caution: this may be a game changer but the way the advertiser treats the user must also change. Ads alone may not be enough to increase response rates. Engagement — I mean outreach to Mary through Twitter where she mentioned the activity — may seal the deal.

Ads, for the most part, may become irrelevant. Even Facebook realized that low click-through rates (CTRs) on the now-defunct sponsored stories were driving conversion. They are now relying on "Impression-based" ads i.e., "I saw the ad" vs. "I clicked on the ad" to determine conversion.

How do traditional media people feel about this? An ad ops person put it this way:

> *"Conversation data may yield us the top 20 people who have a higher propensity to buy. Is this enough? The client wants more volume."*

…to which I responded,

> *"Social data allows you to target very niche groups — the tighter the targeting the better. After all, would you rather have a higher response rate, and spend less on advertising, targeting a more finite group rather than doing a blanket campaign across a larger volume with a standard 0.15 per cent CTR?"*

The value of social data is amplification and use of social strategies for outreach to augment ad performance. It also allows you to find "like individuals" by profiling users from social data results, and targeting them with similar content or offers; this results in BOTH a higher response rate and stronger word-of-mouth effects. This is where you get your volume. It also allows the Marketer to spend more wisely and opens the door to developing sustaining relationships with consumers.

Rethinking Business in the New Digital Customer MUST be at the Core

I had the pleasure of being part of a panel at Mesh a called "Beyond Social Monitoring. "I was in good company with Joel Yashinsky, CMO and SVP of Marketing and Consumer Business Insights at McDonald's, and Scott Lake, CEO of Source Metrics.

The panel provided some amazing insights into best practices that have moved beyond simple listening. An important part of the discussion was the brave McDonald's campaign called "Our Food. Your Questions," which won numerous awards and accolades including Marketing Mag's Marketer of the Year 2012.

The importance of this campaign was to highlight one corporation's move to really understand their customers. A core tenant of direct marketing underlines the importance of targeting the right products to the right customers. However, the evolved one-to-one model professes the customer have a voice that will be heard and acknowledged by the brand. While the results from the data collection largely impacted the brand's reputation, its efforts were also directly felt on the sales side. For a corporation like McDonald's to develop a campaign outside of its comfort zone is a telling sign for other stellar brands to follow.

This quote from *Alex Sévigny*, director of the McMaster-Syracuse Master of Communications Management program said it all:

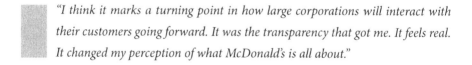

> *"It was a courageous and savvy move that recognizes the importance of creating a kinship with consumers…Trust and reputation are becoming a fundamental part of building a brand and maintaining a brand community. The McDonald's campaign is great in that respect. It's absolutely brave because it required them to give the public a backstage pass to how things work."*

At the same time, McDonald's was able to collect reams of data from their customers– good, bad and ugly perceptions about their food, their service and ultimately, their brand. This data provided a wealth of knowledge that will allow the corporation to take a step back and evaluate future changes to their business.

The quote from *Kristin Laird* of Marketing Mag that stood out for me was this,

> *"I think it marks a turning point in how large corporations will interact with their customers going forward. It was the transparency that got me. It feels real. It changed my perception of what McDonald's is all about."*

In a relatively short-time span, many brands are learning quickly about the impact of errant tweets and "very public" customer service missteps. One brand, that had a lot to lose given years of customer speculation regarding its food, its processes, and negative health claims, chose to open itself up for discussion with its customers about anything and everything they wanted to know.

Joel Yashinsky, CMO of McDonalds, understood that they were headed into the "Lion's den" but faced it head on. I empathized, having worked with a client, another quick-service restaurant (QSR), that had faced years of customer innuendo and backlashes, which were now showing up on forums, photo-sharing sites, Twitter and review sites.

Many brands choose to bury their heads in the sand to avoid facing the detractors head-on. Not McDonald's. It's the reason many of those to whom I've spoken, have come back to McDonald's. And while Yashinsky did not disclose the exact impact on sales during the campaign period, he indicated the peripheral results were positive enough to replicate the same initiatives in Australia.

The reams of data collected from the customer feedback during the "Our Food. Your Questions," campaign provided data points relevant to outside of the Marketing organization. While McDonald's has yet to determine the "measurable" influence of these numbers on the company's bottom line, it's clear that KPI's need to evolve.

Everyone Agrees: The KPIs are all Wrong.

MEASURE WHAT MATTERS

Let me ask you a question: If you lead a business and/or you are responsible for the marketing of your company, what is the return on 1000 Facebook Likes?

Perhaps a better question is...

Did you know that only one to five percent of the people who "Like" your Facebook page[4] actually see what you post? Furthermore, only about 1.5 percent of those who like your Facebook page will ever return to it?

Yet Marketers clamor to get more Likes, almost obsessively, as if these Likes can be traded for revenue. They can't - at least not directly.

What about Twitter followers? How important are they? What exactly should a business expect from increasing their followers?

While many businesses will tell you that they have generated a lead or an opportunity through engaging with someone that follows them on Twitter, few can say that a higher volume of followers directly led them to more opportunities or revenue.

MEASUREMENT IS IMPORTANT, BUT WE MUST MEASURE THE RIGHT THINGS

The smart Marketer has dismissed the value of a "Like" or the "Number of Followers" as a true success metric.

Would you like to have 500 people reading your blog that are in your industry and are potentially consumers of the product or service you sell?

Or…

Would you prefer to have 50,000 readers that are just eyeballs because they have no need to consume what you are selling?

The answer is obvious, but I often hear Marketers and business owners saying, "We need more people to read our content." Wrong. What you need is the right people reading your content.

THE SOFT METRICS HAVE THEIR PLACE

Where engagement is still a hard metric to measure, many in the C-suite still want proven conversion. How do we prove that social can drive sales?

I agree that the soft values like engagement and content have been difficult variables to properly attribute to sales, but an amazing thing about the web is that everything can be tracked.

However, it's about more than just sales. It's everything about social: the content, the conversation, the sentiment and the amplification. Is there a clear path to sales from all these?

Amazing companies like Measure.ly have the ability to track and measure the conversion value of content. It may begin with amplification from the strongest voices in social media, but inevitably conversion, as Josh Merchant, Co-founder and CTO of Measure.ly put it,

 "…comes from those individuals who have the closest relationship to the point of conversion."

This validates the strength of advocates like the micro-influencers for your brand, as Danny Brown and Sam Fiorella point out in their book, "Influence Marketing."

While we're still trying to track coupon redemptions from online to offline to prove that social works, we are missing a very important component: the Customer.

START WITH A PURPOSE

Why are you engaging in Social Media? Why is your company blogging? What are you trying to accomplish?

The answers to those questions are your digital marketing strategy.[5] However, it is important to fundamentally understand these things before getting caught up in how many followers you have, who likes your page and how many readers you have.

So here are a couple of things to focus on:

Target the Right Readers/Followers: You know who the ideal customer is for your business. Focus on connecting with them through social channels and content. With the right audience, your conversions will grow at a much greater rate than they will by just pursuing volume.

Don't Count Followers and Likes; Instead, Build Relationships:[6] The counts really don't mean that much. While they may feel good for your brand's ego, a huge volume of "Window Shoppers" or worse yet, unengaged followers would not translate into anything meaningful for your business.

With so much data and information available to us, it is easy to get caught up in the hype. But our role in the digital sphere is to drive meaningful relationships[7] that translate into customer advocates and revenue.

BE RELENTLESS AT DRIVING CUSTOMER VALUE

We need to go one step further from where we are today. We need to shift focus and be relentless about finding out more about our most valued customers.

Despite the emergence of social media as a necessary channel to inform, companies are still having trouble moving in this direction. The challenges that many CMOs face is that they have not yet evolved in their thinking. Many are still focusing their efforts on the old channels.

Companies continue to focus on selling a product; they haven't emerged from this type of thinking. The abundance of social and mobile data that exists on a single consumer allows many companies (especially those not privy to this information traditionally) to capitalize on this advanced direct response practice more than ever before.

Case in point: Banks are and have always been product centric –both in objectives and compensation. It's the reason why there is a large duplication of effort, minimal cross-product collaboration, huge inefficiencies and inadequate customer engagement. (We will delve deeper into banking in Chapter 12, as an industry that is rich in customer data but may be one of the slowest to evolve.) Banking is not the only industry focused on products. Many verticals operate this way.

The Opportunity Beyond Listening... Beyond Engagement: Build Enduring Conversations with your Most Valued Customers

Companies have traditionally built better mousetraps, expecting the market to follow. Consumer Package Goods Companies (CPGs) continue to innovate on existing products. QSRs follow the same model. While both have the ability to build a 'functioning" CRM program, the limited data access to consumer usage and attitudes of their products "at scale" has limited the degree to which these programs could be truly successful.

It has been even more difficult for franchised models to understand the "local" customer's usage patterns to the degree of identifying those who frequent the store. But now that data exists and can be made available locally, the opportunities are endless.

Yes, companies are listening. Yes they are engaging with their customers. They are taking this one step further to being able to identify Joe Parker, teacher from Bayview Glenn, who stops into McDonald's by Bayview and Eglinton in Toronto every morning to get his large double double and McMuffin? (Note: fictional scenario)

Technology now exists to identify the most passionate discussions: consumer generated content about a brand. We need to go beyond the Like and look at the profiles of our Fans and Followers, our detractors and advocates. We also need to look at their behavior to determine those most likely to inhibit or move the brand message.

We can now piece together and aggregate the check-ins, the picture uploads, the tweets, the reviews and the discussions to find those customers that matter the most to a brand, or have the potential to matter.

But things have to change....

Joel Marans, Digital Marketer at Soft Choice, turned my attention to his presentation that catalogued the 30 Best Creative, Design and Marketing Quotes. In it, I found this quote from Seth Godin:

> *"Don't find customers for your products. Find products for your customers."*

I think we are fooling ourselves into thinking we really know who our customers are.

Where value has traditionally been defined by how much a customer is contributing to the bottom line, the "CRM" school of thought also defines the brand/customer relationship as a "Value Exchange."

In the digital world, this definition has evolved into "Consumers raise their hands and receive content that's relevant at that moment. In exchange they reward advertisers that deliver."

In social, true value exchange should be as transparent as its meaning: A product or service that meets the needs of its customers; something customers are willing to buy and to advocate.

How does this differ from the traditional view? The customer now becomes a partner and stakeholder in defining that product or service. Suddenly, this becomes a variable that can create greater sustainability for the brand. Inevitably, the product-centric company will evolve to ensure that it iterates alongside the market... and becomes less product-oriented in the process.

It's inconceivable to think that this can occur outside of an organization… or so goes the thinking.

In a world that's filled with the sound of billions of brand discussions, companies can no longer ignore these external messages, or their eventual impact on the company performance and reputation.

It's time to rethink business and focus greater time and energy on truly knowing the customer.

REFERENCES

1 http://www.forbes.com/sites/kenkrogue/2012/07/20/the-death-of-seo-the-rise-of-social-pr-and-real-content/

2 http://en.wikipedia.org/wiki/Death_of_a_Salesman

3 http://www.forbes.com/sites/elandekel/2013/01/22/facebook-pages-are-a-bad-investment-for-small-businesses/

4 http://www.socialmediatoday.com/content/facebooks-new-set-challenges-post-prism-concerns-ad-network-problems-privacy-policy-changes

5 http://broadsuite.com/a-small-business-guide-to-digital-marketing/

6 http://broadsuite.com/what-makes-good-online-business-relationships/

7 http://broadsuite.com/return-on-content-marketing-where-your-focus-should-go-b2b/

Marketing and the Holy Grail: ROI

BUILDING A PROPER SOCIAL BUSINESS MEASUREMENT METHODOLOGY
by Olivier Blanchard

One of the most crucial aspects of building and properly managing a social business practice is establishing a measurement methodology that is both legitimate and credible. In order to do that, you need to focus on two basic things: First, measure what matters. Second, measure it properly. If you start there (and don't deviate from the course), you will have a much greater chance of measuring what your program did right, what your program did wrong, and in both cases, how to make things work even better next time.

The problem is that when it comes to social business (and social media as a whole), the measurement waters have been thoroughly muddied by an influx of pseudo-science, charlatanism, and well-meaning but incompetent nonsense. So before you base your measurement practice on someone else's model that "seems" pretty good, let's set some ground rules that will hopefully keep you out of trouble.

1 **ROI isn't everything.**
Repeat after me: Not all social media activity needs to drive ROI. (And by ROI, I mean return on investment; not some alternate social media version of the term but the actual business equation universally accepted to describe the relationship between a financial investment and a financial return from that investment.)

Technical support, accounts receivable, digital reputation management, digital crisis management, R&D, customer service... These types of functions are not always tied directly to financial KPIs. Don't force them into that box. You don't have to and you probably shouldn't.

This is an important point because it reveals something about the nature of the operational integration of social media within organizations: Social media isn't simply a "community management" function or a "content" play. Its true value to an organization isn't measured in the obvious and overplayed Likes, Followers Retweets and Click throughs, or even in Impressions or estimated media value. Social media's value to an organization, whether translated into financial terms (ROI) or not, is determined by its ability to influence specific outcomes. These outcomes could be anything from the acquisition of new transacting customers to an increase in positive recommendations. They could be an increase in buy rate for product x or a positive shift in sentiment for product y. They could be a boost in customer satisfaction after a contact with a CSR or the smooth (and swift) attenuation of a PR crisis.

In other words, for an organization, the value of social media depends on two factors:

1. The manner in which social media can be used to pursue a specific business objective. (Any objective)
2. The degree to which specific social media activity helps drive that objective.

In instances where financial investment and financial gain are relevant KPIs, this can be ROI (a purely financial calculation that measures the relationship between a financial investment and a financial return). In instances where financial gain is not a relevant outcome, ROI might not matter at all.

2 **If you are still having trouble explaining or understanding the intricacies of social media ROI, you are probably asking the wrong question.**

One of the worst questions in the digital world these past few years has been, What is the ROI of Social Media?

It isn't that the idea behind the question is wrong. It comes from the right place. It aims to answer 2 basic business questions: Why should I invest in this, (or rather, why should I invest in this rather than the other thing?), and what kind of financial benefit can I expect from it? Both are valid and perfectly normal. The problem is that the question can't be answered as asked. Here's why: social media, in and of itself, has no proprietary, self-contained version of ROI. You measure ROI in social media the way you measure ROI everywhere else. There's no "trick" to it. It's all Business 101 methodology.

Also, the question is too broad. By referencing "social media," it focuses on a broad swath of channels, platforms and activities that can produce a broad range of returns (and/or none at all), but without focusing on the activities that ultimately drive outcomes. It's a lot like asking what the ROI of email is, or the ROI of digital marketing. Well, it depends: the channels aren't predictors of ROI. The channels are just conduits for activity. What you do with them is what drives ROI.

3 So what should the right question be?

The question, then, should not be what is the ROI of social media, but rather what is the ROI of [insert activity here] in social media?

Remember that you aren't investing in channels. You are investing in campaigns, in content, in engagement, in activity. ROI begins with the spend: what are you investing in? You aren't really investing in Facebook or Instagram, right? You're investing in account management. You're investing in social campaigns. You're investing in community management and content curation. You are investing in activities. Measure that, and the more specific, the better. Here are examples of how ROI should be framed in a legitimate business discussion:

What was the ROI of [insert activity here] in social media for Q3 2011?

What was the ROI of shifting 20% of our customer service resources from a traditional call center to twitter last year?

What was the ROI of shifting 40% of our digital budget from traditional web to social media this past year?

What was the ROI of our social media-driven raspberry gum awareness campaign in Q1?

If you know the cost of the activity and you can determine its impact on sales for x timeframe, you can actually take that to a CFO and a CEO and have a credible conversation about ROI. If your report, however, compares the cost of an activity to the number of likes obtained from that activity, you aren't talking about ROI. As positive and beneficial to the organization as it may be, you are talking about a non-financial outcome. It is crucial to understand the difference between the two.

4 **The cost of asking the question incorrectly.**
What is the ROI of social media? asks nothing and everything at once. At best, it begs a response in the interrogative: Just how do you mean? At worst, where either educational gaps or a lack of discipline can find an in into the discussion, asking the wrong question tends to lead to a loose interpretation of the term R.O.I., which has already led many a social media "expert" down a shady path of improvisation.

Asking the wrong question to the wrong people is how ROI went from being a simple financial calculation of investment vs. gain from that investment to becoming any number of made-up equations mixing unrelated metrics into a mess of nonsense.

In the real world of business, the ROI equation is always the same:

In the world of social media, ROI often turns into measurement soup like this:
Social media ROI = [(tweets – followers) ÷ (comments x average monthly posts)] ÷ (Facebook shares x Facebook likes) ÷ (mentions x channels used) x engagement Huh?!
Equations like this are everywhere. Companies large and small have paid good

money for the privilege of discovering that they don't work. Don't be one of them. Always start by asking the right questions, and make sure that the people answering them are competent.

5 Putting it all together.

Now that we have established that outcomes are not medium-specific but activity-specific, let's talk about the sorts of outcomes you should be looking to affect. (Hint: increasing Likes and Followers should not be your priority if you are running a business. Driving business should be your priority.)

If you aren't immediately concerned with ROI, what is your primary objective? It could be any number of things, so let's look at a new product launch scenario: your new product launches in 6 months. You want to start driving excitement for it in the market because excitement should drive desire, and desire should drive sales when you finally make it available. So for the next 6 months, you aren't going to concern yourself with ROI. That comes later. Initially, you are going to focus on driving discovery, interest, positive sentiment/mentions, purchase intent, positive word-of-mouth, as well as visits to product pages and key content.

In this phase, measure these outcomes against the activity that drives them to see what is working and what isn't (and make the appropriate changes to improve results). In other words, don't just blindly measure Likes and Followers because that's what you were told you're supposed to do. Measure what matters. Shape your program to drive results that matter for your business. Learn what you can from that and keep going.

In six months, when you finally make your product available, start measuring the ROI of that activity then. (Pre-orders are increasingly common now, so start measuring ROI then, if applicable.) How much did you spend on the activities that drive sales?? What uplift can you reasonably attribute to these activities? (Do you have a way of connecting the dots? (Establishing a path from discovery-to-purchase is really helpful.) ROI measures the ratio of cost to gain for the activity that ultimately drove revenue.

That's all it is. Your measurement of ROI should be very specific and focused, but your measurement methodology should incorporate far more than just ROI measurement.

Now let's take a step back and look at the big picture: unless you only use social media to drive awareness for your products and services, it is pretty likely that more traditional marketing means (TV advertising, PR, etc.) will have had an impact on both awareness and sales as well. In other words, social and non-social media will have driven both financial and non-financial outcomes together. The question now becomes which was more responsible for driving outcomes x, y and z?

That's where things start getting complicated, so let's tread carefully.

First, perhaps it doesn't matter what channel or activity drove what. Perhaps it isn't even the right question. Perhaps the right way to look at it is that everything worked well together, that the media and activity formula was effective. Perhaps it was combining social and non-social that ultimately drove awareness and product adoption, and not one channel more than another. Perhaps mistakenly favoring the channel that seems to have driven key outcomes at the expense of another might render your next campaign ineffective. One way to think about this is to use a sports team analogy. Soccer, football, basketball, it doesn't matter. Let's take soccer though: imagine trying to determine which player on the team was most responsible for a win. Naturally, the players who scored goals will turn up at the top of that list, even though they could not have scored without the help of other players, who kept the other team from scoring and/or assisted in scoring goals by passing the ball at the right place and the right time. Now imagine that you are asked to cut costs next year and remove the least valuable players on the team, based on your measurement methodology's perception of the role they played in driving wins. By focusing more of your attention and resources on the scoring players, you may end up weakening their ability to score in the first place, and set your team up for a string of losses. The moral of the story being this: look at the big picture. Understand how the pieces fit. When a multi-channel approach works for you, don't pick at it to remove bits and pieces whose value you might not be completely aware of. Sometimes, overzealous performance measurement can become a means of self-destruction. Learn to trust in the intangibles.

If you really must measure the specific effectiveness of a certain activity or channel, test it. Don't try to measure it over long periods of time; too many layers, too many fluctuations, too many variables. Think biopsy instead of EKG. Run very short, very focused tests at regular intervals and look for a) results, and b) changes, and trends particularly.

Some years ago, a small retailer asked me to help him determine which of his marketing channels were the most valuable to his store. He was concerned that the money he was spending on print ads was yielding negative ROI (more spend than sales revenue) and wanted to know if his hunch was correct. He didn't have sophisticated social CRM software, but he did have a pretty decent standard CRM system that captured customer transactions fairly accurately. Here's what we did: we created special one-day sales events, spaced every 4-8 weeks, so the scheduling wouldn't be predictable. We reached out to the public via all of the marketing channels he was using already: print ads in two magazines, email blasts, in-store promotional displays, Facebook, the website, and the blog. We assigned a unique promo code to each channel. This way, a customer using promo code x instead of promo code y at the point of purchase would tell us two things: 1) that one of the promotional messages had reached him and driven a transaction, 2) regardless of how many of these messages had reached him, the promo code he used indicated which channel had ultimately driven the decision to make a purchase.

This simple system told us the extent to which each channel was valuable to the store in regards to influencing transactions. By performing the same sort of test over time, we were able to 1) determine whether or not the value of each channel was consistent, and 2) if these values were shifting. Regardless of the technology and resources your organization has at its disposal, the principle is equally applicable if you are an enterprise class business or a small one-office operation.

By the way, it turned out that he was right: we found out that although print advertising sucked up the majority of his marketing budget, it only drove 4% of his sales. The most effective channel for him was email. As a result of the data we collected during our ROI biopsy measurement program, he was able to shift his marketing resources and make pretty key cost-benefit improvements to his business. (Translation: he stopped investing in the wrong channels and activities, and focused his attention on improving what was accidentally working for him already.)

It's amazing how much more valuable measurement is when it actually serves a business purpose instead of bowing to vacuous conventions. Don't get me wrong: it's important to measure changes in Likes and Followers and other social metrics (like comments and positive/negative brand mentions). They're indicators of your company's value and relevance in the market, but they're pretty basic, like the temperature on a thermometer, and if you want to really understand what aspects of your communications are working or not, and why, you have to know how to dig deeper, first of all, then how to analyze your results properly.

Returning to the bigger picture discussion we started before I threw in the retail example, it doesn't really matter where you measure your cost-to-gain equation. ROI is media-agnostic: cost is cost. Revenue is revenue. ROI is ROI, regardless of the channel or the technology or the platform. That's the basic principle. To scale that model and determine the ROI of the sum of an organization's social media program, all you have to do is analyze either a) channel value (through biopsy schemes like the one I just outlined) or b) the ROI of a specific campaign or set of activities, then add them all up.

Can it get pretty complex? You bet. Does it require a lot of work? Yes. It's up to you to figure out if it is worth the time and resources, which… is an ROI calculation in and of itself.

6

5 fake ROI practices you should avoid at all cost.

I mentioned that bogus ROI and shady measurement schemes were all too common in the social media space. Let me give you some examples of what to look for, so you will be better equipped to spot them when they come up. Here are some of the most egregious (and sadly, common) examples of what you are likely to find out there:

The Social Media ROI Calculator: Plug your likes into box a, your blog comments into box b, and your twitter followers into box c, click the magic button, and presto! Instant ROI calculation. Magic is so awesome! Except no. It doesn't matter if the calculator is 30 boxes long and asks you for dozens of social media account statistics. That isn't an ROI calculator you are wasting your time on. It's a scam. Unless the calculator is the standard, universally accepted ROI equation, walk away.

The new and improved social media ROI equation: This is the pseudo-academic version of the ROI calculator. Same principle but instead of creating a cool website that lets you plug in your values, the "social media scientist" behind this gem just decided it would be easier to share the equation and let you sort things out. Again, anything that isn't the ROI equation doesn't measure ROI. Be especially vigilant when you start seeing entirely unrelated values arbitrarily combined to fill confused space on a page. Example:

$$[(\text{Likes} - \text{Followers}) \times (\text{Comments} - \text{Likes})] \div (\text{Posts} - \text{Avg Word Count}) = \text{ROI}$$

The alternate definition of ROI: In this one, the social media ninja didn't even try to come up with a measurement methodology. It was easier to just redefine ROI altogether than to learn what it actually is or how it actually works. So now, ROI no longer means return on investment. Instead, it means something else entirely, like return on influence or return on interest. Though alternate versions of ROI don't always result in new and improved equations, they can. For instance:

$$(\text{Value of a Like} \div \text{Impressions}) \times (\text{Followers} \times \text{Follower Value}) = \text{ROI}$$

(Same nonsense, slightly different flavor.)

The rebranded ROI: Not to be outdone by creative interpretations of what ROI might be or should be or could be in the world of likes and "engagement," this particular scheme attempts to remove the I in ROI altogether and replace it with a more convenient and pliable letter. Here, we start bumping into ROE (Return on Engagement) or ROC (Return on Conversations). Fanciful equations tend to pop up there as well but the math is just as absurd as with the other fake ROI schemes. You may even be introduced to terms like "cold metrics" and "warm metrics," and other such nonsense.

Predictive ROI: This scheme is particularly insidious because it often blends the real ROI equation with fabricated values. The most common among these is "the value of a Like" fallacy, in which a social media scientist assigns an arbitrary financial value to a Like, based on some arcane equation not unlike some of the ones we have just seen. If you do a quick online search for "value of a Like," you will bump into a number of these schemes. (Note that none of the social media scientists who have devised their own proprietary ways of calculating the universal value of a like seem to agree on what that value actually is: $3.17? $34.79? $0.03?

Here's a tip: there is no universal value of a Like. The value of a Like is always relative to the company whose Likes are being measured, the types of products offered by this company, the range of price points the company offers, the transaction habits of the individuals whose Likes are being measured, and on and on and on. In other words, the value of a Like for a soda brand and a car manufacturer are not going to be the same. Ever. And even for the soda brand by itself, the value of each Like will tend to fluctuate based on the relative value of the individual responsible for said Like. Let me illustrate:

i.   Compare the value of 10 Likes from a customer who spends $800 per year on soda vs. 10 Likes from a fan of the brand that never makes a single soda purchase and doesn't recommend the brand to anyone.

ii.   Compare the value of 10 Likes from a customer who spends $800 per year on soda vs. the value of 100 Likes from a customer who also spends $800 per year on soda.

In other words, universal "dollar value" schemes for Likes, followers and fans that find themselves plugged into legitimate ROI equations end up infecting good measurement methodologies with bad math. That one is tricky, so remember to check your assumptions: always ask how the value of the Like/Fan/Follower was calculated. (Tip: look for Like/Fan/Follower acquisition costs being magically turned into value. Cost is not the same as value in regards to the relationship between acquisition and transactions, so don't fall into that trap. Also be on the lookout for similar transmutations from cost of Impressions to media value to like/fan/follower value. That one is especially common in advertising and PR circles.)

ROI Denial: Last but not least is the notion that by virtue of being "social," social media and ROI are incompatible. Evidently, because social media is about "being human" and having "conversations" and building "relationships" with people, ROI is not something that companies should even bother with. It would be a nice sentiment if it were genuine, but read it as basic laziness. Fact 1: businesses (the good ones) already make a point of being human and having conversations and building relationships. Social media didn't invent any of those things. Fact 2: A business doesn't stop being a business just because it's nice and friendly to its customers. You can be a social business and be focused on things like growing your business and driving profits. In fact, you should do all of those things. ROI isn't evil. It isn't in any way incompatible with building relationships or being social. So please, don't let anyone convince you that social media and ROI are mutually exclusive. That just isn't true.

I hope this quick little tour of social business measurement, especially in regards to what ROI is and isn't, and how it fits into a healthy measurement methodology, will be helpful to you. As long as you focus on what truly matters, don't fall for scams and erroneous assumptions, and do the work, you should be all right. Just remember that ROI is an extremely specific and somewhat narrow tool in your measurement toolkit. It will always matter to someone in your organization, but it most likely won't matter to everyone in your organization. So measure it if you can, and measure it well, but don't forget to measure other types of business-specific outcomes that will tell you what is working and what isn't. Ultimately, having a breadth of insight into your business is what will drive the best results, both in the short term and the long term.

Olivier Blanchard is SVP Creative and Digital Strategy at KGB Global, a full service digital, social business and analytics agency, and co-founder Kült Digital, which focuses exclusively on digital influencer programs. A prolific blogger and speaker, he is also the author of the bestselling Social Media ROI: Managing and Measuring Social Media Efforts In Your Organization (Que/Pearson), the world's #1 social business desk reference for digital managers and business executives.

Marketing ROI: the Man, the Myth, and the Legend

THE MAN

There may not be a CEO or entrepreneur on the planet that doesn't smile just a little bit when they hear the phrase ROI. In a world that is fueled by obvious returns in periods too short to make meaningful progress (thank you stock market), the idea that measurability exists provides peace of mind to so many of those responsible for the vision, strategy and execution of their respective organizations.

For many aspects of our businesses, measurable ROI is simple. If I buy one more machine and put it into production I can generate X% more products, which will generate Y% more profit. The decision then comes down to a simple question of cash flow. Is the potential return worth the short-term financial risk? This type of

ROI can also be applied to other facets of the business, such as software automation or expansion of the sales force. However, measuring ROI is not always so simple. In fact, in some areas of the business it can be close to impossible.

In marketing, the role is to create customers. Essentially, spending X amount of dollars to create Y number of new customers; a simple equation perhaps, but the formula to determine the success has long been evasive or maybe even impossible.

Before Internet Marketing ruled the roost, the primary measurement of marketing success was how many people "Viewed" your advertisements. From broad scope to narrow focus, the idea was to put your business in front of as many of the potentially correct clientele as possible, and hope for a response.

With advertiser feedback and the evolution of 1:1 Direct Marketing, the science became a little bit better. Yet, without specific user action such as participation in a survey or input of a campaign code, it was still next to impossible to directly correlate the creation of a new or returning customer with a specific campaign.

To some extent the marketing spend was a pseudo-science of sorts that kept entrepreneurs and their CFO's awake at night. Just what was the return on a back page ad in the New York Times?

THE MYTH

With the evolution of digital marketing and social media, the ability to measure has taken a substantial leap forward, as every campaign can be tracked, keyword spend can be seen and conversions can be associated with dollar value returns. In short, it is possible to set up every piece of content, tweet or keyword buy with a means to determine its effectiveness, answering the question; did someone buy something because of this campaign?

In many ways such progress is an epic improvement over the way it was done before. Now, the customer needs to do nothing but "Surf" for us to collect the data to determine the success of a marketing campaign. For some this may be a moment for celebration, but for others, the new and more readily available information merely creates more questions, more unknowns and more uncertainty.

As campaigns become more measurable and the results that ensue become more clearly attributable to ROI, the original question of marketing as a means of creating a customer ends up hanging in the balance. Just because our keyword led someone to a landing page, and then led to a click on our link, and consequently, led to a specific action, is that the reason they bought something?

The most cut and dry response may be yes, but the answer isn't really that clear. Does that workflow from click to buy measure, in any way, the role of content that the ultimate customer may have consumed? Does it say for certain who in the customer's community may have influenced their decision to buy? Is it really safe to say that the purchaser's affinity toward your brand is legitimized by the sequence of events they went through just prior to making the purchase?

Of course the answer may vary based on the nature of a transaction with the specific brand, but I think the attempt to directly correlate the purchase with the campaign strictly to place a measurable ROI on an activity is an obtuse oversight on the part of those trying to do so. This is because marketing has two very unique stages that need to be measured in totality to fully understand ROI, and unfortunately only one part is clearly measurable; the other is not.

The measurable part is the ROI on a campaign; the second is the creation of the aware consumer, the passionate brand advocate and the community that drives earned response to the campaigns. What did building those relationships cost? Can it be measured? Can it be attributed? Better yet, should it be?

Where the science of marketing ROI unravels is perhaps where Marketing's greatest application of effort is needed; creating the relationship that fuels a purchase. Otherwise all of those measured campaigns are going to be nothing more than a beautiful automobile without the gas and oil required to run it.

THE LEGEND

Measured return isn't something that can or should be ignored. It is important to every business to have those tracking results, or improvement would become elusive for every facet of a business. In the world that we call marketing, ROI needs to be seen for what it is, and what it isn't, and complete measurement still (and may always) lack a certain amount of potential as return on relationship. This is an idea with legs, but unfortunately not a formula.

In the future, as sentiment measurement gains traction and big data correlations continue to provide more clarity as to how things that aren't apparent connect, there will continue to be more and more advanced ways to measure the ROI of the entire marketing mix. However, for now it is still as much an art as it is a science when we attempt to draw final conclusions.

What may be the most important take away from all of this is that the desire to connect dots that don't connect needs to be avoided at all costs when trying to measure the ROI of certain marketing practices.

For instance, the value of a Follow, a Like or (gulp) an Impression: Sure you can build an equation that will give you an answer but don't be upset when I pass judgment on you for making ridiculous correlations.

The desire to put a stake in the ground with a flag that says "Marketing ROI" will probably continue to radiate like heat in the Saharan desert, but just remember the mirages that you see when you reach your most desperate points are most likely not real, which sounds an awful lot like Marketing ROI?

Social Media Is NOT About the Numbers!

One of my greatest sources of angst since diving into social media is that new media has yet to prove itself.

For any one company to spend the time to learn about social media, they need to understand the underlying benefits, in particular, "What is social media going to do for my business?"

If I spend "X" dollars doing social, what do I get back in return? Ahh, the dreaded and seemingly yet-to-be-answered question: What is the ROI of Social Media? While social media is a channel, it doesn't have the same traits as the traditional advertising mediums. You have to build a framework and strategy for social media before you can see tangible results.

If you're serious about incorporating social media into your business, it's important to see it for what it really is.

UNDERSTANDING SOCIAL MEDIA

Social media is unique in its benefits and provides more sustainability than most channels out there. In some cases, social media has been put on a pedestal because of the after effects we've seen in case studies citing "viral" activity.
But to be clear, social media does NOT equal VIRAL. Viral activity is a circumstance. It cannot be planned. People who find value and interest in a piece of content will define the extent to which it gets shared. Creating that value and interest is not done based on a formula. In short, those who consume it dictate it: the customer.

So, therein lies the rub! Social media is not an ordinary media channel because it cannot be controlled at the corporate level.... but it can be maneuvered and led down an intended path if it is managed correctly.

Let's start debunking some of these myths:

- **Social Media is NOT another advertising channel:** You may decide to invest in a TV advertising campaign. Once that campaign ends, so does the expense. If you decide to invest in social media, you're investing in relationship building. You can't turn off social media the way you turn off a campaign. Once you start down this path, you need a commitment to nurturing it. Remember, once a campaign ends, the relationships you started do not go away. This image below says it all: Would you rather spend thousands of advertising dollars to eventually get to the potential 2% of the population who would buy your product? Alternatively, Social Media has the unique benefit of targeting consumers already talking about your brand, those that have a higher propensity to buy. The immediate relevance has the ability to spread through word of mouth recommendations.

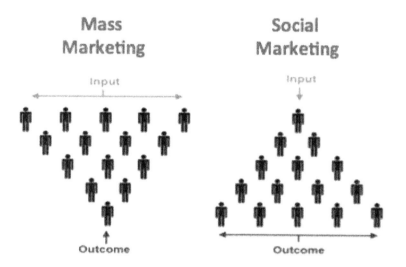

- **Social Media is NOT the magic bullet:** Social media is not the answer to all your business problems. It is a way to build more lasting relationships with your customers. Used effectively, Social Media is a catalyst that can help optimize functions across your organization. Expect to stumble and make mistakes. You need to learn it, embrace it, and make it as commonplace as brushing your teeth.

- **Social Media is NOT immediate:** Social Media takes time. If I were to parallel advertising channels to a cocktail party, Direct Mail would be equivalent to the annoying guy who introduces himself to you and starts talking about himself: "This is what I do? This is why I'm great." You will find any excuse to exit this seemingly one-way conversation.

Social Media is like that guy at the party that concentrates the conversation on you. He may introduce himself but listens primarily about what you have to say. He manages the conversation so there is a clear two-way discussion that provides value for each participant.

- **Social Media is NOT free:** It takes a lot of time and effort to build relationships with your customers. It starts with the cocktail party, the conversation and the eventual exchange of business cards. Trust needs to be built before you are given permission to start talking about purchase. Time and effort do not come free. The cost of maintaining the relationship should be equivalent to the cost of an employee's salary and the hours spent developing this. These days, dedicated community management, content development and deployment all have costs associated with them. The real cost: human capital.

- **Social Media is NOT about the number of followers:** Take this first scenario: Twitter Account X has 8000 followers, follows 10,000 people and has only 200 tweets. What this tells me: This person used some bot to game the follower base, unless there were pretty significant tweets that garnered them an incredible following...most likely NOT.

- **Second Scenario:** Twitter Account Y has 2700 followers; and follows 2400 people and has 11,400 tweets. So, while Account Y doesn't have as many followers, the number of tweets by Account Y reveals a greater level of commitment, which in turn will yield a greater level of engagement. We continuously analyze correlations between twitter posts and resulting follower behavior. We found that discussion drives follower growth. The higher the engagement level, the higher the follower growth. In fact, posting content alone did not highly correlate with follower growth. In some cases, it tended to turn followers away.

Likes, Impressions, and Follower volume are irrelevant if the quality of those elements do not provide business value.

- **On the positive side, Social Media is sustainable.** We've stated this before and this continues to prove itself. If you are committed, if you engage with your audience consistently and add value, you will begin to see significant impact on your business. Consider the traditional campaign model: There is a direct correlation between media spend and traffic and/or sales. The image below reveals the ebbs and flows that result from paid media activity. The more media effort, the more campaign impact. The minute the campaign ends so does the consumer activity.

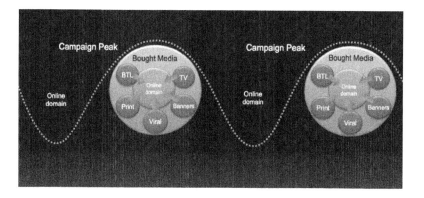

Now imagine what would happen if you decide to continue to engage with the customer (via social media) between campaigns? The effect below reveals a continuous stream of consumer activity even after the media dollars have been expended. Paying attention to your audience and not letting the ball drop reaps tremendous rewards over time. It goes beyond a campaign. It now provides a stepping-stone to true social engagement and improved relationship management.

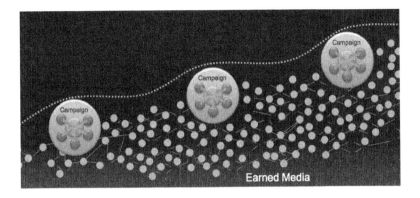

When that happens, you'll not only see your numbers soar, you'll also see your campaign spend become more efficient.

Social Media ROI can be measured. Social Media, if done correctly, can yield results with clear attributions in a short time. And, in the case of Columbia House, targeting the right communities with transparency and value can develop sustainable customer relationships with profitable results.

CASE STUDY:
Columbia House and the Need to Revamp the Brand

This is one community success story that didn't take long to generate signs that it was indeed working. By following social media rules of engagement this proved to eventually work in the brand's favor. The reason this success is so profound is because its Marketing team, while well versed in utilizing Online (search, display, affiliate) Marketing to achieve clear ROI success, did not necessarily see Social Media as a medium to achieve similar results.

Background:

Columbia House was a traditional direct mail company, with strong foundations in measurability, attribution and ROI. These were key pillars that drove its success for many years.

Technology and industry changes i.e. the decline of music CD consumption, Apple's introduction of the iPod, and the subsequent move to cheaper MP3 downloads, left the music industry scrambling to monetize artists and their music.

This, in turn, necessitated Columbia House to focus more efforts on movie sales. Despite its long tenure and strong presence in the movie entertainment distribution business, it had also met with criticism from users in areas regarding claims of negative option, unfair shipping charges, and challenging customer service issues.

YEARS OF CUSTOMER COMPLAINTS

Columbia House was famously known for their "13 CDs for a Penny" Promotion that they ran for decades from the time they started selling Records to CDs and eventually DVDs. As enticing as this was, customers complained about the "fine details" disclosure: While customers only paid a penny for the 13 products, they also had to pay $1.99 shipping for each product. In the end it cost the customer far more than "just" a penny.

What's more, Columbia House had a reputation for sending customers the "selection of the month" products unless the company actually received a return mailer "explicitly' requesting the customer not receive the selection of the month.

Customers had consistently complained about these practices to no avail. It was only when Columbia House initiated some focus group research did they realize how angered many of their customers were.

THE REVAMP

So a new company was started in Canada – with a new business model that responded to many of these consumer claims in hopes of starting fresh, recruiting a new support base and migrating its loyal customer base.

The new company launched November 2008 and its positioning has been evident on their website: CH Canada.com "Welcome to the NEW Columbia House…You spoke, we listened…No more unwanted shipments…"

REPUTATION PRECEDES…

While Columbia House was aware of the focus group findings, they were unaware of the extent of the damage that lay in their wake.

A simple search "I hate Columbia House" netted almost 700,000 search results. Unlike traditional research, the comments were in social media spaces for years… and for the world to see. They remained unchallenged and were never responded to.

Initial social insights were conducted around the brand and its competitors in the weeks before launch to validate the new business model.

What CHCanada discovered was a wealth of passionate conversation both positive and negative about the very topics (…and then some) that instigated the business change. One small site called Ripoff Report with a reported audience of about 100,000 visitors per month housed customer posts that included complaints of customer service, involvement of collection agencies etc.

The company noticed, at the same time, the number strong advocate discussions that had gone unleveraged.

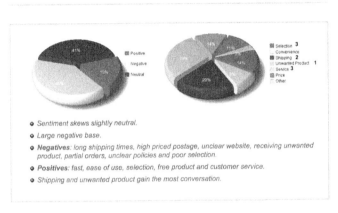

- Sentiment skews slightly neutral.
- Large negative base.
- **Negatives**: long shipping times, high priced postage, unclear website, receiving unwanted product, partial orders, unclear policies and poor selection.
- **Positives**: fast, ease of use, selection, free product and customer service.
- Shipping and unwanted product gain the most conversation.

What CH had realized was that a comment posted many months or even years ago, could strongly influence those who had seen the discussion for the very first time.

These strong conversations could very well hamper a successful launch of the new business model.

In addition, as is the plight of most Canadian subsidiaries, any strong changes implemented locally were still "blips" in the overall map and did little to positively impact the overall Columbia House brand... the US parent Columbiahouse.com that still retained the original business model.

THE CHALLENGE... UNFOLDS

It was clear that this revamped business of a highly visible and established brand like Columbia House had already been marred by a history of deceptive business practices. They needed to overcome this hurdle and convince customers it changed before they could hope to drive to the new model.

The Objective:
- Increase consumer awareness of the new CH Canada brand while emphasizing the differentiation from the old Columbia House
- At the same time, shift consumers' negative perception.

The Prescription:
The key to ensuring a successful launch of CHCanada.com was to provide a brand voice in the social sphere.

The Approach:
- Identify conversations now and begin to go head to head with detractors, clarify misperceptions, eat some crow and gain some credibility for turning around the business model.
- Call on strong advocates for Columbia House brand to help CH build voice within the forums.

The latter, we assumed, would take time. We needed to develop trust with significant community members before this was remotely possible.

BECOME PART OF THE COMMUNITY

So CHCanada began engaging in conversation. We quickly identified three DVD and Blu-Ray forums where strong discourse existed about Columbia House.

The most difficult efforts included confronting its detractors. We surmised that if we could win over the detractors, then that would be half the battle. We assumed those turned-detractors-into-advocates would help pave the way for the new brand to emerge.

Honesty, transparency, and humility were the order of the day. Applying this strategy has allowed forum members to welcome CHCanada to the thread. By letting forum members understand what CH had done to change, and by openly asking people for their honest opinions and questions, CH had been able to eventually build trust.

The Marketing Manager of CHCanada, Rob Weatherall, who was very new to social media, found himself troubleshooting customer claims that had been in the system for some time. One by one, he was able to fix many of the problems that were thrown at him in these forums. He soon found out that this was consuming much of his time. However, in the process, he was slowly gaining the trust and more importantly, the respect of many of these forum members.

Along the way, not all forum members were quick to welcome CHCanada with open arms. It's not surprising that they "Googled" each of the community names to validate who we were and what we were saying.

From time to time we were met with accusations of SPAM and have been banned from sites. But overall, our presence in key forums made an incredible impact on CHCanada's reputation, its organic search listings, and had resulted in ever increasing positive sentiment in favor of CHCanada vs. its US parent.

THE 24-HOUR TEST

Once Rob had reached significant status within the forums, he was now in a position to ask the community for something in return.

He told them about the new business model and wanted their input in helping him develop programs that people would buy. He crowd sourced their favorite movie titles. And when he inquired if there was one thing they wanted out of a promotion, the answer was clear: Free Shipping.

Once Rob had this information, we developed a program to determine how strongly these relationships would return for Rob and CH Canada. The program was structured this way:

- The top 10 movie titles crowd sourced
- Free shipping
- Period 24 hours ONLY: starting midnight Tuesday
- Promotion ONLY in the two forums. We isolated this promotion to ensure we had a clean measurement.

STELLAR RESULTS

Orders started pouring in minutes after the promotion was posted. Within hours the 24 Hour post had been reposted on peripheral forums like Red Flag Deals, Twitter and other Blue-Ray and DVD Forums where CH Canada were less engaged. The CH Community was advocating the promotion like mad. Sales went through the roof in this short time period.

- Compared to other channels: Affiliate and PPC, this social media posting drove the highest ROI at 7%.
- 24-hr free shipping offers yielded 731% increase over average daily orders.
- Total revenue from 24 Free-shipping offers equivalent to 33% of revenue generated for an average month.

Ongoing Testing and Optimization

Once we were able to gain favor among forum members, we were able to develop a few strategies to help optimize ongoing sales efforts.

Social media training for staff participating in social media.

- Set-up Facebook, Twitter, and DVD forum and Blu-Ray forum accounts to highlight ongoing deals; as well as take an active role in engaging with customers and prospects.
- Content Strategy and Management: weekly calendar for promotions, crowd-sourcing and relevant content i.e. new releases, and trailers.
- Influencer Outreach Strategy, research and management – identification of strong voices within influencing discussions to help build CHCanada voice.
- Daily engagement included:
  ◊ Crowdsourcing: asking customers about service issues, product preferences, promotion suggestions etc.
  ◊ Forum/Twitter engagement came to double as a customer service channel.
- Monthly tracking results: visits, engagement, sales by true attribution, optimization opportunities.

STRONG ADVOCACY:

More important than the results was the outpouring of advocacy in the forums

I'm amazed at how much they try to make everyone happy & take in their input.

Just another vote FOR CH Canada. I've had no problem with numerous orders from them, along with great prices, occasional free shipping, and bonus DVDs.

....short version, I give a thumbs-up to CH Canada.... I have no complaints and would easily recommend CHC.

while i haven't ordered from chcanada in quite time, i still frequent the thread and certainly appreciate the some comments and initiative shown by the chcanada staff. when is the last time you saw an amazon or futureshop/BB rep come in and ask us what we like? NEVER!!

This topic cloud is indicative of the positive consumer perceptions surrounding the brand. Within 4 months the new model, CHCanada was perceived as the Blu-Ray provider of choice among influential Movie DVD and Blu-Ray forums

THE TESTIMONIAL

Rob Weatherall, Marketing Manager of CHCanada had indicated,

"Entering into the realm of social networking I knew this was something that needed to be done but was quite skeptical what impact it would have on my

business. Within a couple of months of launching our program, I clearly saw the positive impact this media was going to have. Social networking not only provided an open line of communication with customers, it also provided a product/offer testing arena, an ever-ready focus group, a source of testimonials, and for this business – our highest value customers."

Beyond Sales: The Business KPI's of Marketing ROI

By this point we all know that at the end of the day the top priority of marketing should be to create customers for the business– whatever the business may be.

As a Marketer, you live in a world that is adding channels on a seemingly daily basis, while, at the same time the consumers', attention is being drawn in a hundred different directions, making it increasingly difficult for any brand (especially those without an endless budget) to stand out.

In the end the mission is sales; I think we all agree that when we invest in marketing we seek a return. More often than not those upstairs writing the checks and controlling the budget want marketing to drive more sales. But in a world of short attention spans and unprecedented options are there key performance indicators (KPI's) that should be attached to marketing and social media efforts that span beyond just customer acquisition and sales?

The short answer is yes, there are, and while these new KPI's should, by no means, replace the onus on Marketers to create customers and revenue, they do measure different aspects of a business that are equally, if not more important, for long term performance than their traditional counterparts. In the vastly evolving landscape of marketing, the new KPI's must also reflect the following:

- **Customer Retention:** How successful are we in keeping customers and building repeat business?
- **Customer Satisfaction:** Are our customers happy? How well are we doing at getting them to share their satisfaction to build word of mouth?

- **Product Improvements/Optimization:** Is our community driving ideas to help us innovate? Whether products or services, do we have our finger on the pulse and how much are our customers helping us accomplish this?
- **Employee Productivity:** Does the company adequately equip and empower employees to succeed?
- **Employee Retention:** Are we creating a brand that employees are proud of and a place of work where they can grow personally and professionally?

HAPPIER CUSTOMERS, BETTER PRODUCTS, SATISFIED EMPLOYEES

The business of the future should not simply measure their marketing by the dollar value returns that it generates.

If you look at the numerous studies that have shown the value of a satisfied customer or the return on stronger employee morale, you would have to be crazy to dismiss these items when determining the success of a marketing program.

The question remains: is it possible to measure the direct value of investing in customer satisfaction?

For instance, Zappos, from their earliest days, set out to build the ultimate customer experience. With almost a "Never-say-no-to-a-reasonable (or unreasonable) customer demand," their customer experience teams will do whatever it takes to maintain a happy customer.

I suppose a Marketer may say that is a customer service expense, but I would beg to differ. When an unhappy customers' situation is flipped on its head by a small expense approved by an empowered customer service professional, what you have is an investment in your customer. Furthermore, the cost of replacing a customer is 6x the cost of retention, so why wouldn't we want to keep our customers happy?

Another great example is the way companies like Dell and Starbucks use online communities to drive product development and innovation. Both have invested substantially in building their brand evangelists by making their most loyal customers feel welcome, and by listening to their ideas and input and sometimes even using them for product optimization.

While Steve Jobs may have been known for never putting his ear to the street and just "knowing" what his customers want, he was the exception and not the rule. Companies that can find ways to listen and adapt to their customer feedback can build a new type of loyalty that translates into dollar returns. The challenge again is how do you attribute that to a campaign? Is it even possible?

WHERE MARKETING ROI IS HEADING

In the future Marketing ROI will have to spread its wings to move beyond customer creation and measurable dollar value returns. However, I want to be clear when I say that doesn't mean those activities aren't important, because they are.

The chart below provides a clear picture of where Social Media has evolved in its short lifespan. Laurie Dillon Schalk, Sr. Planner at DraftFCB developed this roadmap to Social Media Maturity that is defining the way business must revamp to better manage the new order KPIs, and at the same time, become a more dynamic and customer responsive culture.

While Social Media has been around for almost a decade, it is still a nascent channel with many unknowns. Organizations continue to learn and discover its true value, but with much resistance. It continues to be managed within Marketing and PR, with the majority of businesses adopting no more than a "Look and Listen" or "Establish a Social Footprint" presence.

Engagement is difficult and takes strong commitment and resource consistency. However, if your organization becomes more engaged you will have the right marketing tools to validate the impacts beyond just follower growth. By this stage, if you've identified the most passionate conversations and the movers of the message you will be rich in the insights. This will allow your organization to begin analyzing impacts of communities, individuals, and content, as they relate to the business objectives. Closer to ROI, right?

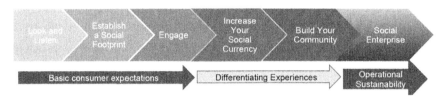

Monitor conversation	Social platforms: FB, LI, Twitter, Foursquare	Define voice and tone	Start conversations	Reach out to brand advocates	Address issues driving complaints
Regular reporting	Media sites: Youtube, Flickr, Instagram, Pinterest	Engage existing networks	Custom response	Empower external advocates	Social commerce
Social media education	Blogs and podcasts, forums and boards	Participate in existing conversations	Non-social content goes social	Empower internal advocates	Develop internal data workflow processes
Monitor growth of emerging technology	Supported by SEO	Respond to wall, comments	Geo-targeting social, mobile	Allow for community defense	Adapt products, services and policies
Clear ownership and governance	Active growth of social asset base	Quality vs. quantity follower refinement	Appropriate staffing (governance)	Location-based community building	Collaboration systems among all stakeholders
	Designate community manager	Design for social longevity	Social and web integration	Identify social influence	Social CRM
Social media monitoring tools		Social marketing tools	Advanced social analytics	Content management and curation	Social Media ROI

By this stage we begin to see some serious impacts on other areas of the business. The creation and continued evolution of metrics that measure the baseline value of more satisfied customers, the involvement of a brand's community in product development and the investment in more satisfied employees – will all become anchor points in the process of building a marketing strategy.

Once your organization has "bought into" Social Media, you will begin to take proactive steps to create more differentiated experiences, like Columbia House. These newly developed practices from identifying the right discussion to developing governance policies begin to open doors to possibilities as technology is introduced to identify and map communities, curate content and moderate discussion.

Next comes the establishment of a social enterprise where operations will become more nimble with the market. Community development gives way to brand advocacy, as much stronger voices advocating for your organization are empowered and nurtured. Slowly the systems, the culture, and the processes begin to morph to respond to a dynamic and unrelenting customer voice.

The new KPIs become the norm that will ultimately impact customer churn, product adaption, customer satisfaction scores, inventory management etc.

Perhaps the biggest difference will be the way smarter businesses big and small will apply the new marketing KPI's to enhance their marketing 24/7/365. Ultimately this will impact the broader business to mitigate customer churn, adapt products to market, improve customer satisfaction scores, and optimize inventory management. Rather than placing a hyperawareness on the peaks and valleys created by a traditional marketing strategy, the evolved organization will be able to build loyalty within the brands' stakeholders.

This is where true Marketing ROI comes to fruition.

Community Takes Time but Consistency and Commitment Unearths Significant Benefits

THE POWER OF RELATIONSHIPS by Tim MacDonald

If you have ever traveled to a small town, you know the kind with one stoplight on Main Street? You probably noticed a gentleman sitting on the bench in front of the general store. He had a few other people engaging him in conversation, sharing laughs or just observing the weather. This person wasn't the mayor, didn't own a business or have a lot of money. What he did have was solid relationships with everyone in town. He could connect people from opposite sides of town who probably wouldn't talk to each other on their own. He would connect people with other people when he knew what they wanted to buy, and knew who was selling it (long before Craigslist and the internet existed).

And for anyone traveling through town, he would become the source of information for where to eat, who could fix your car or where to get the best haircut. Not only would you know where to go, you would also know what to expect once you got there.

Communities have existed well before "online." So many people think social media changed the game, and it has changed the speed at which we communicate and with whom we can connect. It has not changed the core concept of what has made communities work for ages: relationships.

Managing online communities is about building relationships. A salesperson doesn't get measured on how strong their relationships are with customers, only on how much they sell. However, you won't find many salespeople that would deny building relationships helps them in the selling process, and makes it easier to know where your price needs to be, how quickly you need to deliver and who your competition is.

The recruiting departments in companies love employee referrals for two reasons: 1) They tend to refer high performers and 2) it saves the company money. All these referrals come from relationships that your employees have. Your R&D team could reduce costs and time by not having to pay for focus groups and can receive live-time feedback on new features.

Many businesses look at social media as a function of marketing, but when you build relationships you build community. If relationship building is one to one, how does a business scale this? Not by adding resources, but by enabling the community itself to scale.

Look at what No Kid Hungry has done with their social presence. They have listened to their community on social, seen who is most active, who has the most response, and most importantly, who actually does what they say they are going to. They then pick some of the most passionate community members and ask if they want to join the social council. The social council members become advocates for No Kid Hungry. Instead of having one brand spreading your message and building relationships, you now have the brand plus twenty individuals, all with unique communities of their own.

On Giving Tuesday in 2013, No Kid Hungry utilized the relationships they had built with the Social Council and worked raised over $31,000 in a 24-hour period. The conversation using social media for #NoKidHungry had nearly the same Twitter timeline deliveries as #GivingTuesday had. That's 114.7 million timeline deliveries! With over 10,000 organizations participating on Giving Tuesday last year, No Kid Hungry was clearly leading the way with the conversation on Twitter.

Even though this case was a non-profit with a cause, every organization has a group of passionate community members. Don't think yours does? I've seen it with Fiscars (scissors), DeWalt (tools), Applebee's (restaurant), Magento (ecommerce) and many more. If you don't think you have a passionate community, you probably haven't been listening intently enough. Communities are built on relationships. Have you started building yours?

 Tim MacDonald builds communities, not networks, through individual relationships that create movements. Tim believes in Purpose Driven Passion. He's the Purveyor of Purpose at Be The Change Revolutions, the co-founder of Creating-Is, and formerly the Director of Community for the Huffington Post.

The Awesome Power of Community: How I Became the Anti-Marketer

I've told this story countless times but this event played a significant part in my life. It's what Oprah would deem, "my defining moment'... a time that changed the way I thought about marketing, dismissing what I've learned, and began to embrace a new way of thinking. When this happened to me, I became somewhat of a purist and it has brought me to where I am today.

Social Networking is a phenomenon that has gained incredible strength and continues to flourish. An old boss of mine assumed it would die, arguing:

"Social Networks will never be able to effectively monetize themselves...."

He said this when Facebook surreptitiously, but swiftly, found an online audience, whose mindshare was largely captured by the "then" powerful Big 3: Yahoo!, MSN and Google... at the time.

In the last 8 years, Facebook's rise has baffled advertisers, as the next-generation of Marketers learn how to tap into users in this space. A significant shift has resulted where Marketers realize that traditional advertising on the web is slowly becoming obsolete, and appealing to consumers means having to change the mediums, the means, and the methods by which we communicate.

WHERE I CAME FROM

I've worked at both agencies and banks, trying to understand the data triggers that influence people to purchase. When my family would ask what I did, I told them I was in the junk mail business… you remember: the direct mail you received in your mailbox that you usually threw in the wastebasket? That didn't really matter to me because as a Marketer, we didn't need everyone to respond and purchase. We only needed 2% of you to actually raise your hand and say, "I want that." Over the course of time, we could validate that 2% would provide a positive return on the marketing spend.

MY INTRODUCTION INTO SOCIAL

I didn't buy into community instantly although I managed the launch of Yahoo! Answers, one of the few social search products in market at the time. Its premise: Leverage community to provide valuable information based on experience – something algorithmic search could not provide at the time. Google was still largely keyword-based.

Unlike other social search products, Answers did not rely on expert advice from pundits in their fields, but the common person, whose life experiences provided the source of answers to many questions.

WHEN SOMETHING DEEPLY PERSONAL HAPPENS

The turning point for me came when I was attending a Search Summit in the UK, working with other international product and marketing people who were also launching Yahoo! Answers in their respective regions. I received an email from a friend who informed me that my former VP's daughter had passed away from Leukemia, something she'd been battling for 6 years. She was only 10 years old. I had lost touch with my boss over the years but I did remember her daughter, Hannah. While her mom tried to put on a brave face, Hannah was incredibly optimistic about her condition, always willing to talk about her condition in the most positive light. And she was willing to educate others about the advances in medicine that would make her better. Leukemia was not a hindrance to Hannah. It was a bump in the road.

I was saddened by the news and I wanted to reach out to my friend and give her some comfort. I was reminded of a poem that my Mom had shown. It was poignant and yet comforting – about a child that predeceases the parent. It spoke of God loaning the child to its parents for a time and then, at some point, calling the child home.

I emailed my Mom and asked her about it and, while she remembered the poem, she didn't know where to find it. I asked the rest of my family if they knew about it, but the response was same. I was obsessed with finding it. It was important that I give this to my friend. I searched for the poem online not really knowing the author or any of the words — just the context. I did this for some time with no luck.

TURNING TO SOCIAL MEDIA FOR ANSWERS

Someone from my team suggested I give Yahoo! Answers a try. At the time, Yahoo! Answers was very new. It had launched in the U.S. a month earlier and its community was small, yet growing. I was hesitant. I didn't think there was any way that this new community would give me what I was looking for.

With my avenues exhausted I sent my question into the unknown world of the Answers Community, skeptical of what I would receive.

So I waited. The Answers team told me that the average response time was approximately 4-5 hours. It took awhile. One day turned into two as I become more pessimistic about anyone ever providing me an answer. I was looking for a needle in a haystack. I started to question the effectiveness of the platform.

My friend's daughter passed away. What poem talks about God giving us his child for a time & may take him bk?

I don't know the author. I am desperately looking for this poem. It talks about the mother not fretting because the child was here for a while and was happy but will be happy again with God. Can you help?

THE RESPONSE THAT WOULD FOREVER CHANGE ME

The response came 9 days later. And it made me cry.

Best Answer Asker's Choice

Blade answered 9 years ago

I am not sure about the exact one you are looking for but I found another on the internet:

I'll lend you for a little time a child of mine, He said ...
For you to love the while he lives ... and mourn for when he's dead.
It may be six or seven years, or twenty-two and three,

But will you, till I call him back, take care of him for me?

He'll bring his charms to gladden you. And shall his stay be brief,
You'll have his lovely memories as solace for your grief.

I cannot promise he will stay, since all from Earth return.
But there are lessons, taught down there, I want this child to learn.

I've looked the wide world over in search for teachers true,

And from the throngs that crowd life's lanes, I have selected you.

Now ... will you give him all your love ... nor think the labor in vain?

Nor ... hate me when I come to call ... to take him back again?

I fancied that I heard you say ...
"Dear Lord, it will be done!

"For all the joy Your Child shall bring, the risk of grief we'll run.

"We'll shelter him with tenderness. We'll love him while we may.

"And for the happiness we've known ... forever grateful stay.

"But shall the angels call for him much sooner than we've planned,
"We'll brave the bitter grief that comes ... and try to understand." *

Someone out there had the answer. I connected with Blade and she became my first connection across this community. She gave to me something that was incredibly meaningful and important to me. She didn't know me, but when we connected, she told me that when she saw my question, she immediately remembered a poem that had a similar context. It took her little time to find what I was seemingly-forever looking for.

We often talk about the power of community and online relationships that develop without two people ever meeting face to face. Since that moment, I've met countless colleagues and close friends online. I've espoused the notion of community and its strength to influence mindsets and behavior. I have experienced this time and time again. It's what I've come to know and fundamentally embrace. This mindset is shared by others as well. The ability for community to influence purchase behavior and build loyalty for brands is a very real phenomenon.

Brands: Don't Underestimate the Power of Community

Perhaps nothing drives a brand forward more than its community. Knowing that 55% of consumers are willing to recommend [1] companies that deliver great experiences and 85% are willing to pay a premium [2] for those services, who are those "People" making those recommendations? It is your community, right?
One thing I'm certain of is that if I asked most CMO's and Marketing Leaders how they define their brand's community I would get a different answer from each.

This subjectivity is further driven by the wide variance in how different brands are seen, heard and felt [3] by their community. More or less, how connected are they to the brand?

Think about Apple for instance; the company is frequently used as an example due to their powerful brand recognition, but have you considered how influential Apple's community has been on the success of the brand?

To further envision what I mean, think of the last "Apple Fan" that you have talked to about Apple or Apple Competitive products?

What did that conversation look like?

If your experience is anything like mine, chances are the conversation went wonderfully so long as you agreed with how wonderful Apple products are. However, if you dare to question the products, ideas or innovation of Apple to an "Apple Fan," be warned, for you have just crossed into enemy territory. It is almost as if you are telling your child that Santa isn't real, only worse.

What is the catalyst for this insanely powerful connection that Apple has with its community?

By and large Apple isn't a highly social company, so they aren't doing it using standard methods through Facebook and Twitter etc. Apple has brought together a worldwide community by creating a feeling of belonging that its users get when they utilize their products.

Their slogan, "Think Differently" defines their cult-like following because people who want to be seen as creative, broad thinkers can often be found attached to their MacBook inside a Starbucks somewhere; almost as if the presence of an Apple product defines who they are.

For Apple this works. Through their idea of being cool, different and innovative they have built one of the tightest brand communities on and off the web.

However, like you, I know that Apple is an established 'Gazillion' dollar company, leaving us to ask, how do other brands, smaller, newer brands tap into the power of community?

NOT JUST A COMMUNITY, A CLOSE COMMUNITY

Think about the neighborhood you grew up in.

What was it like? Was it urban or rural? Were there many houses or just a few? Did you know your neighbors or were they merely passing strangers?

Regardless of the shape, size and geography, most neighborhoods have some sense of community. However, they aren't all the same. Where I grew up there was a "Community Center" which was a place where folks from the neighborhood would come to congregate.

The closer the community, the more they would work together to get things done: Like the installation of a Stop Sign in a critical area where kids play, or the passing of a referendum to build a new school.

With the shift from more traditional urban settings to modern subdivisions, communities were intentionally created, like the Neighborhood Watch, a Board of Directors and sometimes, their own pool and recreation center.

This intentional community brought all the stakeholders closer by creating greater visibility to what was happening in their neighborhood AND by helping the community see the impact of everyone's involvement.

BUILDING A BRAND COMMUNITY
LIKE A NEIGHBOURHOOD

When you boil it down to its most simplistic form, a community is made up of those who are stakeholders in your brand.

The reason I use the word stakeholder rather than customer is that many people beyond just those that purchase your products and services can become part of a brand's community.

First there are the obvious extensions such as employees and friends. Then there are the less obvious community builders such as those who are interested in learning more about your products and services.

Here is an example:

When I was 14 years old (1995) my favorite car in the whole world was the new Pontiac Grand Prix. They had just changed it to the wide track and as a 14 year old I thought it was one bad machine.

However, at 14, I wasn't legally or financially able to buy a car.

4 years later when I was 18 and I had scraped together all the loose change from under the sofa cushions, I was ready to buy a car. Guess what I bought? The Grand Prix of course!

That is because I had emotionally tied myself to the brand, the car, and the community, and when I was ready to consume it wasn't even a question which company would earn my business.

While my story is just one example, this type of brand loyalty can be seen to a greater or lesser extent with everything from the food we eat to the jeans we wear and beyond.

When people become a part of something, [4] their purchasing sentiment changes and guess what, so does the way they evangelize for your product.

You think someone that likes your product is a good ambassador [5], just think of someone who has bought your product and likes it. That is another great frontier for brand building, which takes us back to building a close-knit community. It requires a setting for cultivation and nurturing, much like a neighborhood, only different to suit the needs of the brand and its community.

COMMUNITY IN THE CONNECTED WORLD

If you think about the example of the neighborhood, you will usually think that a good community is small, tight knit and somewhat directionally aligned.

In the new world, the connected world, where we have communities on our blog, our Facebook Page, our Twitter Account and what seems like a million other places, the idea of community can become pretty daunting.

This is because the "Internet of Things" is profoundly big, and this "Massiveness" is really difficult for most Marketers to break down into something meaningful.

Most often this leads to brands making a few mistakes.

1. **They aim too large:** This is where they go for mere numbers (Page Visits, Likes, Followers, etc.)
2. **They don't engage:** Communicating with a digital community can seem like a daunting task.
3. **They Miss Out:** Online communities are a powerful way to build influential brand advocates [6] but sometimes inaction takes over when brands don't know where to start.

While these mistakes are commonly made, they can be avoided by following a few common sense tactics.

1. **Aim for Relevance:** Rather than shooting for a large community, start by aiming for those that are most likely to buy your product/service now or in the near future. Also, when it comes to online networks, especially social, find out where your target audience is and go there first.

2. **Engage More Than You Promote:** Share your stories, ideas and information, but make sure you allow the community to become part of the conversation. Ask more questions, build more testimonials and case studies, and invite participation.

3. **Start:** Even if your "Start" is small, don't miss the opportunity to build a community by putting your head in the sand.

REMEMBER THAT BUILDING A COMMUNITY CAN TAKE TIME

Apple does have an amazing community of insanely loyal brand advocates. They also nearly crashed and burned on multiple occasions and were saved by the innovation of how music was consumed on a tiny little MP3 player.

For most businesses not named Apple, community takes time and real work to build.

This goes from the core of building products and services that your customers love, to building places for them to congregate and talk about your products.

On the flip side building communities requires brands to also acknowledge their shortcomings and respond transparently when things go poorly.

Think about the kind of community rebuilding brands like Target and Snap Chat will have to do following their security breaches.
Neither of these incidents was intentional by the brand, but in both instances it cost the brand trust, and their community response needed to be monumental to rebuild that trust.

The beauty of community, however, is that when you build it, nurture it and engage with it, it will help your brand in good times and in bad. While never perfect, like your family, your neighborhood or your city, the community that is your brand is one of the most powerful tools in the connected world.

COMMUNITY AT PLAY THE RIGHT WAY

It's clear that community takes time to build. All good things do, but there is a clear path to advocacy, conversion and sustainability. Companies that build communities the right way will find strength in leveraging these relationships to be better as a company, drive better products, develop strong customer experiences and eventually drive sales time and time again.

What does building a community look like? For every business it is unique; in all cases, it means a strategy is required. Let's take a look at an example of the maturation of an online community in the online media and gaming space.

CASE STUDY: Gygax Magazine - When Community Goes Right By Susan Silver

Gary Gygax said "I would like the world to remember me as the guy who really enjoyed playing games and sharing his knowledge and his fun pastimes with everybody else." I wonder what my legacy will be.

As I sat down to call Jayson Elliot, the editor-in-chief of Gygax Magazine, my own feelings towards Dungeons & Dragons were bubbling in my mind. Role Playing Games (RPGs) have an unfortunate stigma for an activity that comes naturally to us as humans. Very young children play games similar to those I play with friends. The main difference is one happens on a playground with a loose structure and our games happen around a table with a player's handbook to guide our choices.

Point forward: I believe everyone is a gamer. This is the attitude I expressed when I met with Jayson for our first phone call. People who play games are my friends. I want to have more friends therefore I want to include more people under the gaming umbrella. Everyone is a potential friend that I haven't met.

This set the tone immediately for what Gygax Magazine's online presence would become.

HOW DOES ONE GENERATE AN INCLUSIVE COMMUNITY SET AGAINST A VOLATILE HISTORY?

There are a lot of issues confronting a brand focused around gaming and in particular Tabletop RPGs.

Edition Wars

Debates around editions get very heated. This was something that we have to be careful about because the magazine is system agnostic. The adventures published are meant to be adapted by reader as needed. These arguments are deeply tied to the history of our hobby. You cannot enter into any community without knowledge of its past, particularly in online discussions.

Creating a Safe Community

We had to set a tone early on that was inclusive of all who have a gaming identity, including those whose voices are not heard in online discussions. This meant creating a safe space where people could express their point of view without being challenged. We worked with the community to let them know there were boundaries and if crossed they would no longer be welcome.

Communications

The gaming industry has become one where the majority of publishers are independent. They have a small, but loyal, cadre of customers. The biggest issue is usually around communications because these companies are often understaffed. Social media is a tool that works for and against us at times.

Gygax Magazine had already existed for several months as an idea shared by Jayson Elliot and his business partners Ernest Gary Gygax Jr., Luke Gygax, and Tim Kask. I had discovered the existence of the magazine only due to a leak. This put the magazine at a disadvantage because it garnered interest but just wasn't ready yet. The inquiries were flooding the inboxes of staff and this became my first challenge to overcome.

COMMUNITIES DEVELOP ORGANICALLY BASED ON THE CHOICES THAT WE MAKE

I was not concerned with growing the community at first. The leak had caused an influx of PR opportunities and we needed to leap on them while the momentum was there. My primary tasks were responding to individuals, the press, and building our relationships with key stakeholders. My goal was to sustain what we had garnered through luck and use it to promote our company. But we were a company without a product.

It became clear that the magazine was still a few months or more away from being complete. While the staff hoped for a January 1st 2013 deadline, due to many factors, that was no longer looking possible. Our community was growing at a healthy clip without much influence from us. Our next challenge was keeping people happy while they waited for the magazine to go on sale.

One of the great things about RPGs includes the talents that develop the storylines, game mechanics, characters, and illustrations. These worlds are born through collaboration between peers. This is enduringly true from the perspective of game publishers and those who play the game. We work together to bring life to these settings.

Our first social media marketing campaign was simple: highlight our contributors and share resources that would show off their portfolios.

The biggest gains for the brand for this campaign came from our growing social media numbers. We were racking up Likes, comments, and Follows. It became clear, through the data, that Facebook was our strongest channel and that became the cornerstone of our community strategy. We were creating an online presence that demanded attention beyond what was in the magazine. We were showing that we also understood the online gaming culture.

WHEN DO YOU HAVE COMMUNITY?

When I started with Gygax Magazine in December of 2012 the social media accounts already had a following of 1,000. People had gathered, but their motive of following was to receive updates on the progress of the magazine. This was not enough for me. Community isn't about numbers. It is about creating a space where the individuals share at least one connection, the emotional investment in your product.

I will say, at this point, we had captured the curiosity of those in the gaming hobby. People were waiting in anticipation for our next move. This kept our engagement rates high from the get go. This also meant that the magazine was more of a spectacle than anything else at this point.

The real challenge of building the community was connecting this group together with something more enduring than our future product. We all know that a company's offerings will evolve over time. The customers you have today will not look like the ones you will have tomorrow. Your company is going to grow and you need a thread that people can follow from your first product to your latest.

I didn't want our community to be based upon the experiences of those who already play. We know we are awesome. I wanted to know what would feel most welcoming to someone new to the hobby. I made a key assumption: treat our community as if everything was new. I thought carefully about the rites of passage related to Dungeons & Dragons (D&D). I went over my own history, retracing the path that led me to becoming a player.

What had felt most welcoming? What is that every gamer needs?

Every RPG requires some element of random chance and D&D represents this in the form of a unique dice set: the d4, d6, d8, d10, d12, d20 and the percentile die.

A person's first dice set is incredibly personal. There is an industry within gaming responsible for the production of these dice sets. They came in all manner of sizes and colors. Some are even made from unique materials like precious stones. Chessex and Game Science are two companies that specialize in manufacturing dice for RPGs.

I made the request for the community to send in pictures of their dice collections. These posts on Facebook proved to be our most viral and were the first to gain active comment threads. It turned out people loved comparing their own collections to those featured.

DID WE HAVE COMMUNITY YET?

Yes, I felt that there was telling evidence of this fact. People who commented began tagging their Facebook friends to respond. They were actively recruiting people to our page. We didn't ask them to, it just kept happening. We soon found that our Facebook presence was beginning to transform from a place to get information into a place where people went to hang out.

I began to notice a strange pattern. The majority of traffic to Facebook was not coming from people seeing updates in feeds. Our community actively sought out our page and would spend time responding to or liking new updates. People who already liked the page were coming through to see what they had missed.

I believe this is why the Gygax Magazine Facebook page continues to thrive despite the crisis of Facebook Zero. We've only experimented a few times with paid ads, but they didn't perform. Without a doubt, our community grew organically based on the enthusiasm of the people who banded together to personally promote our page.

THE GAMING FAMILY

Gary Gygax's words exemplify the attitude of players. Gamer is just another label, a stereotype, and no one person in the hobby fits the outside perception held by people. We certainly have our issues, but you find they are similar to what you encounter anytime a group gathers together. At heart, we are people with a fun hobby that we want to share with others because it is meaningful in our own lives.

That is why I was first drawn to Gygax Magazine. I wanted to preserve that legacy. I took a proactive approach by showing the ways gaming empowers people doing good in the world.

I shared stories about:
◊   Educators using RPGs to teach
◊   Kids who use gaming to raise funds for charity
◊   Cool or unique places related to the hobby that people could visit
◊   DIY projects
◊   Plays, movies, and books inspired by D&D
◊   Little know history or origins of games

I especially enjoyed sharing the stories of parents who were playing D&D with their children.

These are stories that you don't always see in mainstream media, but are very real examples of how this hobby enriches people's lives.

I would like this to be your take away as you begin building a community of your own. The cognitive and emotional aspects of behaviors are also associated with the data they generate. When performing an analysis do not neglect to consider the hopes, dreams, desires and frustrations of your customers. As you begin to make choices there will be a real emotional impact on the members of your community that will also influence their behavior. That is a relationship that needs to be respected and nurtured.

Community building is hard. Sustaining community takes much more commitment. We know this. We've done it. From the viewpoint of someone who has extensive community experience, Susan Silver, this provides perspective of a Day in the Life...

COMMUNITY MANAGERS ANTICIPATE NEEDS: WHY YOU MUST DEVELOP YOUR COMPANY RADAR By Susan Silver

Community managers fulfill a very important niche in the work place, not unlike the company clerk Radar O'Reilly in M*A*S*H. The company clerk's real name was Walter, but he earned the nickname Radar for his sixth sense, which allowed him to anticipate the needs of his commanding officer before he was asked. His other talent was the ability to warn the doctors and nurses of incoming wounded by sensing approaching helicopters. In a similar fashion, your community manager is on the front lines of your business vigilantly attending to the needs of the customer and company.

"All community managers manage some form of digital/social community, but the best ones inspire those communities to take action, and they take proactive steps to become better representatives for their brands."

– Six Tips for Better Community Management on #CMAD (Community Manager Appreciation Day) 2013 [7]

The term Community Manager means different things to different organizations, especially if they are not clear on what managing a community is all about. Here it is plain and simple:

Community managers anticipate needs by listening to customers, acting as customer advocates, and expressing the values of their company culture.

COMMUNITY MANAGERS CREATE BEHAVIORAL MODELS BASED ON COMMUNITY CHATTER AND DATA

At the heart of it, a community manager's role is that of active listener.
They monitor conversations about their company wherever they occur and are usually the first to respond. These conversations make us aware of the Zeitgeist of our communities. Simply put, the Zeitgeist is the spirit of your community and includes the attitudes, beliefs, culture, and prevailing opinions contained within them.

I will admit that I am using the definition of Zeitgeist loosely here because it actually refers to a period of time or an age. But there are moments in time that community managers' note. We pay attention to the milestones and points of growth of our communities. We can look back and analyze what methods lead to success in those moments, which allows us to create a model of community behavior.

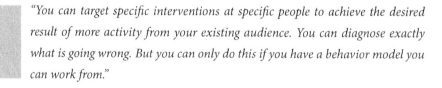

"You can target specific interventions at specific people to achieve the desired result of more activity from your existing audience. You can diagnose exactly what is going wrong. But you can only do this if you have a behavior model you can work from."

Applying Behavioral Models to Online Communities [8]

COMMUNITY MANAGERS ADVOCATE THE NEEDS OF CUSTOMERS BEFORE IT IS REQUIRED

A good community manager will not only be available for crisis communications, but will act before one starts.

I found the following presentation on slide share fascinating. Jenise Fryatt identifies an important requirement for a community manager.

"It is essential that your community manager be hypersensitive to the 'energy in the room,' so to speak."

7 Traits of Highly Effective Community Managers [9]

It sometimes only takes a simple comment to stop a flow of negative commentary from customers. Only someone embedded in the community can do this because they understand the nuances of the culture within. They understand the history of that community and can appropriately gauge its reactions to incoming messages.

COMMUNITY MANAGERS EXPRESS COMPANY CULTURE AND CREATE SOCIAL NORMS THAT REPRESENT VALUES

I was lucky to get a ticket to the first CMX summit. It was a historic event as the largest gathering of community managers from around the world and across different markets. One presentation stood out to me in what it had to say about creating rituals in communities that bond members. This was given by Emily Castor of Lyft. She explained how every Lyft ride ends in a fist bump.

Not only did this make me smile, but I am also reminded about the importance of human touch in psychology.[10] Lyft has tapped into that deep reservoir of the ways humans make social connections and integrated that into their brand.

What makes rituals important is that they are passed down through generations. The rituals you start with your customers today will most likely continue to exist after you leave the company. In that regard they are self-perpetuating, becoming the foundation for your future interactions with the community.

COMMUNITY MANAGERS ARE PIVOTAL MEMBERS OF YOUR TEAM

Here is a fact about M*A*S*H you may not know; Gary Burghoff is the only actor that played the same character (Walter "Radar" O'Reilly) in both the film and TV show. Radar was the pillar and heart of that story. The farm boy form Iowa that kept everything together when the rest of the characters were falling apart.

In the same way, your community manager is building the foundation for your future business. They hold up the brand reputation through their interactions with the community every day. Most importantly, they are taking what they learn from these conversations and converting them into actionable decisions to accelerate the growth of their companies. This is exemplified when looking behind the scenes of Tosca Reno, a celebrity brand and media company that experienced both sides of community and ultimately found a balance that led to the results they were looking for.

CASE STUDY: Tosca Reno – The Sustaining Power of Community

I've had the immense pleasure of working with Tosca Reno[11] in the past few months. I remember being approached by Deb Von Sychowski and Kim Phillips, Co-founders of Patch Design, design agency for Tosca Reno when they told me of this exciting new opportunity to resurge the social strategy for

an already exciting brand. I read the brief and right away was enamored with
this icon – not only because of what Tosca had accomplished later in life – but
because of the success she had achieved in spite of some incredible personal
struggles and heartbreak.

This is about the strength of a community built and nurtured by Tosca Reno and
her two children, Kiersten and Rachel Corradetti. For those who question the
virtues of an engaged community– more importantly, for those who question
the ability of community to drive significant momentum–you need to read this.
I promise you, it's a lesson from which everyone can learn.

> *About **Tosca Reno**: Tosca Reno is the New York Times bestselling author behind*
> *"Your Best Body Now" and the "Eat-Clean Diet" series. She is also a certified*
> *Nutritional Therapy practitioner. At the time of writing this case study, I worked*
> *with Tosca Reno on the launch of her new book, "The Start Here Diet".*

THE STORY

I never get tired of hearing this story because it comes from a position of
strength and inspiration. From *Tosca*,

> *"You know in the last 3 years… my family has lost a son; we have lost a father*
> *and a husband and we've even lost a business. And those are enough, in many*
> *people's lives, enough to decimate them… to wipe them out… and even to con-*
> *sider never coming back. But what kept me going was the idea that I would*
> *[come back]…."*

And come back she did. Tosca Reno and team, with Patch Design, re-launched
ToscaReno.com on April 15, 2014 with a bang. Many would say the results on
the week of launch were absolutely astounding:

◊   9.81 MM Reach

◊   152K Clicks

◊   2.8 MM Reach on Twitter

◊   2.5 MM Reach on Facebook

◊   5,712 Unique Conversions in one day

◊   40% Conversion Rate

The strength of the website drew staggering numbers. More importantly, NO paid media went into driving these results. Instead, we developed a strategy that spoke to the needs of Tosca's audience, and leveraged the strength of this already-engaged community.

THE BEGINNING: BUILDING THE COMMUNITY

When Kiersten returned from a trip, she was asked by her boss to manage her mother's social media platforms: Facebook and Twitter. Virtually unknown to the social media world, Kiersten found herself without a guidebook. All she had was her wits and trial and error. She started posting and was able to keep track of what worked and what didn't.

"To this day I still find the best stuff is always the stuff that comes directly out of my mom's mouth. Her fan base has a 'Spidy-sense' for when it is someone else. Plus, my mom is actually hilarious, and the things that come out of her mouth are out of this world, and generate a lot of buzz all by themselves!"

GROWING TWO COMMUNITIES

At the time Tosca Reno had written a new book, The Eat-Clean Diet, the team realized that in order to leverage and help sell the new product, they needed to create separate accounts for The Eat-Clean Diet and Tosca Reno, as a brand.

Kiersten noted the challenges in convincing the company to provide resources for social media. Eventually she was able to work with a small team to help offset the incredible workload.

"Coming up with new, interesting content was also challenging. In the beginning, I would post the same content in every profile. I quickly learned that was not well received by our readers, so I started creating content schedules, monthly campaigns, and mining all of her old content to repurpose. In addition to Google Analytics and various tracking sites, I had my own tracking system to see what worked, when and what didn't. When I started doing this, each platform responded with praise."

Kiersten also found that as the community grew, so did the negative posts. She eventually grew a "thick skin" and killed "each negative post" with "kindness" which would usually stop the trolls.

It took about a year and a half to start reaching exponential growth for both accounts. Today, @ToscaReno and @EatCleanDiet have approximately 42,000 followers each.

COMMUNITY: THE DAILY GRIND OF GROWING AND ENGAGING

Kiersten realized the importance of responding to everything and this became an essential strategy.

> "Anything we could do to make their lives easier we would do. You have to give to get! I also enlisted my team to make social media profiles on Facebook, Twitter and Google+. I would send out a weekly newsletter of things to post. Once we started doing this along with the campaigns and schedules, our team had a lot of fun!"

The system wasn't refined but it showed signs of working. It wasn't long before Kiersten and team were able to identify the most active and engaged users. This was the potential for the Ambassador community.

GOING DARK ON SOCIAL

Despite the successes, the company had to shut down and that included social media. Kiersten felt the backlash from the community:

"...it was awful. They blamed my mom for everything. Everything buzzing around her networks was filled with lies, assumptions and rumors. I had strict instructions from the lawyers to stay quiet. I couldn't respond to anything and we weren't allowed to post. It went against everything I stood for on so many levels."

"First and foremost, she's my mom and I wanted to protect her from the negative backlash. Second, it was my job and my passion. I was devastated to see something I had nurtured from the beginning suddenly slammed with slanderous content. My mom found me crying over it several times over the summer. "

Eventually the negative sentiment died down. Slowly, Kiersten and team began to realize who their real advocates were – the ones who stuck with Tosca Reno despite all the negative incidences. Kiersten heeded some smart advice from her Strategic Communications professor, *Nancy Hobor*:

"...when it comes to your most engaged stakeholders you have to take a risk even if that means going against your lawyer's advice. Instead of asking "why not", you ask, "How can I do this?"

Crisis communications, as Kiersten found out, became an important element to the strategy. Being proactive on social media goes much further than just being reactive.

RETURNING TO SOCIAL AND THE COMMUNITY REACTION

Tosca Reno returned to social after months in hiatus. Rachel Coradetti, now had to run community, while her sister, Kiersten headed off to university. As Rachel noted,

"The task at hand was to promote a book that was written well before the death of my stepfather, Robert Kennedy, and before the bankruptcy, meaning it was out of context. Furthermore, it was with a new publisher, who we had never worked with before. Finally, social media was in the hands of a part-time employee with very little experience in building social networks."

Overall, Rachel was pleased to see that the community was happy to be acquainted with her again. However, people had pointedly questioned the company about its bankruptcy and the sale of the magazines. These had to be addressed. At this point, Rachel, Kiersten's sister, resumed the duties as the community person. She soon realized that the fans were genuinely concerned.

They even inquired about the "Kitchen Table" – a forum built by Tosca's team that allowed members to support one another through advice, sharing and engaging discussions.

The team did their best to engage and respond to as many questions as they could. Soon they found an even more positive community.

FAST FORWARD TO THE LAUNCH OF "START HERE DIET"

To promote Tosca's new book, we decided to leverage the strength of Tosca's communities on Twitter and Facebook to launch her new branded website. We were putting all our eggs into one basket– Social Media – hoping it would pay off.

As per above, the results were astounding. Rachel, Kiersten and Tosca's team were "ecstatic, relieved, and grateful beyond measure." They weren't surprised by the strength of community. It was always there. They "just needed to find a way to bring it back again".

The level of engagement is starting to come back a year after the bankruptcy. There are kinks that Rachel has indicated still need to be worked out. But Tosca's "voice is clear and consistent." It continues to be trial and error but now we have measurement tools that provide us with performance for all of Tosca's content and her social media efforts. We now have a formula to determine what the market conversation trends are all about, and what discussions are driving discussion and website traffic.

THE LESSONS

For *Kiersten*, she realizes there are many paths to the top of the mountain, just like there are many approaches to social media. What has worked for her and her team includes an approach to be

> "...real, and authentic ...finding the sweet point with your audience that jives with them... Listen and respond".

As *Rachel* put it,

> "Overall, communities are resilient, and my mother has been able to build a strong, healthy community even through heaps of personal turmoil with genuine, impactful messages."

IN THE END, THE BRAND BECOMES STRENGTHENED...

It's clear that growing and nurturing a community takes an incredible amount of time and effort. Like all relationships it has its amazing moments but it is also wrought with volatility. The advocates, however, always rise to the top, no matter how few. And this is what will strengthen and sustain a brand.

For many companies, the role community has been erroneously associated with merely maintaining a presence on social media. So yesterday! For companies still stuck on this perception, you need to move with the times and understand the more vital presence community managers.

A COMMUNITY MANAGER'S VIEWPOINT: IN SOCIAL MARKETING ACT WITH INTENTION OR DON'T WASTE MY TIME By Susan Silver

I frequently encounter clients that want to "do" social marketing because they have a Twitter or Facebook account, and in turn they attempt to reduce my role of community manger to merely posting status updates.

There are valid reasons why your marketing team wants you on social:
- Generating data for analysis
- Responding to customers that post their opinions publicly online
- Incentivizing customers to make purchases

But honestly, that isn't really all that I should be doing for you as a community manager. Nothing listed above requires loyalty on the part of your customers[12]; it may provide you with information and some customer service, but it should not be your main focus on social.

My main goal when working with clients is to set an intention for their community; a vision of sorts [13], which creates a movement with which individuals can belong. I find ways to connect brand goals with the very human needs of acceptance and respect.

Community, at its best, unites customers with various backgrounds into a force that can be mobilized under your banner.

SOCIAL MEDIA LEADS WITH AN OPEN HEART

In my role as a Community Manager, I take a position of compassion, empathy and mindfulness. [14]This is because I know that my community is made of individuals and my role is to create an inclusive place where they can belong. I need to encourage them gently to share their true thoughts with us. This means doing research to find out just what resonates with our core customers.

But some clients are at odds with this process, wanting to dominate their customers with marketing messages. They want the most efficient way to open up their customer's pocket books. Unfortunately, community does not work that immediately. In community, the company takes on a more passive role eliciting customer feedback and allowing them to be key decision makers at times. The community manager allows this to happen organically by creating a space where open communication can occur.

This is why community works so well for the companies that embrace it. [15] Community empowers customers. It is a win–win situation, but for it to work the company must cede some control.

WHY SOCIAL MARKETING IS SCARY

I see this fear when I talk to clients because it is in their body language. The crossed arms and sideways glances tell me that they aren't sure, but they really want to try this 'social thing'.

I want to acknowledge that and say that the fear is well justified. The social mob is a real thing that exists. Amy Tobin outlined this in her Social Justice series. [16] I am not going to sugar coat it. Here are a few of the fears that I have encountered from clients and how they prevent community from working:

1. I am not worthy of attention. You might think that you have done nothing yet to earn community. You are wrong. You already have a community although you may not have customers. That community is the internal team.[17] Believe in your work and celebrate it! That enthusiasm will spread every time you encounter a new customer. You'll be growing your social presence much quicker than you would have expected.

2. I don't want to give competitors an upper hand. Hiding from social is a disadvantage in a competitive space. It is only going to hinder you because your customers won't get the chance to hear your voice. A big advantage of social is that it allows you to differentiate your company from competitors. [18] It allows you to share the values that make you unique. Community becomes an important part of your branding.

3. What if I Say the Wrong Thing? This is a big one. It is also the root fear that I had when I started working in community management. I was afraid to talk to customers. It is hard to make a counter-argument. There are times when you are going to make mistakes, but you have to deal with them and learn from the experience. It takes many conversations that equate to deliberate practice [19] to overcome this.

This is a recent encounter on the Gygax Magazine Facebook page.

Bob Swindell Um, no. In its present form, it looks like something hastily photoshopped by a high school student. A few ideas to improve for your next revision:
1. Every planet is the moon? Unoriginal. Every planet should be different, preferably in keeping with the theme of the game it represents.
2. Planets should be clustered together in galaxies for shared publishers.
3. Genres (space opera, dystopian future, high fantasy, Western, paranormal, super hero, etc.) should be kept along a general radial line as much as possible in keeping with the different galaxies of publishers. I.e. Boot Hill and Deadlands should be near each other.

I'm looking forward to seeing the next incarnation of this poster.
5 hrs · Like

Gygax Magazine Thanks, Bob - we'd love to see your version. Please put one together as a submission if you're interested, email djinn@gygaxmagazine.com
Commented on by Jayson Elliot [?] · 5 hrs · Like

Treat every interaction you have as if it were your first. Be modest. When you encounter a challenge find a way to turn that into an opportunity for community contribution.

The worst sin in social is neglect. You may not handle every situation with aplomb, but you will get better every time you do it. Most importantly, you will wow customers with your responsiveness and care.

SOCIAL MARKETING IS A COMMITMENT YOU MAKE TO YOUR CUSTOMERS

Community Management doesn't work if you are not willing to commit. I know clients waiver about taking the plunge. Some days it seems that we are working as a strong team, but they may change their mind a few days later. I've come to expect it. I know that I am doing all that I can for our mutual success. I don't hold any grudges about it. That is business and there is a bottom line that must result in increased revenue for the company.

Keep in mind that marketing is a numbers game, but it is also about the wealth of human emotions. Making your company accessible via social media opens up your ability to listen to your customers' needs and receive qualitative feedback on how you are doing.

When you start with a deliberate strategy for your community efforts then you can measure results! Real data about how your efforts change the behavior of your customers. Don't judge the worth of your community until you have been doing it long enough to see results. Every month re-group and adjust your efforts.

FeverBee estimates that starting a community from scratch can take 9 month or more. [20]

- If the intention to make social work for you is not there…
- If you don't see value in relationships….
- If you believe that social cannot lead to sales…
- If you are reactive and not proactive when it comes to communication…

Then don't hire me. I will not be able to do anything for you.

You reduce our community manager's effectiveness when you take away their agency. They must be able to set a strategy and act on your behalf. [21] That takes a lot of trust, but it is also what makes these communities enduring. Don't take the process lightly.

One Platform that is leveraging page community fans the proper way is Crowdly. Dan Sullivan, Founder, understands that focusing on those who ultimately love your brand will yield stronger results as opposed to spreading the love across your entire base.

Interview with Crowdly: Engaging Your Most Passionate Advocates

When I met Dan Sullivan, Founder of Crowdly, I was very interested in his platform and how he was leveraging the Page Fans to enable Brands to get the most out of their Facebook Fans.

Where Facebook continues to incentivize brands to buy more ad space to maximize their exposure, Crowdly's proposition is simple: Surface, rank, and create segments of your fan base to find the most influential people and identify the advocates who love you most....

Build a direct, owned channel to your top advocates and drive more word-of-mouth through public or private 1:1 offers, rewards and recognition, and exclusive content.

Understand what is driving advocacy now and do more of it.

I have dubbed Crowdly the anti-Facebook within Facebook, a platform that really builds on the authenticity of brands to connect, and initiate interactions with customers. I sat down with Dan to talk more about Crowdly and where this is all going.

These days it's about identifying your greatest advocates and keeping them. Retention is a much harder initiative these days. Acquisition is baked. Do you agree?

> *DS: Absolutely. I think brands that thrive are the ones that are able to mean something to the people who really care about them. If a brand can't understand or express why it should matter to that core group of its potential advocates, how can they expect to win the interest of the broader market?*
>
> *I think how people define acquisition has become more nebulous as well. If you're defining acquisition as a new visitor, email opt-in, or social like, all you're*

getting is a very brief introduction, a small amount of attention. You're getting
an opportunity, perhaps, to start to matter to some of those people. Acquisition
as an end goal has us shaking hands and then immediately walking away.

Please tell me the premise of Crowdly. How did you get started? What was the impetus?

DS: *Crowdly exists to connect brands to the fans who love them most. The large brands we work with have such a huge asset of existing advocates who carry that brand out into the world with tremendous earned credibility and effectiveness.*

We saw a huge, nearly universal problem though, where brands didn't have the tools to see beyond the aggregate data, they could see comments but they couldn't see the people behind them.

They knew they must have great advocates somewhere in their 1 Million Fans, but they had no idea who they were, or how to connect with them. Crowdly is built on the premise that people matter. We can turn our platform on for any brand and show them who all the people are amongst their 1 Million, who their top ten thousand fans are, what they do and why, and give them great ways that they can connect with those advocates in a targeted, authentic way to get more out of their word-of-mouth strategies. For the brands we work with, that matters.

How does Crowdly enable the connection between brands and fans?

DS: *I think there is a shift happening in how we define customer service, and particularly in reconsidering where a company's most effective touch points with its customers might be.*

I think companies are implementing really effective strategies that go beyond di-

rectly communicating only to troubleshoot with customers who have had a bad experience. That traditional customer service model is at best aiming to take a small subset of negative customers to neutral.

If my brand new TV starts to shoot sparks and smoke, a good brand can and should work to effectively solve my problem, but I'm probably still not going to sing their praises when my friend Dave asks for a recommendation, even if the company spent a thousand dollars to quickly resolve the issue.

Imagine there's another friend in that same conversation also with a recently purchased TV from a different brand that had not burst into flames. He posts a picture on the brand's Facebook page of his mounted TV, exclaiming his excitement to break it in at an upcoming movie night next week. That fan gets a surprise package, with a note from the manufacturer saying they're glad he's excited, and here's popcorn and Twizzlers for him and four friends for his movie night, at a total expense to the brand under $20. What do you think Dave's next TV will be?

Brands get hugely more return for the smaller efforts that take customers from passively happy to actively advocating than they do focusing on the few percent with a negative experience, and I think we're seeing a shift in strategies that reflect that.

How are brands utilizing Crowdly? Do you find it's moving away from campaigns, and rather, focusing on mining insights about their Facebook fans and taking action to nurture relationships?

DS: We're not a campaign driven purchase for our brand; we're typically an annual license. They might have an upcoming large product release or initiative that they know they want to leverage their authentic advocates for that has brought us into consideration, but none of them are of the mindset of 'great, that worked, now we'll never need advocacy again, let's turn it off'.

A pillar of the platform is that we enable brands to build a permanent direct channel to their core advocates, which get more valuable over time. Earning the engagement of those advocates is very valuable; you'd be feeding a very leaky bucket if you're not retaining that value between campaigns.

I've only had one VP of marketing that was completely opposed to the value of investing in relationships, and the deal fell apart because of it. He said, "If these are already our advocates and they're already advocating, we've already got them; we don't have to do anything else. Why does it matter who they are?" I countered that I've been with my wife for 17 years but I still bring flowers home occasionally. He said he didn't believe in flowers either. I asked him if he was married, and he said he used to be. Three times.

How does Crowdly identify a superfan? What are the measures/features you use to allow brands to optimize relationships?

DS: We're looking beyond just frequency of interaction to really focus on influence. It's great that someone wants to chime in with "awesome" every brand post, but it's much less valuable than someone who talks about the values of the product, how it allowed him to fit more healthy sit down meals with his family into their busy schedules.

We look at not just the actions of the fans, but really on the reactions that they garner. Are they generating a chain of Likes, shares, and comments from other people that shows they're actually driving influence about that brand?

I think brands also need to find the balance between finding the valuable opportunities to uncover more passive positive fans and turn them into advocates, and falsely viewing engagement as a pipeline, where they have to push to convert every passive curator to active content creators.

There are many different types of good advocates and many reasons why people want to be advocates. A brand needs to understand the difference and provide a good experience for each type.

Do you find your clients using Crowdly more for marketing or customer service or a hybrid?

DS: *We're generally pretty firmly in marketing. One aspect the platform facilitates is more effective direct and 1:1 connections, and I think marketing departments have definitely shifted to seeing this as an important strategy for them, not just the job of customer service.*

Generally the touch points and circumstances where they come in are different, and they work alongside a separate dedicated customer service department. From a PR perspective, brands might use the platform to identify and foster a core group of active brand defenders who are doing a great job quelling an untrue rumor about the brand, or thank champions who are actively addressing purchase decision questions from other fans.

From a brand perspective, they're using our insights to understand the positive and negative sentiments, often informed by what CS is seeing that are shaping brand perception. Our partners have varying layers of integration, but I'm still seeing these as largely separate functions.

Have you received results on the impact of customer sat scores, employee churn? What about acquisition?

DS: *I think there are some core commonalities that most brands look to in understanding the effectiveness of their word-of-mouth and advocacy, such as engagement, reach, and favorability, but there are also some goals that do vary brand to brand.*

We haven't had a partner that's had customer sat or employee churn as a key measurement for advocacy yet. For a brand like Hilton Honors, they were able to reach out to their 550 most engaged advocates to reach nearly three million friends of fans with authentic stories told about the brand.

For other brands, we've been able to help them seed a new product launch into the hands of paying advocates at 1/3 the cost of their previous customer acquisition. We can also tie loyalty cards into social profiles, so going beyond surveying a handful of people on purchase likelihood to attempt a correlation, we can directly attribute social advocacy to purchase in a way that's never been possible. We're extraordinarily data driven, and can usually give our brands all the core metrics that they're using to measure their initiatives, as well as a few more they didn't know were possible.

What's your vision for Crowdly? Where do you see this evolving in the coming years?

DS: I want to build a great, growing company that means something to the people who work here and to the people who choose to work with us as customers.

Our industry moves quickly, so we need to be even quicker to stay ahead and keep our lead, but I want to avoid fashionability and glomming on to the flavor of the week as we grow (looking at you 'Yo').

We are focusing on connecting the brands to those that love them is an enduring purpose. I see it as an inevitable evolution as digital moves beyond high volume audience to high value engagements and the concept of what a brand is becomes increasingly decentralized and co-owned by those that care about it.

Ten years from now, our technology, platforms, channels, and structure of the marketing organizations to which we sell will have changed substantially, but that need for authentic connection will not. We'll still be trying to solve that a little better than we were able to do the day before.

This is a pivotal chapter. It was important we provided strong case examples as well perspectives from people who live Community day to day. Where the corporate naysayers try to poke holes in the value of Social Media and its impact on business goals, what we've demonstrated is that when done properly, the efforts to develop and nurture a community can have profound effects on the business.

REFERENCES:

[1,2] http://www.business2community.com/customer-experience/customer-experience-important-advertising-infographic-0726258#pUDWCtU4rkZjerB8.32

[3] http://millennialceo.com/social-media/company-digital-personality/

[4] http://millennialceo.com/social-media/building-online-relationships-customers-clients-community/

[5] http://mycmgr.com/brand-ambassador/

[6] http://millennialceo.com/social-media/2014-age-brand-influencer/

[7] https://www.sprinklr.com/social-scale-blog/six-tips-for-better-community-management-on-cmad-2013/

[8] http://www.feverbee.com/2014/01/applying-behavioural-models-to-online-communities.html

[9] http://www.slideshare.net/dnnsoftware/7-traits-of-highly-effective-community-managers

[10] http://www.psychologytoday.com/collections/201303/the-power-touch/touch-louder-words

[11] http://www.toscareno.com/

[12] http://www.entrepreneur.com/article/233680

[13] http://www.thindifference.com/2013/05/29/visionary-leadership-belongs-to-everyone/

[14] http://www.v3im.com/2014/05/social-media-community-management-basics-leave-your-opinions-at-home/

[15] http://www.entrepreneur.com/article/226003

16   http://arcompany.co/social-justice-a-paula-deen-recipe-for-disaster/

17   http://sherpablog.marketingsherpa.com/marketing/employee-run-twitter-deliver-value/

18   http://www.americanbanker.com/bankthink/great-branding-comes-from-the-heart-1067975-1.html

19   http://www.wired.com/2011/03/what-is-success-true-grit/

20   http://www.feverbee.com/2013/01/the-online-community-lifecycle.html

21   http://arcompany.co/community-managers-anticipate-needs-why-you-must-develop-your-company-radar/

Making Content it's Own Kingdom

WHERE CONTENT LEAPS AHEAD OF ADVERTISING
by Michael Brenner

Where is content headed? The explosion of channels we all use to gather, consume and share information is having a dramatic impact on the methods of modern Marketers. This is putting much more focus on the content brand Marketers create ahead of the channels they use. TV, Search Engines, Facebook, Twitter, Instagram - none of these destinations are nearly as interesting as the content that flows across them.

Consider that, as consumers, we largely don't answer cold calls, watch television ads, respond to unwanted emails, click on banner ads or appreciate disruptive marketing techniques of any kind. And this is having a dramatic impact of the landscape of agencies, publishers and brand advertisers that fuel the creation of much of the content we seek on TV, online and the remaining print vehicles some consumers are clinging on to.

Today, advertising agencies are absorbing the impact of programmatic buying (where publisher banner ad inventory is bought and sold to brand advertisers in an online marketplace). They are reeling from the increasing consumer backlash against the interruptive techniques they have pioneered for nearly 100 years. Their response is to get back to what they do best: creativity, design and storytelling. Agencies are tapping into their core and becoming storytelling masters. They are leading their clients to think in bold, new, and more human ways. Publishers are clearly feeling the pressure of consumers' shifting information habits from print to digital and mobile content experiences. Even the oldest, most respected traditional publishers like Time Magazine and the New York Times are considering how they can sustain themselves as viable businesses.

A new breed of publishers is tapping into the needs of modern consumers by creating content in many formats – long and short, shareable, informative, and even entertaining. These "social news" content leaders include both newer players like Buzzfeed and Huffington Post, and Vice as well as more traditional news outlets like the BBC and The Guardian who have shifted the content they publish to reflect consumer habits.

These publishers are all seeking new ways to generate revenue from a new breed of Marketer: one that understands digital, social, mobile consumers. Marketers also need to hone their storytelling craft if they want to compete in the battle for customer attention and reach their audiences.

At a recent marketing event, actor **Kevin Spacey** told a crowd of content Marketers,

> *"Actors and Marketers - we are all the same. We are trying to reach an audience with stories."*

The future of marketing is all about storytelling. And the skills required to be successful will look more like that of actors and directors, publishers and film producers who know how to create great content, how to tell amazing stories, but also who know how to win the war of distribution.

But the real trick to becoming an effective storyteller is embodied in extreme customer centricity. It goes against the basic human nature of an enterprise to put customers first. The modern business wants to sell. It wants to grow. And it believes that it needs to push its way into the buyers trust.

As human beings and consumers, we know that this approach won't work in the long run. We know that we need to put customers first. We need to think like human beings and we need to fight inside the business to show that taking an extreme customer centric view can produce business results.

This is why marketing is hard. This is why most marketing is highly ineffective. 99.9% or more of banner ads are ignored. And yet Marketers continue to increase the budgets for online digital display. This approach is not sustainable.

So it all comes back to storytelling. Brands will learn to partner with agencies and publishers. And they will work together to refine their narratives.

Brand stories or longer term narratives that resonate with consumers will focus on creating emotional connections based on business' higher purpose – why they do what they do, and how that impacts their customers, employees and society at large.

Storytelling and corporate social responsibility will stop being labeled buzzwords and will become business imperatives as consumers connect with the brands who do it well and who do it consistently.

Where is marketing headed? It is running fast in the direction of content and storytelling. The future of content will embody these traits:

- You will see an increasing need for marketing to push back on corporate cultures to invoke "extreme customer-centricity."
- Brands will create internal structures that resemble publishers (editors, writers, designers). Some will go so far as to create entire divisions like Red Bull Media House that even seek to turn a profit from their content
- Budgets will shift out of paid promotion like advertising and into owned content hubs that seek to attract audiences with stories people want to consume and share across their social networks.
- Brand content will follow consumer trends to be more visual, helpful, and entertaining.

- Leading brands will hire comedians, producers and actors and begin creating top-ranked shows like Netflix did with "House of Cards."

The future of marketing explained above may sound like a far cry from the folks you see today who blow up balloons at your events, fly around the world with expensive ad agencies to take a few photographs in exotic locations, or manage the budgets of the telemarketing agencies who still cold call millions of people every day.

But the future will be better for all of us. One where brands bring new stories and new formats to consumers like P&G did with soap operas; One where we see less clutter from advertising we don't want; One where companies that don't figure out their larger purpose are punished for their self-serving behaviors.

The future of marketing is bright. And it's all about stories that connect with us in a human and an emotional way; stories that inspire our minds and touch our hearts.

Michael Brenner is the Head of Strategy for NewsCred. Recognized as a Forbes Top 40 Social Media Marketer, a Top Content Marketing Influencer and Most Mentioned Marketer on Twitter, Michael is an accomplished marketing speaker, author of the B2B Marketing Insider blog, and a frequent contributor on leading publications like Forbes, The Economist, and The Guardian. Michael is an experienced marketing executive, most recently serving as Vice President of Global Marketing and Content Strategy for SAP where he developed an award-winning thought leadership blog for SAP called Business Innovation. Michael is also a co-founder of social news site Business 2 Community. Follow Michael on Twitter (@BrennerMichael)

Content has Changed Marketing Forever

Social media strategists continue to warn Marketers to provide more customer value, and move away from me-me-me messages about the company. Marketers now have to rethink the approach to messaging to gain increased consumer mindshare.

Marketers are used to focusing on the sell message. Marketers have traditionally used revenue as the success metric to gauge program effectiveness. Now, this new approach: "value = the new currency," is drastically changing the ad game.

All the platforms are implementing some variation of this: Facebook's (now defunct) sponsored stories and Twitter's Promoted Tweets. It's clear that the purchase funnel has been extended and Marketers need to focus on content that gains the customer's attention well before they are even thinking of purchase.

Interview with Daniel Robinson of Antelope: The Real Value of Content

I spoke to Daniel Robinson, President and Founder of Antelope, [1] a Content Measurement and Strategy Platform. At that time he was working on a solution many Marketers sought: understanding and measuring content's value to the business.

These days, content is king. Consumer attention is moving away from blatant advertising and focusing more on content value. You came from agency where the traditional thinking was to develop awesome campaigns to highlight and sell a product or service. Are advertisers getting it right?

DR: There's always going to be room in the market for a smart campaign or a captivating TV spot. But as consumers increasingly shift their attention to digital channels; it's important to realize how this media is being consumed.

Today, one in six minutes online is spent on social networks. On Facebook, over 40 percent of that time is spent consuming content in the news feed. As users expand their networks, and those connections produce more content each day, Facebook is challenged with prioritizing billions of pieces of content into a news feed that is relevant and timely for users. Their ad revenue model depends on it.

Consumers now expect this same treatment from brands on the social web. This demands an engaging content strategy that lives and breathes the narrative of a brand each day.

How did you conceive of Antelope? What was happening in the market that drove you to develop your concept?

DR: *I'm a data junkie. I have always been enthralled by how new data sets can give companies a competitive edge. As a digital strategist in Toronto, I was privileged to build the social media strategies for some of Canada's most recognized brands. At the time, I turned to social listening platforms like Radian6 and Sysomos to help craft those strategies.*

What I found was that those tools took a very bottom-up approach to social analytics. They were great at uncovering what consumers were saying about brands, but did little to measure what brands were saying to consumers.

Antelope looks at social analytics from the top-down by measuring what brands are saying to consumers. Our platform and analysts synthesize engagement signals (i.e. Likes, Comments, Retweets, YouTube views, etc.) into actionable social media strategies. We combine proprietary technology with a unique strategic framework to enable our clients to make sense of and take action on the findings.

Social Media ROI is a huge factor that seems to prevent brands from stretching the limits with social media. Part of the issue with content is that there isn't a direct correlation to driving consideration or purchase. How do you respond?

DR: *I've seen plenty of examples of tangible ROIs being derived from social marketing, but it's still early days. It's a billion-dollar nut that everyone in this industry is trying to crack.*

At Antelope, we try to shift our client's mindset to considering social media's impact on their overall advertising spend. Our platform enables brands to answer critical questions like: How much content do I need to be creating? When's the best time to post my content? How did my competitor grow their Facebook page? The insights that roll out of these findings empower clients with strategies to extend their earned media reach. We then map this earned media reach back to an equivalent paid media spend.

Content is still an evolving medium. The emergence of native advertising now allows brands to test the value of content that appears in an ad format and location. This article from Forbes, notes "Uh-Oh--Survey Says Most People Find Facebook and Twitter Ads Misleading."[2]

The majority of respondents indicated that the native formats on Twitter, as well as FB Sponsored stories, had no impact on perception of the brand advertised. Is there a place for content in advertising or should it remain an earned media component?

DR: Most consumers find advertising misleading. This article does little to benchmark how content marketing compares with traditional marketing, nor does it suggest that it's ineffective. I think Facebook's attempts through [their tests] Sponsored Stories and Twitter's Promoted Tweets are clear indications that social networks are doing their best to combat the mistrust consumers have with advertising.

There has always been a sliding scale between where an ad creates vs. diminishes value. Historically, ads could diminish value because they had their audience trapped into watching commercials in exchange for their favorite programming. In social, your brand's message is competing against hyper-targeted messages directed to who your consumers are and what they care about. If your brand's message doesn't create value here nobody is going to notice. Content marketing at its core is about adding value to advertising.

Appealing to the customer's interests and trying to create trust is an about-face for the marketing community. It also is a longer lead cycle. How do we balance the content plan with traditional tactics that are closer to the true corporate objectives of driving sales leads?

DR: This challenge varies from industry to industry. We've worked with fashion labels and sports teams who were blessed with a deep pool of content opportunities; the challenge then became filtering that content into a strategy that balanced engagement with driving sales. We've also worked with brands that sell toilet paper and insurance packages, where the challenge became manufacturing interest by determining content with which consumers were most likely to engage.

We start with a deep dive where we analyze the content of our clients, their competitors and best-in-class brands in similar markets. We determine the content that resonates best with consumers and generate KPIs to measure success. We then balance engaging content with offers and sales incentives to map to objectives.

Is the banner ad dead? Mindshare is eroding and access proliferation is narrowing the consumer attention span as more devices, more channels, more sites are introduced. Where do you think the demand will be in the next five years i.e. by way of content vs. ads?

DR: Social networks have captivated the world by producing a new form of media that targets user's interests at an unprecedented level. Mark Zuckerberg's quote "a squirrel dying in front of your house may be more relevant to your interests right now than people dying in Africa," encapsulates this phenomenon perfectly.

Personalization is what makes social media compelling, and as we connect with more people and brands, more opportunities will arise to increase this personalization. One-size-fits-all banners will die to make room for more personalized and targeted messages. It's quite clear that this progression is already well underway. Since Facebook's IPO, we've already seen quite a few new targeting capabilities open up as Facebook considers how to balance revenue growth with consumer privacy concerns.

To win, Marketers are going to need to understand how they can use data to increase personalization with their consumers. They need to invest in people to make sense of this information. We haven't even cracked the surface on what's possible with big data, and the ones that do will win.

Can Content Help Reach and Build Relationships with members of the Purest Form of Social Networks?

I had the distinct honor of speaking at ForumConn in San Francisco. This event was dedicated to providing online forum owners with tips/tools and best practices for managing, growing and monetizing their forums. Ironically, the forums and boards, which lit the initial fire for social networking, were left behind as more prominent channels like Facebook and Twitter sped past.

An online forum, one of the earliest and purest forms of social networking, by definition:[2]

> *"Is an online discussion site where people can hold conversations in the form of posted messages... early Internet forums could be described as a web version of an electronic mailing list or newsgroup (such as exist on Usenet); allowing people to post messages and comment on other messages. Later developments emulated the different newsgroups or individual lists, providing more than one forum, dedicated to a particular topic."*

This event was an eye-opener for me. In many ways I found it ironic that the online forum, the purest form of social networking, the very definition of community had remained true to its intent, even today. It had not yet evolved to modern day where its sustainability required the very solutions that websites and brands have been introduced to: search engine optimization, online influence, social media integration and monetization.

The forum owners, with whom I spoke, were passionate about their jobs. I sensed some pretty strong frustration among them; one had told me he worked over 100 hours a week in multiple roles: the moderator, the business development guy, the Marketer, the web owner. The consistent gaps were noted across each of these discussions:

- The top priority was to protect the communities. This meant minimizing disruption.
- There was a need to understand how social media could drive awareness, hence more users.
- The need to be able to make money from the forums while keeping the community intact was also a challenge.

Most of the attendees were comprised not only of forum owners, but also media and tech start-ups, which provided some pretty innovative and insightful suggestions in response to the challenges stated above.

BRANDS ARE INCREASINGLY BECOMING AWARE OF ONLINE FORUMS

This was one insight that many of the online forum owners were unaware of. I presented a case study that proved to them that some of the strongest and most compelling discussions were not on Facebook or Twitter. In fact, some of the biggest retailers are beginning to realize that there are engaged communities that reside predominantly in forums and boards providing amazing insight into product/ service development, and company sentiment.

These discussions are raw and unfiltered. Actively listening to what's happening within these forums provides a wealth of information for companies. One of the forum owners argued that these discussions were so niche that brands probably would be unwilling to pay attention to a community thread of 200 people discussing a specific topic. I argued that Marketers would be more willing to spend time in a targeted discussion with fewer people than be exposed to a market full of noise and discourse with no specific focus.

I also indicated that people who are more passionate about certain discussions have a higher propensity to share it outside of their immediate network. The dynamics of most communities also needs to be considered. According to Charlene Li and Josh Bernhoff, authors of Groundswell, within any given social network, 13% are creators of content, and 19% a responders or reviewers of content.[3] The remaining 78% have the potential to consume the content, be influenced by it, hence share it among their own networks. This is the classic word-of-mouth effect that can potentially reach what Malcolm Gladwell has coined, "The Tipping Point."

I've seen and analyzed instances where purely passionate discussions have seen a few reposts of information to other forums, blogs, and Twitter amplifying the message even more and ultimately driving, not only website visits, but purchases as well.

BRANDS STILL DON'T KNOW HOW TO ENGAGE EFFECTIVELY IN SOCIAL MEDIA

This continues to be a challenge, despite the growth and understanding of content. A few of my peers have had some success when it comes to persuading brands to see the value of social media and engagement in its true form. There are some brands that still believe they have control. Despite its warning, many brands remain unaware, nor are they willing to admit that they need to change the way they deal with customers.

For those who heed the warning of the *Cluetrain Manifesto*, it professes:

> *"Networked markets are beginning to self-organize faster than the companies that have traditionally served them. Thanks to the web, markets are becoming better informed, smarter, and more demanding of qualities missing from most business organizations."*[4]

This is why brands are starting to pay attention.

Here is an example of forum traffic and engagement from one of the forum owners with whom I spoke:

- 152 active discussions
- 6,522,000 discussions
- 84,402,000 posts

As the owner stated earlier, the discussion topics were very niche but for a brand it was highly relevant. And brands are asking for ways to have access to these engaged discussions, at the very least, to obtain the valuable insight.

I have worked with brands to navigate through these "tight" communities, careful not to interrupt or upset its members. I've realized that communities ripe with complaints and anger towards companies have welcomed brands openly, knowing that a company has finally heard them and is willing to listen.

TECHNOLOGIES ARE ENABLING THE CONNECTION BETWEEN BRANDS AND ONLINE COMMUNITIES

I was happy to hear several technologies talk about how they are helping bridge this gap:

1) *Tyler Tanaka* of Nativo [5] spoke of his content platform targeting brands. Here is a description of the product:

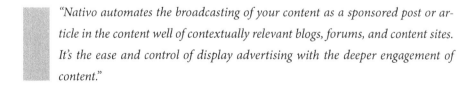

> *"Nativo automates the broadcasting of your content as a sponsored post or article in the content well of contextually relevant blogs, forums, and content sites. It's the ease and control of display advertising with the deeper engagement of content."*

Brands still don't understand dynamics of online communities. Nativo allows the brand to leverage the incredible power of storytelling that goes along with content, place it in the native location, blogroll and engage directly with the forum in ways that are positive. Tyler points out that brands want to spend money. They want to scale their marketing campaigns while still maintaining relevance.

Current display media performance isn't where it needs to be, especially from a consumer engagement standpoint. Nativo uses a natural language processing engine to match brand content with just the right audience. The semantic engine will index the content in the forum, to understand the relevant conversations happening so the brand can reach these discussions by posting engaging content, video, articles, and/or images.

The focus is on content, not advertising. Brands who want to engage cannot do so without risking their reputation. This technology does not disrupt the community nor interfere with the existing monetization.

2) Enthusify was a platform that powered marketplaces for automotive, sporting, and hobbyist communities. The platform, which had recently shut down, provided secured marketplaces for niche communities.

Its premise was to develop a marketplace where communities could provide an exchange of goods and services, a larger "bazaar-type" environment generated from engaged members, immediately open to business in a protected market.

For Enthusify, the value for the seller was:

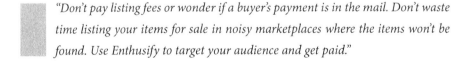

> *"Don't pay listing fees or wonder if a buyer's payment is in the mail. Don't waste time listing your items for sale in noisy marketplaces where the items won't be found. Use Enthusify to target your audience and get paid."*

The value proposition: Generally only forum members are the buyers and sellers. In addition, buyers can find listings in a forum and related forums that are members of the Enthusify network. Listings, as with most social media, will also show up in search engines. Additionally Enthusify advertised listings through display ads that appear on sites related to the buyer listing.

The reason it failed: The platform was not progressive enough. This premise kept the communities intact and closed-off from the rest of the world. It did little to perpetuate community outside of the original niche.

WHERE BRANDS AND COMMUNITIES COLLIDE… IN A POSITIVE WAY

I see a time when brands will begin to seek out forums, eager to get to know the very people who have a lot to say about them and their products. Forums will be baked into media plans for the purpose of engagement, product optimization, marketing opportunities and, for the most part, pure relationship building.

It's clear that major media companies like CBS Interactive, Gum Gum, Vibrant Media, Say Media, Vigilink are wielding their respective influences to build truly contextual media that broadens the definition of advertising from brand to consumer-centric.

And when that time comes, the forum owner will begin to reap the benefits of his efforts. I've come to realize that social media, for all its purity, cannot continue as they are; Social Networks need to make money. From the outset Facebook realized that it must become profitable. However, Facebook will be the first to tell you that it is not easy. What networks achieve without disrupting or destroying the community will be interesting to observe.

Can LinkedIn be the New Kingdom for Content?
By Andrew Jenkins

When it comes to content, LinkedIn would be the least likely platform that users think about. However, lately this business network has changed the game.

The LinkedIn platform continues to grow in membership, time spent and dominance in B2B activities. According to LinkedIn, 1 of every 3 professionals in the world is on LinkedIn, with 200,000+ professionals joining daily. Those same professionals have also driven the growth of 1.5M discussion groups.

LinkedIn's Executive Editor Dan Roth introduced the Influencer Program, helping to enrich the user experience, increase time spent and foster sharing and conversation. According to LinkedIn, the average Influencer post drives more than 31,000 views and receives more than 250 likes and 80 comments.

FAR MORE THAN JUST A RECRUITING TOOL

Many people have viewed LinkedIn as nothing more than a job board or the online equivalent of the Chamber of Commerce. While LinkedIn gets a substantial amount of revenue from their recruiting solutions and job-related services, the platform sees six times more engagement with content versus jobs.

Brands are devoting more time and energy to LinkedIn, which translates to 2.7M company pages so far and the use of company updates, Slideshare and Groups to distribute company news and content. LinkedIn has established connections to 1.3M publishers for LinkedIn Today. Add to that the acquisitions of Slideshare and Pulse, the news aggregator, and you have the makings of a content juggernaut.

CONTENT: THE BEAST THAT MUST BE FED

Many organizations find keeping up with content demands to be the most difficult part of their social media and marketing endeavors. LinkedIn recognizes that and took the opportunity to introduce their new Content Measurement System to help brands make the most out of their content, better understand the right content they should be using, and target it more appropriately. Brands get a sense of engagement and reach, and are more related to their content. The system is tied to buying advertising. While the emphasis of the conference was on content, users will be increasingly forced to pay to have their content seen by their target audience.

Trending topics information provided by LinkedIn also helps brands with their content marketing strategies.

LINKEDIN PUBLISHER

In addition to The Influencer Program the addition of LinkedIn Publisher gives every single member of LinkedIn the potential to become not only a publisher, but also an influencer. Essentially, once the program is rolled out to everyone, LinkedIn is enabling members to publish their own content and convey their thought leadership.

To date, people have used their own blogs, embedded media in their profiles and shared complementary content to establish themselves as curators of content and experts in their respective areas.

In the case of blogs, people have hosted them elsewhere and readers had to leave the LinkedIn environment to read them; but now with Publisher, readers can stay within in the LinkedIn environment and authors get the supporting analytics to track their progress regarding their professional branding efforts.

CONTENT STRATEGY

Yes, content is getting much more airplay but understanding what type of content resonates is still a challenge for businesses. This section provides some guidance.

WHY CONTENT? TO EDUCATE!

Question: What would you say the real importance of content for businesses? Is there anything more than just lead generation?

The simplest answer that I consistently give to clients is that the number one purpose of your content should be to educate. While the outcomes and goals of content marketing and social media may be to drive engagement and earn new leads, by far the best way to do this is to educate your clients about the things that are most important to them in the buying decision.

Usually when someone goes out to the Internet looking for content, they are at some phase between 0 and 90 percent through the buyer's journey. This means that they are basically self-educating on a topic so they can have a better idea about what they want and/or need prior to reaching out to a vendor to supply it. Therefore, by and large, what they are hoping to do with the content is get educated.

This is why companies that create content for their target audience in a way that is educational and compelling will always have the most success. Again, targeted and educational components are key. Once you have the right content and you are driving it in the right direction, you are in a position to try and cast a wider net. But getting more eyeballs on content by the wrong audience is really not worth anything.

In the end, your content marketing efforts should be driven toward education. Understand what your buyers need to know that will help them move to the next phase of the journey. Hopefully when they get to the next phase they will be thinking of you.

Ze Art of Storytelling

I had the distinct honor of being part of a panel entitled Ze Art of Storytelling at Podcamp[7]

"Without storytelling, con¬tent is nondescript, uninspiring and, frankly, a waste of time and energy."

~ Mark Evans, Contributor, Forbes

The premise of the session:

Compelling story telling is the foundation for building strong social relationships and brand advocacy. Persuasive, shareable, and detailed, your brand's story will create deep consumer connections. And yet, many brands do not tell stories well. We explored the core of storytelling, what brands must do to unleash their stories and also how some brands are managing to get their communities to tell the story on their behalf.

STORYTELLING HAS BEEN AROUND FOREVER

People are moved by emotion and the power of the narrative allows individuals to emotionally connect to an object or event. Researchers have long acknowledged that

"...classical language regions, like Broca's area and Wernicke's area, are involved in how the brain interprets written words." [8]

In fact it has been suggested that entering "descriptive" words, words that spark the imagination, can have the effect of altering the way information is processed. The more that people are absorbed in a story, the more the story changes them.

Here's some context: In a meeting when we are presented with dry, factual details and arguments we are more critical and skeptical. Without an interesting lead in or background, we may even become disengaged.

But when we are absorbed in a story, we drop our intellectual guard and this seemingly leaves us defenseless. Now our emotions take over and we become increasingly engaged.

STORYTELLING HAS BECOME MORE RELEVANT TODAY

Storytelling is the differentiator, especially in times when consumers are being bombarded with brand messages everywhere they go: via email, TV, print and now– advertising on their social streams.

This information overload is propelling people to "switch off." Companies must now figure out how to effectively engage consumers in a brand's stories, and use the construct of the narrative to create powerful connections.

In addition, given the number of social media tools, people have the power to fill in the gaps and create their own stories about anything and any brand. They stitch together fragments of information and attempt to draw their own conclusions. It's becoming clearer that companies cannot necessarily afford to sit back and let the consumer decide what they stand for.

There's a risky price to pay, especially if the truth is distorted. Storytelling has the potential to inspire and create meaningful connections that will ultimately benefit the brand.

David Ogilvy once said,

"A great ad is one which sells the product without drawing attention to itself."

THE STORY IS THE HERO. THE PRODUCT IS MERELY A SUPPORTING ROLE

This Audi Superbowl Ad: "Prom" does just that.

How many adult males have connected with the "father", throwing the keys to his "younger self" and remembering when he was in his shoes?

How many of us have played the role of the high-school boy going stag to the prom, parking in the principal's parking spot and having the gumption to approach that "girl" and kiss her.

We may not have lived it but we've enacted it a thousand times in our minds. One individual put it nicely:

> *"Great storytelling includes conflict and resolution".*

Audi successfully connected each and every one of us to the high-school kid and his act of bravery. In turn, we unknowingly had a much closer connection to Audi, the brand.

THE BRAND VALUES MUST BE REFLECTED IN THE STORY

This Lincoln ad included curated tweets by Jimmy Fallon to generate the story the #SteerTheScript campaign.

It featured a man sitting in a chair in the middle of a field explaining the crowd-sourced nature of the spot, a young woman driving an MKZ, a hitchhiker, an alpaca farm, some turtles, bikers, and a wedding. I had to watch this twice to understand what they were trying to convey.

Some indicated "confusion" about the message. It didn't resonate with them. It also did little to convey Lincoln's beliefs or positioning. It left those things to be conveyed via user-generated content and it failed badly.

Laurie Dillon-Schalk noted that total engagement garnered was about 3800 tweets, mostly generated during the time of Jimmy Fallon's show. An ad that gives up that much control to the public is risky.

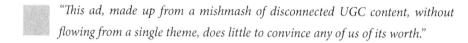 *"This ad, made up from a mishmash of disconnected UGC content, without flowing from a single theme, does little to convince any of us of its worth."*

THE BEST STORIES GO BEYOND ADVERTISING

You want people to connect to your brand? Seed the idea.

Begin the first chapter, establish your brand values, and develop a narrative that connects your customers to those same values. But don't stop there! Weave it into everything you do: your website, your blogs, your internal communications, and your dialogue with your customers.

Allow it to branch and morph and grow. And let your audience interact with it and develop their personal stories. Your story can develop into endless chapters, within months and perhaps years.

The only example that fits this to a "T" is "Red Bull Stratos."[9] Creating engagement at scale, and being able to resonate with and connect "emotionally" with the consumer was established beyond comprehension. Red Bull has been now been lauded as a "media" company, a distinguished label that describes its ability to drive inexplicable reach and resonance.

The results:

- 2,000,000 unique consumer actions
- 1,000,000 distinct Stratos participants
- 2,000,000 new subscribers acquired in 15 days
- 820,000 pieces of positive content created
- 400% increase over average length of consumer engagement
- 50,000 distinct links shared
- 61,634,000 trusted Impressions generated

Build Trust in 5 Steps with Content Marketing

After all is said and done, what is content marketing really all about?

Sure it is about telling the story of your brand and answering questions that your customers have about your products and services in a "non-salesy" fashion, but deep down brands that do content marketing well do it for something more.

The brands that do content marketing better than their competition realize at the end of the day it is about building trust.

Whether you are creating content for new prospects, current customers, industry analysts or someone else entirely, the real purpose behind those efforts should be to build a higher level of trust between the consumer of the content and the brand creating it.

CONTENT MARKETING EVERYWHERE MAKES TRUST KEY

If you stop to consider the fact that there are 347 blog posts[10] created every minute, you will probably come to the conclusion that we have entered the age of information overload. Beyond blogs, there are videos, Facebook and Twitter posts, and, of course, all of the information that comes our way over email.

Beyond the new content being created and shared online every day, we are exposed to a massive amount of advertisements in a given day. In fact, the average Internet user will see about 5,000 advertisements each day. [11]

With so much information being created for and thrown at us each day, it is important to remember what will really make us stand out.[12]

Some companies will argue that it is the frequency or quality of the content. [13] I believe that both of those things play a role, but would tell you that they are less important than you may think.

For most brands, especially those that don't have endless financial wherewithal to spend on their marketing efforts it comes down to creating content that builds trust [14] between the brand and the consumer.

Talking about building trust through content marketing is one thing; doing it effectively is another.

If you are a brand looking to increase trust between your company and those you are creating content for, then I believe the following five steps are the key to building greater levels of trust with your audience:

1. **Define Your Audience and Outcomes**
   Brands must always be thinking about whom they are writing for [15] and why they are writing. It is much easier to build trust (and sales) when the right reader is given the right content. Then brands must think about why they are writing. I suggest they ask themselves, what is the goal of our content marketing [16]campaign? If trust is the object, then make sure not to push too hard, too soon.

2. **Determine Content Type, Frequency and Location**
   While the type, frequency and placement won't in itself build trust; you

have to think about whom you defined as the audience and show that you
are interested in them. If your audience primarily seeks content via email
then make sure you make it available to them. Trust starts by putting the
information they want in places where they can benefit from it. Great
content marketing that isn't seen will not build trust or anything for that
matter.

3. **Share, Promote and Engage**

   Part of the process of building trust is making sure that the word is out
   that your content is available; there is a fine line between helpful awareness and spammy promotion. Make sure that sharing is done on the
   platforms where your audience is active. Further, curate content carefully
   and help the reader quickly see why they may want to consume the content. Finally, if a reader takes the time to engage with the content, whether
   they share it on Social Media or comment on it, make sure to reach out to
   them to let them know you appreciate their support and to see how else
   you may help.

4. **Make Connecting With Your Brand Simple**

   If you do all the work to create great content, then you should be highly
   motivated to make it easy for someone to connect with your brand. However, I see them get this wrong all the time. They make it far too difficult
   to find their feeds or their social bookmarks. Make sure it is very easy
   for interested readers to become more meaningfully connected to your
   brand through email, phone, RSS or other means. After all the work to get
   people excited about what you are doing, don't push them away by making it hard to connect.

5. **Analyze Responses, Optimize and Pivot**

   You may be thinking: What does analytics have to do with trust building?
   The reason this step exists is because great content Marketers take the
   time to monitor what is working and what isn't. Brands must look at the

content to see what is being viewed, shared and engaged with. If certain content is drawing a great response while some is largely being ignored, then brands should pivot to create more of what their audience is connecting with. This doesn't only drive more readers[18], but more opportunities to build trust with an audience.

These five steps, like any process worth doing, take time. One of the biggest downfalls most brands face when executing their content marketing strategy is that they don't set proper expectations for how long the plan should take to work.

While we all know that trust can be built quickly, more often than not, it takes time to establish. With this in mind, most content marketing campaigns won't work until trust is established; therefore, adequate headway must be given to trust building efforts.

One thing I can tell you for certain: Once high levels of trust are established between a brand and the consumer, the sales process becomes much less cumbersome. With trust, business moves from a "Prove-it-to-me" debate to a "Help-me" dialogue, where both sides benefit.

Brands that focus on consistently informing their audience about the items they are most interested in knowing are off to a great start for establishing higher levels of trust. Once informed it comes down to being active, connected and available for the customer to learn and find out more. Then brands must continue to self- actualize and ask themselves: Are we providing the content our audience really wants and adjust accordingly?

Trust is a process, a worthy one, but a process nonetheless; build it and everything about your business can and will become easier.

Will Content be Going Away Anytime Soon?

With 3 of the largest platforms continuously optimizing formats to respond to user acceptance, plus the emergence of native platforms to develop new connections between communities and brands, it's clear that content will continue to morph in this new communication space.

The principles of trust, education and value will mandate brands shed their old habits and practices, in favor of newly accepted norms dictated by the very audience they want to reach.

Build Content for Context to Influence a Community

CONTENT MARKETING: LIKE BUILDING A BUSINESS ALL OVER AGAIN

You spent how many years building your business?
You mean…it didn't happen overnight?
Exactly. While there is always an anomaly, chances are, your business, like so many others, took time to build.
So what makes your content marketing strategy any different?

Your Blog Wasn't Built in a Day
Truth be told, it's not that simple.

A content strategy has to be backed with a commitment to creating the content that your current and ideal customers will want to read.

People are exhausted by the "Sell Job" they encounter–day in and day out. What they seek is information that will help them make better purchasing decisions, either directly or indirectly.

That means that consistently delivering quality content is the only way to win in the long run. Obviously, coupling content with best practices for the search engines will help create the synergistic effect that we are looking for.

What is certain is that you can't write one or two posts (even if they are terrific) and expect to move the needle.

The only thing those first two posts signify is the start of something critical to your business long term.

WHY YOUR BUSINESS NEEDS CONTENT MARKETING

Did you know that businesses with a blog drive 55% more traffic [19] than businesses without one?

I actually thought that number was pretty low, but nonetheless it is a reflection of the "average" increase in traffic for a company that blogs versus a company that doesn't.

Basically, a company site without a blog is likely just a lot of stale "marketing" content that reads like a billboard.

This is where "Context" comes into play.

MAKING IT MAKE SENSE – CONTEXT MARKETING

Content drives more traffic. Context drives the right type of audience.

And the difference, while subtle, is significant.

Having 5,000 visitors to your site in a day may sound great.
Having 5 visitors to your site in a day may sound terrible.

But would you rather have 5,000 visitors that never buy anything, or 5 that are great candidates for what you have to offer?

When you blog, you create content, but when you create the right content you create context. This will help you make someone want to take action.

A FORMULA FOR DIGITAL SUCCESS?

Content + Context = Meaningful (Useful) Content

Now, when we add a layer by consistently building meaningful content, the formula further expands and will look more like this…

Meaningful Content + Consistent Production + Engaged Community = Influence[20]

Influence drives behavior, and in the case of most businesses, the decision to buy something.

But here is the kicker: The formulas, while overly simplistic, are still very representative of the work that needs to be done. And like the business you have built, your online presence, and more importantly, your community, is built over time by providing meaningful content that continues to feed the minds of those thirsting for it.

When your audience sees you as the source for the information, it is quite likely they will see you as the source for procurement.

After all, we buy from the people we like, and the people we trust–which is exactly who you will find in a well-built community. However, at the heart of most online communities is content. This is why content is more than just a part of the "Evolved" Marketer's ecosystem, but rather a kingdom in itself.

REFERENCES:

[1]   http://antelopeinc.com

[2]   http://www.forbes.com/sites/roberthof/2012/11/05/uh-oh-survey-says-most-people-find-facebook-and-twitter-ads-misleading/

[3]   http://en.wikipedia.org/wiki/Internet_forum

[4]   http://www.cluetrain.com/book/

[5]   http://forrester.typepad.com/groundswell/images/2007/04/24/ladder_3.gif

[6]   http://www.nativo.net/

[7]   http://2013.podcamptoronto.com/sessions/ze-art-of-storytelling/

[8]   http://www.nytimes.com/2012/03/18/opinion/sunday/the-neuroscience-of-your-brain-on-fiction.html?pagewanted=all&_r=4&

[9]   https://www.youtube.com/user/redbull

[10] http://mashable.com/2012/06/22/data-created-every-minute/

[11] https://www.thinkwithgoogle.com/collections/zero-moment-truth.html

[12] http://broadsuite.com/differentiate-business-content/

[13] http://broadsuite.com/which-more-important-content-frequency-or-quality/

[14] http://broadsuite.com/can-you-measure-return-on-trust/

[15] http://broadsuite.com/do-you-target-content-for-your-audience/

[15] http://broadsuite.com/use-content-marketing-to-build-community/

[17] http://broadsuite.com/content-engagement-move-beyond-just-promotion/

[18] http://broadsuite.com/b2b-marketing-measuring-what-matters/

[19] http://www.forbes.com/sites/danielnewman/2014/04/10/the-role-of-influence-in-the-new-buyers-journey/

[20] http://leaderswest.com/2013/09/04/infographic-companies-with-a-blog-get-55-more-traffic/

Big Data: Making Things Easy for Marketers and Companies

THE PROMISE OF DATA by Amy Vernon

What's not to love? It's Big. It's Data. Marketers love numbers. Numbers are data. Marketers love big numbers.

OK, let me take a step back. I know that's not what Big Data really means.

But the problem is that so many people buzzing about Big Data don't really know what it means. It sounds like a huge pile of numbers. And those numbers can quantify what you're doing. Marketers are always being told they need to quantify their efforts – show how that Facebook page is contributing to the bottom line, how all that work on SEO is driving traffic, how having that Twitter account is aiding customer service.

The fact of the matter is the data that's available now is so much deeper and more detailed than it's ever been. There are privacy battles yet to be fought over this data, and consumers have a love-hate relationship with it.

We all prefer seeing ads for things that actually relate to our lives. At the same time, we find ourselves a little creeped-out when that dress we almost bought follows us around the Internet for weeks via retargeting campaigns unless we clear our caches. And when Gmail serves us up ads that are a little too closely related to the email we're reading? It feels like we're in a George Orwell book, Big Brother breathing down our necks.

As Marketers, we love all this data, because we can target our efforts to the people who might actually be interested in what we're peddling, rather than spraying it all out there and hoping we hit some targets.

We have become the product. We've been told that for a while, about Facebook, Twitter and other platforms that provide us with what seems like an amazing service for free. If you're not paying for it, you're the product, right? How else is Mark Zuckerberg going to pay his bills if he's not selling us all to the highest bidder (literally)?

Think about how much Google, Facebook and Apple know about your personal tastes and interests. Everything you've searched for and emailed is there, somewhere, on a Google server. Facebook tracks everything you like and have ever posted. Apple knows every piece of media you've ever purchased – every song, every TV episode, and every movie.

And, yes, there are other players, but the big three are the ones that really matter. It's a good thing they don't like each other all that much, otherwise imagine the complete picture of each and every one of us they could put together with their combined databases.

We're now adding a layer of physical and health information over all that, too – Fitbits and Fuelbands and Shines that track our every step, our every breath, our every heartbeat. So we're mixing our health information with our interests and demographics.

Never before has there been such a complete picture of whom we are as individuals available simply through data.

As I noted, there are a lot of privacy issues relating to this data. But I'm not going to focus on that right now; many others have and will examine those potential landmines.

There's an amazing amount of power behind this data. We can find things much more easily – think of the "people who bought this also bought ..." feature on Amazon. The ability to discover something new that others with the same interest have bought is powerful, for both consumers and business. I always look at those suggestions. Even though I rarely purchase from that list (that has more to do with me and my purchase patterns than the utility of the list), I consider that feature a bonus, not an annoying advertisement. It really is no different than the ads that come up in Google when I search for something – it is Amazon's algorithm crunching the data and coming up with something else I might want to spend money on.

The main difference here is that it's more closely aligned with what I actually want to purchase than Google ads. And it's at the point of purchase, when I'm more likely to click on "add to cart."

That's the direction all this data is moving in – a more personalized experience online and in real life. If you have the Walgreens app on your phone, it knows when you have walked into one of its stores and can serve you up real-time specials. Though I don't believe it's yet incorporated into your spending patterns, I can see it eventually being synced with your purchases on your loyalty card and maybe even your prescriptions.

As Hessie and Dan discuss in this chapter, many companies feel overwhelmed by Big Data. The reason is simple: so much of it has come so quickly. We're simply unprepared for all these bits and bytes that are pouring in.

Yet it offers us all such incredible opportunities. Companies that do not begin to figure out how it's going to parse this data will fall behind, and quickly.

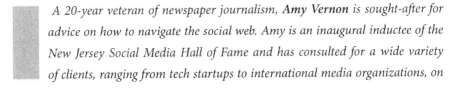

*A 20-year veteran of newspaper journalism, **Amy Vernon** is sought-after for advice on how to navigate the social web. Amy is an inaugural inductee of the New Jersey Social Media Hall of Fame and has consulted for a wide variety of clients, ranging from tech startups to international media organizations, on*

how to harness their community, develop shareable content and put in place best practices in their digital strategy. Amy has blogged for VentureBeat, The Next Web, Network World, and Discovery.com's Parentables. She's also a wife and mother and lives in New Jersey.

Big Data Creates Win/Win for Businesses and Consumers

FOR BUSINESS BIG DATA IS A BIG DEAL

The new marketing meme, "Big Data" has captured everyone's attention. Did you know that 90% of the world's data[1] was generated in the past few years?

The rise of social, online behavior, user content generation, not to mention increased mobile activity, has contributed to the mountain of datasets that have grown so large "they become awkward to work with using on-hand database management tools." (As per Wikipedia).[2]

Every minute on the Internet there are more than 2,000,000 Google searches, 685,000 Facebook updates, 200 million sent emails and 48 hours worth of video uploaded to YouTube. Not in a day or a week, but in a minute.

That is a ton of information to process, and frankly, most companies are struggling with what to do about it.

How have these data sets become so large? Like this:

Almost any current technology can collect data. Information is captured the moment devices are enabled: RFID (Radio Frequency Identification Readers) or Chip readers from credit cards, mobile-sensing devices, aerial sensing technologies, software logs, cameras, microphones–and now, Near Field Communications (NFC) [3] and iBeacons as mobile payments take the stage. The more prevalent the use of technology – especially mobile– the more exponential the data volume becomes. As this article suggests:[4]

> *"The continuing global data explosion, which some say will reach 8 zettabytes by 2015, is demanding a new, smarter approach to storage. It must be one that infuses infrastructures with greater automation and intelligence to store data in the most strategic places, make it easier to access, and enable greater insights to be gained."*

In fact, one survey found that 70% of companies are overwhelmed by the amount of data coming their way, and only 25% of businesses had a plan to deal with big data. What makes big data even more complex, especially for small business, is that not all data is created equal.

While some data comes in structured formats, such as sales data, web statistics and marketing lists, much of the data comes in free form or what is referred to as unstructured. This data is much harder to utilize and leverage than its counterpart because it is comprised of the information inside of presentations, images, videos and blog posts. Both of these data types are seeing tremendous growth, with structured data growing at a rate of 60% year over year, and unstructured at an even greater rate of 80%.

Wikipedia estimates, "The world's technological per capita capacity to store information has roughly doubled every 40 months since the 1980s (about every 3 years) and every day 2.5 quintillion bytes of data are created".[5]

The richness of the data makes any analyst salivate. Just imagine how this could be applied. I was at South by Southwest (SXSW) when a panel of pundits spoke about Big Data: Powering the Race for the White House:

U.S. Republican Race of 2012: Twitter was a major source of data aggregation for the Republican Race in the U.S. At SXSW, It was noted,

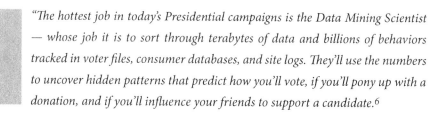

> *"The hottest job in today's Presidential campaigns is the Data Mining Scientist — whose job it is to sort through terabytes of data and billions of behaviors tracked in voter files, consumer databases, and site logs. They'll use the numbers to uncover hidden patterns that predict how you'll vote, if you'll pony up with a donation, and if you'll influence your friends to support a candidate.*[6]

The rise of public opinion–stored in platforms like Twitter, Google, Facebook, etc. provides enough intelligence to influence the campaign development, timing, geography and even the color of the campaign signs.

As you can see data is becoming more powerful than ever, impacting some of the world's most watched events. What about the everyday business, and of course, marketers? Where does Big Data fit into their world?

Every Day Business Uses for Big Data

With so much available information there is a tremendous opportunity for companies that can identify and isolate key pieces of information that help improve their business.

Just imagine how this could be used in positive ways: Consumer products and services will now be adaptable to customer needs.

Everybody has his/her own personal preferences when it comes to movies. Netflix already captures your movie genre preferences and makes recommendations on recent shows/movies you have watched. It is already capturing which devices you are using to watch these shows, and when.

In addition, Netflix uses Facebook's Open Graph to provide you with friend activities, ratings and recommendations. Marrying that data with TVTag [7] for example, validates the original information and supplements the user information with commenting, share data, as well as potential prospects.

When combined and correlated, these snippets provide insight that now allows Netflix to optimize their movie offering to you, and ensure that you're a satisfied customer. It can also capture the comments and shares from those watching the movie in order to drive messaging to attract new users.

HEALTH CARE AND THE AGING BOOMERS

Now predicting incidences of disease and finding cures are within reach. Healthcare can be a major beneficiary of Big Data.

Hospitals and general patient care information have been traditionally gathered and stored manually, in file folders. That information was then transferred to microfiche.

The health industry, no matter how archaic its traditional information storage, is slowly beginning to digitally archive information.

A McKinsey Global report[8] released last year reported, "effective and creative use of big data could create $300 billion in value for the US healthcare system. Two thirds of that would be in reducing US health care expenditure."

But I believe the most significant movement for healthcare is in analyzing patient cases and records, and determining commonalities, prescribed procedures and outcomes that can be applied in similar cases. Imagine if Big Data were able to provide supplemental learning for scientists and doctors.

By and large, however, the majority of healthcare information is locked away in a document – a patient's medical records. Privacy protects this information, as it should. Balancing the needs of the individual with the society at large is a strong consideration that Chapter 8 seeks to tackle.

FOR MARKETERS, THINGS HAVE GOTTEN A WHOLE LOT EASIER

For the database marketer, forget about A/B testing. Analysis of real-time data enables predictive algorithms to increase the certainty of future initiatives: development of products, services or processes.

Personally, I love the fact that we don't have to rely on statistical significance to extrapolate results. There is enough information in Big Data and in "real-time" to make analysis much more meaningful.

No more spending on expensive subscription reports from the likes of comScore and Nielson, which rely heavily on panel data and statistics to "seemingly" extrapolate to a population behavior. This clearly doesn't work all the time but there hasn't been an alternative, until now.

I can see having the ability to tap into markets already using my product, and gaining the insight needed to validate whether I'm targeting the right audience right NOW. The future screams, "Let the data show you who's already using similar products" and that will dictate who truly wants and needs your products.

Now Marketers have a whole lot more information about customers and potential customers. Traditional CRM allowed Marketers' access to customer:

- Purchases
- Returns
- Complaints
- Transaction history
- Customer service calls/resolution history
- Standard demographic information

Now, supplement that with customer social data:

- Where he goes

- What he does
- What he likes
- What he loves
- What he hates
- His close friends
- What he shares
- What he buys
- His hobbies
- What he searches for online
- What he says

… And so on…

Marketers can even capitalize on what's happening with competitors to obtain more robust intelligence into current online activity, social discussions and consumer sentiment, and be able to adapt and flex campaigns to maximize opportunities. At the end of the day, both the company and the consumer win.

Technology and data collection is inescapable. For businesses and organizations of all types it is now mainstream, and policies are beginning to change to ensure proper disclosure to the user.

Why Small Brands Need Big Data

While these are just a few of the ways Big Data can be used to drive better business decisions, it is becoming more and more clear each day: businesses that can use information to better manage decision making will be at a distinct advantage.

The emerging problem is that data visualization is expensive and as one Harvard Business Review article [9] points out, we are going to be moving to a world of Data-Haves and Data-Have-Nots. It is going to be based on financial wherewithal, an area where many smaller organizations come up short.

The information outlined above represents the quandary of not just small business, but of all business, so let's drill down one level further. What is the biggest challenge for Small Business looking to take advantage of big data?

BIG FACTS, BIG DATA, AND SMALL BUSINESS: SOLVED BY CLOUD, SOFTWARE AND TOOLS

The truth is that Big Data for small business is no Longer "Mission Impossible." According to Phil Simon,[10] author of some of the leading books on Big Data including Too Big To Ignore: A Case For Big Data and The Visual Organization, "I found that plenty of small and midsized companies are doing interesting things with data, and they aren't spending millions on it."

Simon goes on to say in an article:[11]

> *"True that in the past, companies seeking to tap into big data needed to purchase expensive hardware and software, hire consultants, and invest huge amounts of time in analytics. But trends such as cloud computing, open-source software, and software as a service have changed all that. New, inexpensive ways to learn from data are emerging all the time."*

In short, what Simon is saying is that if you are a business, big or small, there are manageable ways to approach big data where you can garner some pieces of information that may very well set you apart from your competitors.

Some recommendations for Small Businesses looking to tap Into Big Data:

- Take the time to understand your goals for Big Data. Are there a few very specific pieces of information you seek such as customer demographics or attrition metrics? Making big data goals smaller can make the potential of implementing a Big Data program more realistic

- Look at data on demand sources like Kaggle, where you can choose the size of the project and the amount of extractable information you seek. Much like a Priceline "name your own price."
- Finally, leverage data brokers with competitive rates. Many traditional data brokers have become more reasonable with mounting competition and therefore offer highly useful data at prices that smaller organizations can afford.

Big Data has a place inside of every organization, but it is more than that; it is truly disruptive. For Marketers, it is evolutionary because it isn't just another thing to talk about; it is a game-changer for the future of business communication.

Big Data Means Big Disruption:

HOW DOES BIG DATA INFLUENCE HOW WE COMMUNICATE AS CONSUMERS?

With this much information being published each minute it can mean many things to the way we, as humans, will communicate into the future.

In the simplest terms, the growth of big data means that we will be far more focused on self-education in the future. With so much rich and useful data available to us we are going to know more about any topic we choose by simply employing search and consuming the results.[12]

Having said that, we will also be more challenged to separate the information that is most valid and relevant, and what is being sold to us. As a society we trust Google[13] to provide us with the relevant content we need. However, with the increased intelligence via smarter search algorithms and the continued advancements in

SEO techniques by Marketers, it is hard to determine whether we will really get better search results for us, the consumer, or better search results for the Marketers/Google. After all, we will find what they want us to find, no?

AS MARKETERS, WE WILL HAVE
GREATER ACCESS TO CONSUMERS

Big Data will also be a powerful tool for brands to more accurately connect with the consumer of their choosing.

In the earlier days of the Internet, it served as a platform to get messaging out, but it was incredibly difficult to target the message. This has gotten better with search, and proliferated further as consumers became more social and willingly revealed more of their thoughts, attitudes, beliefs and behaviors.

In the future, as the power of big data gets reeled into something simpler to use and easier to deploy, consumers will see their entire life experience become more aligned with the information they most desire to consume. This may mean custom retail shopping experiences, television channels dedicated to the individual consumer, as well as predictive analysis that has greater accuracy than any methods used today.

Big Data won't only change the way we live, it will disrupt our entire life experience online and off, and the funny thing is that many of us won't even know it.

The predictive nature of big data opens the doors to many possibilities. We explore one such technology that uses big data to understand the variables that trigger trends. Does it have the ability to predict the virility of such trends?

TrendSpottr: Playing with Viral Possibilities

One of the most powerful videos of 2012, "Gangnam Style," was released in July 2012. On December 21, 2012, according to Wikipedia "Gangnam Style" [14] became the first online video to record a billion hits. As of January 6, 2013, the music video has been viewed over 1.13 billion times on YouTube, and it is the site's most watched video.

Now imagine for a second having the ability to foresee the phenomenon of reaching 1 billion video hits, let alone 1 million. If you did have that power, what would you do with the information?

Here, I profile Mark Zohar, President and Founder of TrendSpottr.

When I met with Mark, he told me about the Gangnam Style video and TrendSpottr's ability to predict, while views were well under 100K, how much this cultural pop video would catch fire when it hit the mainstream.

What fascinates me about your technology is its ability to consistently predict trends before it hits the mainstream audience. What factors come into play that detect a piece of content's potential to be picked up by TrendSpottr?

> *MZ: TrendSpottr's predictive algorithms analyze data streams in real-time to identify content that exhibits the attributes of viral growth. Such factors as the frequency, velocity, acceleration and amplification of content are used to predict trend data. By spotting emerging viral content within minutes of its origin, TrendSpottr is able to predict which information is most likely to trend, hours or even days before it has gained mainstream awareness.*

> *When I think of trend data, it is about tracking the movement of information – vast amounts of data -- over periods of time. Google Trends, for example, has amassed volumes of search data to accurately display what the world is searching for. There are varying opinions as to whether Google Trends' algorithm has the predictive gusto to accurately determine outcomes accurately using search data.*

Trendspottr differs because it only uses real-time data, which means the relevancy of information, has a short lifespan. What is your stance in determining trends via user searches vs. content shares? Secondly, how can you consistently predict trends when your algorithm is dealing with a relatively short period?

> MZ: *TrendSpottr's solution uses advanced algorithms to analyze real-time data for predictive trends. We are living at a time when consumer sentiment, political unrest and viral memes can spread like wildfire. TrendSpottr serves as an early warning system to alert businesses, governments and consumers to these impending trends before they have "tipped". This has proven to be of immense value to our partners and customers.*
>
> *TrendSpottr is currently being used for crisis and issue management, viral content discovery, predictive influencer analysis and ad yield optimization. Google Trends offers a very different yet complementary solution for identifying trends. While Google Trends provides interesting historical trends using search data that may inform the future, there is nothing inherently predictive, algorithmic or forward-looking about this solution. Some of our customers use Google Trends in combination with TrendSpottr to provide them with both historical search trends and real-time predictive insights.*

What recent trend was Trendspottr able to accurately depict? Take us through an example of that "moment" when content reaches that "tipping point".

> MZ: *A recent example was the photo the White House released where President Obama and McKayla Maroney[15] posed together with their "not impressed" faces. The photo was taken on Thursday November 15 but was released early in the morning on Saturday November 17th.*
>
> *TrendSpottr picked up this photo within minutes of it being published on Saturday and issued an "Extreme Alert" to our customers indicating that this image was likely to go massively viral. In fact, TrendSpottr was able to predict that this*

photo would go viral within the first 35 tweets and accurately predicted that the photo would generate over 4,000 tweets within the next 5 hours.

Several of our customers used the predictive alert they received from TrendSpottr to launch customized content marketing and social ad buying campaigns that incorporated the Obama photo and that resulted in huge content sharing metrics and click-through rate (CTR) conversions.

Up until recently, the concept of "predicting virality" has come into question. Viral cannot be created. Something has the potential to go viral based on the relationship between individuals. The value of that content and the context by which it is passed between users will determine its spread to beyond their immediate social graph. NOW, we not only can predict VIRAL content, it seems to me there is a formula to develop it. What's your stance on this?

MZ: I'm wary of claims that there is a formula one can follow to develop viral content. While there are some best practices we can learn from content that has gone viral (e.g., time of day publishing, media type, content messaging, etc.), almost all viral content is surprising, serendipitous and non-formulaic; think "Charlie Bit My Finger", "Golden Eagle Snatches Kid" and even "Gangnam Style". These are all examples of content that went viral because it resonated with people at the right time and without a specific formula or call to action beyond "this is worth sharing".

I believe that manufacturing viral content is the equivalent of capturing lightning in a bottle, and let us hope it stays that way.

While no one knows how to make content go viral, what makes TrendSpottr invaluable is its ability to spot viral content at its earliest acceleration point and allow anyone to capitalize on this momentum.

You are providing a looking glass into the future. I see strong uses for journalists on the hunt for the "hot story," or for companies trying to stay ahead of the competition

or keep up with their customers. What other groups do you see benefiting from TrendSpottr?

MZ: *In addition to journalists and news organizations, TrendSpottr is being used today by large brands and PR agencies for real-time crisis and issue management. For example, one of the world's largest PR agencies was able to use TrendSpottr to identify and act upon emerging issues and trends related to its customers' sponsorship and ad campaigns during the London Olympics.*

Financial services companies, including hedge funds, investment managers and financial news organizations, use TrendSpottr to gain early and predictive insights about individual stocks and macro-economic events that may impact financial markets.

TrendSpottr is also being used widely by content and social Marketers to discover and share timely, trending and relevant content that will resonate with their audience. We have heard from many content Marketers that TrendSpottr has helped them scale their content marketing initiatives and has resulted in significant increases in their social metrics and KPIs.

Another key customer group is advertisers who use TrendSpottr to predict the most effective keywords for their ad campaigns and optimize their ad spending based on emerging trends.

Other customer groups include governments, non-profits, media and entertainment companies and social analytics companies that license our API to integrate TrendSpottr with their existing suite of products.

I can see immense value for enterprise especially when combining your technology with customer transactional information. Being able to predict sales outcomes, reputational impacts from social data, customer service and sales data will allow organizations access to knowledge that will strategically impact the business overall. Is this an area you are developing solutions for?

MZ: One of our key partners is Salesforce.com. TrendSpottr is integrated with Salesforce Marketing Cloud and the Radian6 social analytics platform. This coming year we will be working on extending our integration to include other Salesforce applications, including Salesforce CRM and Salesforce Chatter. We are also starting to work with other enterprise customers and partners to integrate TrendSpottr with their business intelligence platforms, enterprise data networks and web analytics data.

With technologies such as these, perhaps we are much closer to not only predicting, but perhaps also developing formulas to create trends.

Predictability's strength will be key in enabling businesses to make use of its information to maximize business outcomes. As the next section attests, the inevitable next level called Social Business will reference Big Data as its foundation.

Big Data and its Direct Impact on Social Business

I attended a Social Business Summit presented by the Dachis Group (now Sprinklr) in New York sometime back.

The experience provided me access to some pretty forward-thinking professionals intent on building the next phase of Social Enterprise.

The rise of big data means that change is inevitable – it's already happening at the consumption level and the increasing speed at which we're collecting this information. But in order for everyone to really leverage the benefits of Big Data, business needs to change.

The case examples from IBM, Newscorp, Harvard and even Fox News revealed some pretty significant strides in our ability to define implementing social business practices in this new frontier; couple that with the fact that these are tier one organizations, and these examples are all the more compelling.

Jeff Dachis, former CEO of Dachis Group [16] (now Sprinklr) said it well:

> *"We have moved from an era of mass communication to a mass of communicators... with more people trusting the communicators."*

Brand managers now live out in the wild, where their customers are. *Dave Gray*[17], Former Partner at Dachis, pointed out,

> *"The ever-improving digital infrastructure and social networks are causing profound social change that increases competitive intensity...the only sustainable competitive advantage is the rate at which a company can learn."*

This, in turn, elicits two questions:

1. How do we engage with the mass of communicators -- the vendors, customers, consumers -- in a trusted, authentic, and transparent way?
2. How do we, in turn, properly integrate the reams of communication – more importantly the meaningful data – and translate that into organizational performance?

When I look at Social Business as an evolution, it's hard to dismiss traditional practices that have long built and pushed forward processes that have become the mainstay of successful organizations. The eventuality of this emerging service economy brings with it substantial change that many organizations are hesitant to embrace, let alone acknowledge.

In Canada, social media is still emerging. While many brands are willing to include social media in their marketing strategies, it is still largely a campaign component.

While there is a Canadian latency effect, I'd be hard pressed to believe that a large percentage of businesses in the US don't share the same mindset.

The fact of the matter is the phenomena that is social business brings with it inherent business risks, a complete change in mindset, and a cultural shift-none of which will happen overnight.

Scott Neumann, IBM's Social Business Evangelist, spoke about the need to "Activate and create a smarter workforce."[18] This entails:

TRANSFORMING CULTURE AND PROCESS

This means hiring the right people to embrace change. In a sales culture, where individuals are pitted against each other to drive performance, cooperation is rare. Can we effectively align the workforce to operate cross-functionally, break down silos, and more importantly, reach a consensus?

Gray pointed out companies can't easily adapt because of conflicting objectives between departments e.g. profit vs. sales volume vs. attrition.

This also means designing a dynamic model that flexes based on customer outcomes. It's not only about technology; it's about culture. We need to create a culture that can share its mistakes as easily as its wins -- and learn from its mistakes. Can we easily embrace failure in cultures where only success has typically been rewarded?

These two factors alone are hard to come by. You need to establish a culture of sharing in order to effectively engage externally. The mind-set shift required to evolve the organization is substantial.

CONTROL BECOMES ANOTHER BARRIER
THAT THE C-SUITE IS UNWILLING TO RELENT

IBM Social Business presented this viewpoint:

Lead by creating a world of possibilities

- Make everything social and bring your brand to every experience
- Eliminate the guesswork
- Get creativity from everywhere

An organization cannot run effectively if it bows to the whim of the masses at every turn. This iterative model needs process, priority, corporate governance, and an overall mission to ensure proper guidance. A balance needs to be established. And, it relies heavily on analysis of this big data to extract relevant meaning to the organization.

Dave Gray[19] pointed out, "A control system must have as many states as the system it wants to control." This is what he coined, "The Law of Requisite Variety." The way to deal with this complexity: [20]

- **Reduce Variety:** provide a scaled-down product/service offering
- **Absorb Variety:** reorganize for variety instead of trying to contain it.
- **Create Autonomous Pods to address real-time needs:** groups that have authority to represent the company and are given accountability measures.

Chris Crummy [21] , Worldwide Director of Sales at IBM, indicated:

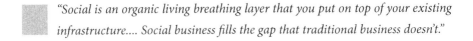

"Social is an organic living breathing layer that you put on top of your existing infrastructure.... Social business fills the gap that traditional business doesn't."

And therein lies the rub: The fundamental discipline of social business is measurement. Dave Gray pointed out, however,

"...it's important to identify constituencies; understand what motivates them, then measure and comprehend how they contribute to overall organizational performance."

Until we set the parameters to measure this, adoption will be slow.

In many ways, it's a chicken and egg scenario: the current approach to engaging in social is a fail. Brands are failing to scale authentic engagement. The reason: resources. Increased resources will not be committed without proper performance attribution.

The new world would argue, "Social engagement will contribute to the new ROI."

In a space that's evolving rapidly, Marketers are realizing numbers are slowly taking a back seat to the inherent value of garnering consumer and market insight.

After all, the new world order relies on doing everything right for your existing customers. Service, these days, has become the new economy. Unless we understand our customers more holistically: what motivates them, what makes them happy, how they feel about our products and how they feel about us, acquisition becomes much more difficult.

Social business seems like a "Pollyannaish" view of the evolution of business. A totally transparent organization may be unrealistic. Mitigating current organizational politics, silo-laden structures and internal competition will definitely stifle this evolution. However, changes are already underway.

As per David Gray, [22]

"There is no way to proceed without dismantling some of that precious infra-structure."

We continue to explore this topic in more depth in Chapter 12, The Inevitability: All Roads Lead to Social Business.

REFERENCES:

1. http://en.wikipedia.org/wiki/Big_data
2. http://www.sage.co.uk/business-advice/running-a-business/infographic-small-business-big-data.html
3. http://en.wikipedia.org/wiki/Near_field_communication
4. http://www.storagenewsletter.com/rubriques/systems-raid-nas-san/ibm-smarter-storage-initiative/
5. http://en.wikipedia.org/wiki/Big_data
6. http://schedule.sxsw.com/2012/events/event_IAP10797
7. http://TVTAG.com/
8. http://www.mckinsey.com/insights/business_technology/big_data_the_next_frontier_for_innovation
9. https://hbr.org/2013/12/small-businesses-need-big-data-too/
10. http://www.philsimon.com/
11. http://www.amazon.com/Visual-Organization-Visualization-Decisions-Business-ebook/dp/B00IKGM9NM/ref=sr_1_1?ie=UTF8&qid=1394660408&sr=8-1&keywords=phil+simon
12. http://millennialceo.com/technology/business-insights-simple-approach-big-data/
13. http://millennialceo.com/leadership/forget-rules-engagement-changed/
14. http://en.wikipedia.org/wiki/Gangnam_Style
15. http://newsfeed.time.com/2012/11/18/barack-obama-and-gymnast-mckayla-maroney-strike-the-not-impressed-pose/
16. https://www.sprinklr.com
17. http://twitter.com/davegray
18. http://twitter.com/scottneuman41
19. http://connectedco.com/about/
20. https://www.flickr.com/photos/davegray/6463738227/
21. https://twitter.com/ccrummey
22. http://connectedco.com/about/

We're Going Back to the Mom and Pop Store: Where We Value the Statistically Insignificant

RETAIL BACK TO THE FUTURE by Denise Lee Yohn

So much has changed in the retail sector in the last 10 years – the major players, distribution channels, use of digital technology, role of brands, and store formats. A consistent theme across all these changes is the shift away from mass merchandising and mass marketing.

From boutiques selling handcrafted wares, to craft breweries, to farmers' markets and personal eBay stores, we're seeing a re-birth of the mom-and-pop shop. Even at national chains, "stack 'em high and watch 'em fly" has been replaced by curated shopping experiences and personalized interactions.

Two intersecting developments have led to this new age in retail. Most people now seek out low-tech/high-touch experiences, and relationships with friends and brands as a counterbalance to the way technology has infiltrated every part of our lives. Advancements in technology -- connective consumer technologies including mobile, social, and location-based, and advanced media capabilities including profiling, targeting, and predictive modeling -- have made it easier and less expensive for companies to advertise and connect with customers on a more individual basis.

Retail has become more personal, local, and relational.

Personal – "It's All About Me"

People now expect retail to be all about them – their individual needs, preferences, purchase behaviors, and lifestyles. No longer settling for being anonymous customers, people want customized products, personal service, and individualized offers. Personalized product recommendations and individually addressed communications are the norm. Retailers must go beyond these basics to truly meet people's desire for the personal touch.

Apparel retailer J. Crew has introduced "Very Personal Stylists" – people who help you pick out the right styles, assemble a collection of items for you to try on at home, shop for gifts, and deliver purchases to you. The company developed the 24/7 on-demand, complimentary service to differentiate its shopping experience and deliver greater value to its customers.

The meteoric rise of Uber, the ridesharing service (in spite of the media's attention to its questionable practices) has to be attributed, in part, to how it's transformed an anonymous transaction into a highly personalized journey – from the options of standard service vs. Uber X (every day cars) vs. Uber LUX (luxury limos) vs. carpooling, to the pictures of the drivers and riders that are exchanged when a ride is confirmed, to its human customer service representatives and community managers.

Retailers need to be personally relevant to customers, or they'll be ignored.

Local – The Corner Store

Wal-Mart and Whole Foods may be as different from each other as two retailers can be, but they share a growing emphasis on local as a growth strategy. Wal-Mart has increased its technology capabilities and shifted its media dollars to reach customers locally. Whole Foods aims to source 20% of its products locally across the chain, and it works with local suppliers in practically every category it sells. In addition, each store hires local marketing staff that communicates with customers through social media, engages with local influencers, and hosts community events at the stores.

Other retailers are also finding that customers are starting to value factors like convenience, community involvement, and local appeal more than the consistency and dependability that used to drive their brand choices. So companies are now including more locally-sourced products in their assortments, participating in community events, designing their stores to reflect their neighborhoods, and promoting their stores as community gathering places. They want to feel like the corner store, even if they're a national chain, because it makes the brand feel more human, more real.

Relational – Not Just a One-Night Stand

Retail is no longer a location; it's an experience. Retailers have been talking about the importance of experience for years, but it's always been in the context of the in-store experience, online experience, service experience or some other tie to a point in time and space. Now retail is everywhere, anywhere, anytime -- thanks to digital technology. That means that people are always in some stage of shopping (even if they don't know it) and retailers must weave themselves into people's daily patterns.

Moreover, a purchase is no longer simply a transaction; it's a communication. With cashless payments, emailed receipts, and subscription purchases, when customers pay now, they are giving retailers important purchase information and the ability to access personal information. Customers who engage with brands via social media or mobile app give companies even more valuable information. Despite privacy concerns, most people expect retailers to use their data responsibly and to use it to serve them better.

These developments have produced tremendous opportunities that savvy companies have seized, including Taco Bell, who targeted specific social influencers to seed a successful new product launch. CVS enhanced its Caremark Pharmacy Service with digital communications and processes to help customers better manage their prescription needs.

It's likely that retail will continue to undergo significant transformation and become even more personal, local, and relational. Mom-and-pop shops were retail's history. Now they're its future.

> *Blending a fresh perspective, twenty-five years of experience working with world-class brands including Sony and Frito-Lay, and a talent for inspiring audiences, **Denise Lee Yohn** is a leading authority on building and positioning exceptional brands. Denise is the author of the new book What Great Brands Do. (Jossey-Bass).*

United Bakers: Toronto's Oldest Restaurant is Connected with its Customers

I've been going to UB (the nickname for United Bakers Dairy Restaurant) for many years.

My brother married a wonderful girl named Irene, who works there with her amazing mom Helen Zellermayer, Manager of United Bakers. It was here that Mrs. Z. introduced me to the delicious pea soup when I was near term with my son Nathan (11 years ago), and promised me that this pea soup would give Nathan a nudge to come into this world.

Sure enough, Nathan was born the very next day! I often come back to UB with my family, or when I'm headed downtown.

I stop by to see Helen, Irene and many of the wonderful staff and make sure I pick up some of their Challah bread, their famous Latkes or yummy cookies. If it's for a quick coffee or a meal, Helen, Irene and many of the staff make sure they stop by to greet me, and sometimes take the time to catch up.

I've never seen ANY quick service restaurant deliver faster service than UB. It has always been fresh, hot, and delivered with a smile.

I've been coming back to UB for over a decade, and I always see the same employees, happy to be part of this amazing restaurant. My experience prompted me to write about UB, their history and what makes them such a successful and renowned landmark in Toronto today. Philip Ladovsky, owner of UB, was kind enough to lend me some of his time.

When I decided to write about UB, it became even clearer how rare companies like this are. It brought me back to the summer of 2012 when we put together a conference called SocialMix.

We hosted *Gary Vaynerchuk (Gary Vee)*, who spoke about the importance of companies succeeding in what he coined, "The Thank You Economy." What he said resonated with me:

Acquisition is a commodity… but the most limited supply in the world is Effort!

"Getting customers is cake… acquisition has been mapped."

Behavioral and data scientists are figuring it out. They are getting a better understanding of the buying cycle and have integrated this into customer touch points.

At the end of the day, there is only one game we'll be playing: Retention. That means true effort and human caring from the business come into play. And that is hard, especially when it is not a natural tendency. "What if that company has done nothing to show they care? Would you stay?"

He states,

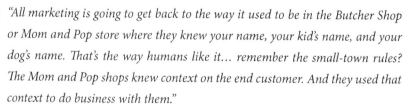

> *"All marketing is going to get back to the way it used to be in the Butcher Shop or Mom and Pop store where they knew your name, your kid's name, and your dog's name. That's the way humans like it… remember the small-town rules? The Mom and Pop shops knew context on the end customer. And they used that context to do business with them."*

WHERE IT ALL BEGAN

United Bakers just celebrated their 100th Birthday in 2012. It was a testament to what they've accomplished.

In 1912, a young couple, Aaron and Sarah Ladovsky, opened a bakery/coffee shop in downtown Toronto. They had just arrived from Poland, and were intent on making a living in Canada.

Their plan was to bring in the "flavors of life they left behind." They set up shop at 156 Agnes Street, then the "heart of the Jewish Ward." They hung out a sign that read "5 cent Coffee House."

They called their new business THE UNITED BAKERS, and sold their breads and meals prepared on the premises; soon it became a popular place.

Their patrons were all immigrants to Canada, from new arrivals to those who had established themselves. At this point in history there was an influx of immigrants from Central and Eastern Europe arriving in Canada; the Jewish community was expanding.

Many a newcomer to Toronto enjoyed their first meal at United Bakers. From the start, United Bakers was a haven of stability in a turbulent new world.

The patrons relished the hospitality of United Bakers. The flavors of the Old World were comforting:

 "...Simple, country-style Polish cooking, with the emphasis on delicious and filling comfort foods...The recipes used the basic vegetables they had been raised with – peas, beans, onions, cabbage, potatoes – peeled, chopped, diced and

cooked slowly, until the aromas and flavours that connected them to their past were coaxed from the pot – often enhanced with a pinch of 'secret' ingredients like parsnip or paprika and always, with a little sugar"

Immigration expanded as newcomers worked to bring their families to Canada. This required extra support from organizations back home in the form of emergency loans, insurance, sick benefits etc. Aaron Ladovsky returned to Poland to offer monetary support for the arrival of new Torontonians and encouraged others to take advantage of the opportunity.

Over the years, United Bakers prospered and it "became the hub of political and social activity," attracting everyone from factory workers, businessmen, artists, writers, poets and people from all walks of life.

"Payment was based on the honor system: you came to the cash register, recited what you'd eaten, and were charged accordingly. Many times, a patron, short on funds would eat for free. The Ladovskys didn't turn anyone away, and trusted that the people they helped would one day be able to provide for themselves, and for others too,"

FAST FORWARD

The strong foundation upon which these traditions were built continues to this day. United Bakers has long since moved from its Spadina location and now has a well-established business at Lawrence and Bathurst in Toronto.

Given its history you would assume that the Ladovskys would opt to expand the business. They have not. As *Philip* explains:

"We are in one location because we decided long ago that we want to oper-ate our business personally, and that means being there in person. Imprinting

a service philosophy upon a large and ethnically diverse staff requires rules, guidelines and training; but there is no substitute for the presence and personal participation of an owner. We have a wonderful team of managers who are in constant and close contact with me and with my sister Ruth. But we consider it our privilege — and our responsibility- to be here to set the tone."

"GREAT CUSTOMER SERVICE, AREN'T THOSE WORDS SELF-EXPLANATORY?"

At UB there are many regulars – the same faces I recognize every time I set foot in the restaurant. I asked Philip what makes customers keep coming back? He indicated that customers are people who have decided to spend their money at your business.

Service is the role the business must play in meeting the customer expectations. UB encourages their staff to be themselves, and that motivates them to take personal interest in their customers. As *Philip* states,

"Great customer service is almost unquantifiable: who can anticipate the myriad expectations customers have in their imaginations? But great is a pas between the two parties, and this has everything to do with attitude: if your interest is satisfying the customer, and making them feel at ease, you have the right attitude. Training can help smooth the edges of your approach, and can teach the server/ staff the most efficient and inexpensive way to achieve customer satisfaction, but there must first be an attitude of willingness to serve and a desire to satisfy."

THE TESTIMONIALS

I scrolled through their website and found patron stories from 1940s that have given lustre to the history of United Bakers. Here are a few noteworthy ones:

In 1948, I travelled from Germany and arrived at Union Station in Toronto. After my long journey, I walked out of the station and looked around to figure out where I was going to head next. A gentleman came up to me and asked me if I would like to have breakfast at one of the finest restaurants in the city. I happily accepted his invitation and he took me to United Bakers on Spadina where I ate my FIRST Canadian meal. It was the first real hamaishe breakfast I had since being liberated from a concentration camp in Germany. This was such a memorable and important moment in my life as it was my first true experience with Toronto and Canada. For the last 64 years I have continued to return to United Bakers at least once a week and enjoy great dining with my family and friends. Every time I return it brings back the wonderful memories of my first day in Canada and my first meal at United Bakers.   Milton B

I am now in my 85th year. When I was a boy of 8 years of age, I lived at 308 Spadina Ave. in an apartment above a dry-cleaning store. A few stores north there was a "United Bakers" store. My Mother would send me twice a week to the bakery to get bagels. It was a small store with about six tables. Customers would come in for coffee and a bagel. Mr. Ladovsky, the owner, would give me hot fresh bagels – what a delight! He was a gentle soul and cheerful and I remember it was a joy to go there. We still continue to go to the Lawrence Ave. location for lunch or dinner with our children and grandchildren, who also enjoy the haimishe atmosphere and the delicious food. Jack B.

I grew up in the Kensington Market area and going to United Bakery with my parents was always a special treat. After we moved to North York the trips were less frequent. When UB opened at Lawrence Plaza my Mom and I were thrilled (Dad had already passed on). It became a special place for Mom and I to meet weekly for lunch or dinner. My Mom passed on a little over a year ago. In her later years, even as the dementia got worse, the one place she would remember was UB. I took her there until the very end. She would always make me wait for a booth to become available and she would always look around and marvel at how busy it was and tell me how she and my Dad would always go to UB when it was downtown. I would always have to take home an order of the pea soup for her before we left. The soup and egg and onion were what she always ordered. I hope you last another 100 years for future generations to enjoy. Joanne S

LEGACY IS GREATER THAN CURRENCY

On the UB website, it states,

"We probably knew your grandparents, and we'd like to know you and your children too".

Philip notes that he enjoys a wonderful advantage: his grandparents gave his family a "seven decade head start".

Ruthie & I appreciate our good fortune at the position we've inherited serving as a meet & eat destination for many, many people. We love what we do, and we hope to continue to work with our staff and our customers to maintain UB's niche as" the restaurant that feels like home."

After all, in the profound words of *GaryVee*:

"Caring for the end user who is buying our products… is ALWAYS the right thing [to do]. The ones who WIN feel it, execute and they tell others how they did it…The world is changing. The eyeballs and ears of our customers are going in different places. If you're not there you're going to lose."

Quid Pro Quo: The Ultimate Dance Between the Brand and Consumer

The sustainability of today's business in a world increasingly controlled by the customer seems daunting for many businesses who are used to and, in many cases, hell bent on, maintaining the status quo with respect to how they market their products and communicate with their customers.

The pundits are saying this:

In order to adapt to the market of tomorrow you, as a business, have to listen to what your customers are saying. You have to make it a priority to build your business around the customer, NOT the other way around.

So one would assume that the more you know about your customer, the better you can target messaging to them in ways that will optimize how the communication is received.

This is the reason why many Marketers are encouraging brands to develop relationships with their customers. Here's the glitch, though…

…CONSUMERS DON'T WANT TO HAVE RELATIONSHIPS WITH BRANDS

In last year's Corporate Executive Board (CEB) study [1] of the 7,000 consumers, 23% have said they have a relationship with a brand. However it was also discovered, for most consumers, increased interactions don't drive relationships and often work against purchases.

What the researchers discovered was, without realizing it, many Marketers are only adding to the information bombardment consumers feel as they shop a category, reducing stickiness rather than enhancing it.

I had an interesting discussion with Doug Stephens[2], Author of The Retail Revival and Kerry Morrison[3], CEO of Norm. We all agreed that the value of Big Data is slowly becoming the Holy Grail to business, hoping to find the sweet spot that can determine what drives a consumer to buy. However, consumers are ever wary of the amount of information that is available to business especially in the face of the NSA scandal.[3]

Whether this will compel government to make business more transparent about the information they collect OR allow the consumer to have more control over what personal information is shared remains to be seen.

The truth of the matter is that it's difficult to break habits. Whether this and the next generation will be more closed off from social networks is not a realistic expectation. Payment systems and mobile will increasingly compound this wealth of data.

No one is really immune to the inevitability of the data solutions for business as this sort of intelligence becomes increasingly prevalent.

On the other side of the fence…

BRANDS DON'T HAVE THE PROCESSES THAT ALLOW FOR A RETURN ON RELATIONSHIP

Doug Stephens said it best,

"The CEO, who has 5 years to retirement, is not going to be the maverick and attempt to develop new ways of doing things, especially where he's in unfamiliar territory."

Companies typically operate within a defined period. Employees are compensated based on performance. Objectives are defined and results are collected within those timeframes.

- Sales;
- Retention;

- Customer Satisfaction;
- Churn Rates

These are the standard measures to benchmark company and individual performance. However, as everyone knows, relationship building takes time.

The value of content, interactions and other relationship drivers will take time to impact the larger organizational goals. In these cases, results begin to develop beyond the set timeframe a company is willing to allow.

I've often been frustrated with clients who expect immediate impact for engagements they've initiated in short order.

The company of today is unwilling to modify existing systems and process to accommodate the new mediums and their promise of nirvana.

WE'VE COME TO A CROSSROADS

So, if brands don't have the wherewithal to make the appropriate changes AND if customers don't really want to build relationships with brands, how do we get there?

TRUE ACCEPTANCE AND PERHAPS, AN AGREEMENT

If we, as consumers, can't stop the collection of our data, can we perhaps have some control over its usage?

If you, as a customer, understand that we are collecting information about you, will you give us, the business, the information that we need to make your experience better?

We touched on this notion during our discussion. Kerry Morrison noted, in the beginning when they were devising the premise of Norm.

We have these amazing social platforms where users are telling us precisely what they want, what they need, problems they're having and no one was listening...Why can't businesses connect with us on a personal level, not as demographic data, but as unique individuals?

If you stop to consider this, everything is morphing to an environment geared to the individual. The hyper local environmentwhere everybody knows your name (That was the Cheers motto, remember?), what you like, and where you go – is more attainable now than ever before with the help of social intelligence.

CAN SOCIAL INTELLIGENCE ACCURATELY AND CONSISTENTLY INFER A CUSTOMER'S PROPENSITY TO PURCHASE?

Doug and I tended to disagree. I would assume what a customer says he'll do may be the case probably 80% of the time. **Doug** noted,

> *"If you look at my tweets, you'll probably assume I hate Air Canada because of how much I complain about them. In reality... I always fly Air Canada because of the points."*

So, is behavior largely the dictator of brand affiliation and purchase propensity? I would argue that the data could tell a different story.

Language (mentions), in combination with behavior (visits, transactions, check-ins, pic uploads) can determine the extent of a person's affiliation with a brand, and predict their purchase propensity.

Natural Language has come a long way to detect aspiration vs. intent to purchase within sentences. Technology has gotten so sophisticated that the ability to use past behaviour/mentions as a predictor of consumer outcomes exists today.

THE QUID PRO QUO: NIRVANA

The business will use intelligence to know more about the customer, and may inadvertently bombard customers with offers, content etc. they don't want to see. However, if there is no relationship and the customer largely ignores the communications, then neither party is better off.

The balance lies in ensuring that the consumer doesn't have the business by the nose. On the flip side, business must understand, in aggregate as well as at the consumer level, the information that impacts parts of the purchase cycle. If there is no relationship, then both have to come to an agreement of give-and-take.

- What do I, as a business have to do to retain you, as a customer?
- What am I, as a customer, willing to give you, the business, to keep me satisfied and coming back?

I straddle the fence on this one.

As a customer, I want the best product and the best service. I want it at my convenience and at the price I'm willing to pay. No, I don't want to be solicited but sometimes I'm willing to look at offers that are relevant to me at that time.

I WANT THE BRAND TO KNOW "ME"

The solution comes down to communications.

Whether it's called a "relationship" or not, there has to be some sort of communication that allows each party to get what they want.

If Big Data is to provide insight, it will allow brands to understand these things:
- how their external factors influence their purchase behavior
- who they turn to for advice for the type of product sold by the brand
- the reason they want or don't want that product

Doug Stephens spoke about a time when, if brands don't make drastic moves to "understand" their customers, channel preferences, and how they want to be communicated with, then the onus will be on the customer to be the control channel that dictates information they want to disclose, and how they want to be communicated, etc.

For that CEO who has only 5 years to his retirement, perhaps it is too late in the game for him. He can't see the forest for the trees, or, if he does see the forest he doesn't want to risk taking an un-trodden path to get to it.

I still believe, however, that companies out there want to do the right thing to create a sustainable business. CRM is a reliable model that is reinventing itself in the social channels. This is what the new vanguard is all about. It doesn't have to stifle a business but can allow it to evolve in other ways.

As for relationship, it's just a word.

At the end of the day, it's an understanding that aligns both the business and customer on the same plane. It's this understanding that sustains the business and keeps the customer coming back.

As we begin to explore technological advances in this area, the new normal for relationships is born out of the data from social and mobile behavior. I explored one such technology from Kerry Morrison, Founder of Norm.

Norrrrmmmm!!: You Want to Go Where Everybody Knows Your Name

It became a familiar place to me. Thursday nights I would often turn on the TV set grinning, anticipating the funny quip that Norm Peterson threw out as he was greeted at Cheers! Here's how a typical banter would unfold:

"Normmmmmmmm!
Sam: How'ya doin' Norm? Whaddaya know?
Norm: Not enough!"

"Normmmmmmm! ...
Coach: What'll it be Norm?
Norm: Fame, Fortune, Fast Women?
Coach: How'bout a beer?
Norm: Even Better!"

This became a second home–a place to stop by everyday to catch up with the same crowd. Frasier and Norm always had their favorite places at the bar; Sam and Coach knew instinctively what their regulars preferred to drink. The customer stories were their stories. Cheers became a place of comfort. I don't think anybody every really talked about the food… because that's not why people stopped by. If anything, it was familiar…. it was comfortable.

Earlier, I wrote about United Bakers of Toronto, praising the 101-year-old restaurant's ability to be true to its customers and take care of them, always exceeding their expectations and going out of their way to satisfy the customer and making them feel at ease.

WHEN BECOMING BIG BECOMES UNWIELDY

When national brands swallowed up the Mom & Pop stores and redirected customers to the new way of shopping, service was less personal, but it was compensated through increased selection and abundant inventory. However, over time, where abundance made it more difficult for customers to choose or find products, service has become paramount.

ENTER NORM

So... the reason for the headline: Kerry Morrison, Founder of Norm[6], has a firm belief that the differentiator in today's connected world is the ability for a company to take care of and nurture the customers they have. I asked Kerry about his view on the importance of Customer Relationship Management (CRM) today and using social intelligence to enable this next phase.

"I think CRM is of paramount importance in today's marketing and business world. While traditional broad marketing with billboards, print ads, television commercials and the like aren't going anywhere soon, no one can argue that these formats are of the past and the future, more effective way of managing, selling and interacting with customers begins by knowing more about them. With the rise of social platforms we have this unbelievable opportunity to hear exactly what consumers want, what they need and the key becomes managing that deluge of personal information and making it accessible and actionable."

The rise of the social customer has also given rise to communities, friends, and recommendation sites having profound influence in their purchase decision. Companies have gotten too big to think about the individual customer. To quote, a friend, *Stewart Hayes*,

> "Companies have ignored the statistically insignificant."

These days, that same customer has the ability to bring down Goliath. I always come back to United Breaks Guitars[7] incident. The truth is that we've now come full circle, and these days in order to get a customer and keep them you have to go beyond just meeting their expectations.

WHERE NORM ELIMINATES THE GUESSWORK

Companies now have abundant information about their customers, "outside of the traditional transactional-based information." They now have access to deeply networked communities, enhanced profile information, behavior and propensities provided by social data. A colleague forwarded me this article, "The Reason So Many Brands Fail on Social Media Is That They Don't Actually Talk to Their Customers" [8]

The study reveals the wealth of data on customer desires being generated by this strategy is helping organizations work more effectively, and achieve better results. Social customer management doubles the percentage of sales leads that result in actual sales, relative to traditional CRM approaches.

HOW NORM ENABLES THIS

Kerry notes that in early conception, the technology was a method that aggregated all of the publicly available personal data that existed across a wide variety of social platforms and presented this information back to the business in real time. The goal: Improve Customer Experience.

Today, Norm is being adapted as a social analytics, profiling and planning tool, which culls together insights that have far reaching implications on a business' operations, products and customer management systems. *Morrison* adds…

 "When you add in our ability to track more and more location data through both in-store devices (wifi and iBeacons) and mobile handsets, we're seeing a level of consumer detail unimaginable just a few years ago."

WHERE NORM WAS BORN

Kerry speaks of the impetus that drove the Norm concept: Norm was born from a very rudimentary experiment that Kerry conducted at a restaurant in Vancouver using real-time Twitter monitoring to monitor customer feedback and improve customer service:

"A customer tweeted that the steak she received was cold. The staff noticed the tweet and immediately rectified the situation, acknowledging the complaint, happily replacing the meal with a warmer one and giving the customer complimentary wine in the process. Needless to say, the customer, quite embarrassed at the time, was pleasantly surprised and could not stop talking about that restaurant in the coming days. What we found though, was that in building a system that watched over and collected data from a number of the major social platforms, we were, in fact, creating these very detailed customer profiles on individuals. We saw where they went, with whom they interacted, how they spoke. From there it was very easy to envision numerous use cases in providing that learning back to enterprise customers."

SCALING SOCIAL RELATIONSHIPS: THE SECOND HOLY GRAIL?

If we're reverting to small town rules again, then technology has to provide the ability to bring those perceived "statistically insignificant" to the forefront. Many companies are beginning to recognize this.

Denise Lee Yohn (who you heard from at the start of this chapter) wrote this article in the Harvard Business Review: "Megastores Want to Be Mom and Pop Shops… Sort Of". In it she writes,

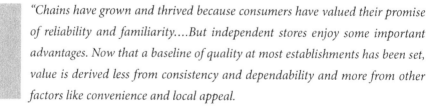

"Chains have grown and thrived because consumers have valued their promise of reliability and familiarity.…But independent stores enjoy some important advantages. Now that a baseline of quality at most establishments has been set, value is derived less from consistency and dependability and more from other factors like convenience and local appeal.

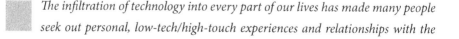

The infiltration of technology into every part of our lives has made many people seek out personal, low-tech/high-touch experiences and relationships with the

companies they patronize. At the same time, connective consumer technologies, sophisticated customer profiling, and targeted predictive modeling have made it easier and less expensive for companies to advertise and connect with customers locally. Independent stores have capitalized on all of these changes."

For Kerry and his team at Norm, reception to this concept of hyper localization is enormous.

We're still in the early years of social, mobile and location data becoming so intertwined and every single company we've met with is struggling to make sense of the volume of feedback / interactions / issues being raised in this space.

Businesses are recognizing the opportunity in having this direct line to consumers, but they're not sure how best to structure their messaging, how to monitor and measure the response or how to monetize these connections.

Perhaps we will not replicate the environment like Cheers, but we have the ability to come awfully close! Corporations are starting to recognize that paying attention to customer comments, interests and preferences–once deemed "irrelevant" by brands– becomes the competitive differentiator that yields more sustained customer relationships, and creates a much stronger company in the process.

Now we enter the World of Omni-Channel, where the ability to meet customer expectations must scale. The increasing reliance on data intelligence, supply-chain management will be critical to service this evolving channel.

The Omni-Channel Experience: Marketing Meets Ubiquity

With the rapid growth of digital consumption and what seems like daily proliferation of social media channels, Marketers are faced with more choices than ever when considering how they want to reach the consumer.

191 | WE'RE GOING BACK TO THE MOM AND POP STORE: WHERE VALUE THE STATISTICALLY INSIGNIFICANT

With each choice comes a certain amount of risk as Marketers, choosing to put a heavy investment in one channel, may miss the untapped potential of another, leaving smaller margin for error as highly informed consumers have become acutely aware of how to seek out information, poll their networks and complete transactions across a plethora of interactive channels.

With this transformation has come a new set of rules, breeding Marketers with a hybrid capability to not just focus on one type of marketing whether it is direct, digital or retail, but rather a Marketer that understands experience, and how consumers are seeking ubiquity. From their cell phone to the desktop to an in store visit; we are entering an Omni-Channel world, where consumers seek an Omni-Channel experience.

WHAT IS OMNI-CHANNEL?

Besides just being another marketing term or "Buzzword," Omni-Channel is a reflection of the choice that consumers have in how they engage a brand, and therefore is best represented as how brands enable their clients and consumers to use these channels to engage with them.

Whether the purchase experience starts online or via a catalogue, the customer has innumerable options as to how they may want to move through the buyer's journey with the brand.

Marketo, one of the leading Marketing Automation providers gives a solid explanation of why Marketers need to think Omni-Channel:

"Marketers now need to provide a seamless experience, regardless of channel or device. Consumers can now engage with a company in a physical store, on an online website or mobile app, through a catalog, or through social media. They can access products and services by calling a company on the phone, by

using an app on their mobile smartphone, or with a tablet, a laptop, or a desktop computer. Each piece of the consumer's experience should be consistent and complementary."

OMNI-CHANNEL AND THE MULTI-PATH PURCHASE EXPERIENCE

According to MIT's report, "Beyond the Checkout Cart," more than 80% of store shoppers check prices online.

If you think about the above data point, this shows the rapid evolution of Omni-Channel. Customers are going from screen to store and store to screen as they engage in buying behavior and for many consumers it doesn't start and stop there.

If you consider what a multi-path experience in an Omni-Channel environment really looks like, you may find yourself in an experience much like the one I had the other day.

I remember this past summer (2014) my oldest daughter Hailey's club soccer season was about to begin. As a 12 year old, she was growing so quickly that it was hard to keep up with her needs, and we had just realized she needs another pair of soccer shoes.

Knowing we were just about to go on vacation, and that as soon as we returned we would be full swing into the season, I jumped on my mobile device while we were wrapping up a dinner out, and I started scanning a popular online soccer site for shoes. I found a pair that I thought she would like and I added them to my cart.

I returned home and jumped on our iMac to show Hailey the shoes and she didn't like what I had chosen, so we picked out a different pair and put them into the cart. But I knew that my wife probably had some type of discount code so I told her we had to wait for her mom to arrive home so we didn't miss out on any discounts.

Life went on. We were distracted and somehow wound up completely forgetting about needing to order soccer shoes until about 24 hours later. I was tinkering on my iPad at that time when I received an inbound e-mail reminding me that I had items waiting in my cart. In that email there was also a discount code that gave me free shipping and a small discount on the purchase if I added certain items to go along with it.

From mobile to desktop to tablet, my experience took place across many channels, which is more common than you may think. It was also personalized, which is the real differentiator of Omni-channel marketing.

THINKING 1:1 BY THINKING OMNI-CHANNEL

When you closely consider the experience I went through trying to buy a pair of soccer shoes for my daughter, you realize that in a world where there are so many channels and ways to get to the consumer, the Omni-Channel experience isn't about the mature one–to-many marketing methods that so many of us know.

Television, newspaper and radio, if you were to advertise across all of them, that would be multi-channel. Omni-Channel, however, is about 1:1 experiences across the gamut of devices that consumers use.

Whether B2B or B2C, the 1:1 experience is what Marketers need to think about when considering the deployment of Omni-Channel because what makes the method so irresistible is how it takes shape based on the consumers behavior and uses your clicks, interactions and data to mold a shopping experience that is personalized.

OMNI-CHANNEL, NEW KPIs AND MOVING BEYOND SALES AND MARKETING

Perhaps one of the untapped potentials for Omni-Channel is moving it from a shopper's journey to a total customer experience.

When looking at the new KPI's for measuring marketing ROI, we brought items such as product development, customer satisfaction and employee engagement into the discussion.

While these items aren't directly attributable to revenue, they are highly correlated to a company's bottom line as for example, a satisfied customer tends to defect less and spend more.

So is it possible for Omni-Channel to address the total customer experience and drive customer satisfaction? If by engaging and determining how much an Omni-Channel experience improved a customers' journey, it is possible that the investment in the experience across a wider sample yielded improved customer sentiment, which in a world full of big data, can ultimately provide clarity in how brands can tweak and massage their Omni-Channel efforts to yield better business results.

1 http://www.retailwire.com/discussion/16071/consumers-dont-want-to-engage-with-brands

2 http://about.me/dougstephens

3 http://twitter.com/kmore

4 http://arcompany.co/the-nsa-privacy-and-the-blatant-realization-nothing-you-do-online-is-private/

5, 6 http://normapp.com/

7 https://www.youtube.com/watch?v=5YGc4zOqozo

8 http://e.businessinsider.com/view/520c1a5b1e240a9c3f2ae15c528672cf7332c1685a00001b/adb57cd4

9 https://hbr.org/2013/10/megastores-want-to-be-like-mom-and-pop-shops-sort-of/

The Dichotomy of Privacy and Increasing Data Transparency

THE PROBLEM WITH PRIVACY by Jure Klepic

There is an old saying that you should act first and ask forgiveness later. It means you can always get your way, no matter what the impact may be on others, as long as you are contrite once someone gets hurt. Some social media entrepreneurs have taken this adage to heart. They roll out a wonderful new product, get millions of users on-board, and then think about privacy considerations. Someone feels his/her privacy has been breached, which results in a huge media uproar. A contrite apology is issued with the promise to "never do this again." Problem solved, right?
Well, not exactly.

We're in an era where suspicion lurks around every corner. We have to rely on a low-level NSA employee to leak information that lets us know how much our privacy has been invaded before the government admits anything. Google is inventing more online ways to let everyone see where we live, while Google Glass lets us spy more effectively on each other in the real world. Facebook's privacy guidelines change so often, it's a wonder anyone can understand what they are "entitled" to on their site.

There are many reasons we need to preserve some privacy in this online world. It's not just that we're worried about somebody hacking into our personal data and stealing our identities, which are always serious threats. We're also concerned about safety issues for our families and our homes, or letting the world see when we've made a colossal mistake.

In the business world, threats from corporate espionage could make the difference in billions of dollars of products sold.

On the other side of the privacy debate is just how much information we want to see or know about others. There are some things that should just be left private and not exposed for the whole world to see. Will people be inspired to act better or worse if they know they are being watched all the time?

With the introduction of the World Wide Web and the social media universe, we're getting closer to a point where human beings lose one of our most important rights - the right to privacy. We feel like we have become naked mannequins in a worldwide window display.

Marketing's Private Nightmares

Marketers have always dreamed that if they had access to every pertinent detail in our lives, then they would be able to precisely target their marketing messages. Of course, nothing is ever that simple. Where do the lines blur between having access to data and using it responsibly? Intrude too much and consumers will strike back. Telemarketers thought having everyone's telephone number was wonderful until consumers pushed back and demanded "do not call" laws.

For each privacy incursion, there is a stronger reaction from the consumer side.
The coveted Millennials are particularly skeptical of brands. They dislike being targeted, especially on social media, although they might be willing to give up personal information for a strong enough incentive. Perhaps it would make more sense if privacy concerns were given more attention before introducing new products, services or communication platforms. Just because Marketers have the ability to access more personal data to offer their line of goods doesn't mean they should.

The solution lies not in blindly accumulating more data, but in garnering real understanding. Providing a name and contact information doesn't automatically transfer the right to use that information. When a customer orders some baby clothing for a friend, does the website assume that customer has a baby so a full-out marketing assault can begin, or would it be better to simply ask, "Would you like us to send you more information about baby clothing?"

Consumers still have an expectation of privacy, even in the online world, and trust corporations to use the information they choose to share wisely. Does it build trust to add a statement such as, "Yes, I'd like to receive more information" in a small font at the bottom of a sales transaction, with a box that is already conveniently checked? Would it be so awful to say, "We'd like to send you information on products and services we think you could use or enjoy. Is that okay?" Or, get on board with the social media universe to reach out, connect and engage consumers so they will want to share information with you.

Follow-through on the promises you make, and only send information that is insightful and helpful. Sometimes you can even send something educational, without trying to sell anything at all! Businesses shouldn't wait until the government steps in to resolve the privacy debate. Marketers need to learn to use private data responsibly, or the consuming public will make sure they can't use it at all.

*A prolific speaker, writer, marketing and social media innovator **Jure Klepic**, specializes in marketing strategy and social media innovation for consumer business. As the Marketer behind successful brands like Givenchy, YSL, Chanel, Lancaster, Jure looks at products differently to boldly crystallize marketing strategies that strongly resonate with consumers. He knows the secrets of what it means to be a social media influencer and uses this knowledge to bring innovation to marketing plans. Jure believes that social media is one of the fastest society-changing phenomenon seen in our lifetime, and is raising the flag to make sure that communication convenience doesn't trample privacy.*

Privacy, Policies, and the Future of the Internet Economy

Social will not go away. The proliferation in mobile will continue to perpetuate and feed increasing data volumes into the already burgeoning cloud. In the last few years, the increasing firestorm around privacy has built a much stronger, more informed consumer base. Facebook's privacy missteps have hastened legislation to put a halt to rogue social platform practices as social networking has forced its way into the mainstream. This has created a domino effect that unravels the questionable government practices that seek to mine these growing data sets, without proper disclosure to the consumer.

Prism and the NSA have opened a Pandora's box to every minor privacy indiscretion that now threatens the very technologies and practices built to support this new communication revolution.

This chapter documents the rise of Privacy in an online world where proliferation of user information continues to grow exponentially. It also details some of these critical events, their impact on consumer confidence, and ultimately user behavior on social networks and on mobile.

There Is No Privacy on The Internet Of Things

In August 2014, there was a tremendous amount of content published about the massive privacy intrusion that is Facebook Messenger. With the ability to intrude into the lives of its users, it isn't a surprise that the new download inspired such strong opinions, and many recommendations to not download the app.

The silver lining in all of the online dialogue about Messenger is that it brought to light the issues that surround privacy of data. Further implicating what some of us have always known: "When the service is free, the user is the product." Make sense?

In other words, when companies like Facebook create applications that we use in our everyday lives, for free, the real price is in what we sacrifice for the right to use the application for free, our data.

INTERNET OF THINGS, BIG DATA AND JARGON, CONTEXTUALIZED

Perhaps the only word more used and abused in the tech space than "Internet of Things" is "Big Data." In itself, Big Data means very little. It is merely the massive collection of information that resides out in cyberspace, waiting to be somehow organized, visualized, contextualized and "Ized" in some other TBD capacity.

It comes down to what you do with it, otherwise it is like an English major staring at endless strings of PHP or Java: totally meaningless.

However, using Big Data has created a revolutionary approach to marketing. It is our online behavior that helps brands and organizations learn about us in ways that they can contextualize and apply to their marketing strategies.[1] Since this became apparent, Marketers have been seeking ways to exploit it. In a world where the web is moving from a search state to a semantic state, it is without question our data that makes this possible. In a later chapter about the collision between search and social, we introduce the semantic web and the marriage that is taking place among Big Data, Semantic Search and User Generated Content that is shifting the way we explore the web.

If you recognize this possibility, you will quickly realize that for the web to be semantic, it is dependent upon us as users to feed it our data. And in order for the web to collect our data we need to voluntarily (if not knowingly) give up our privacy so websites and brands can sell and use it to create this new online experience.

OUR PRIVACY DIED WHEN WE
GREW OBSESSED WITH FREE

With Social Media[2] users numbering well over a billion, and a growing mobile and wearable trends that put us online almost around the clock, we are ever connected and endlessly sharing our every thought.

This feeling of connectedness undoubtedly gives many a sense of community and happiness, as it is through the sharing of our everyday lives that we are able to garner the feedback we seek and the validation that we crave.

However, if we are fooled, even for a moment as to what all of this is really about, the desire to be tethered without wires and connected without cost, then we are delusional.

I, for one can say that I have almost never read the privacy policy of an application I downloaded. As a Millennial I suppose this puts me in the group of about half of us that are okay with trading our privacy for a potentially better experience online. [3] Whether having more targeted ads and content during our everyday browsing is really a better experience is yet to be seen.

As a society, it really came down to our insatiable desire for free. Free content, free social media, free productivity tools and free games. We want to be connected and we want to play with the latest games, toys and widgets, but we, by and large, don't want to trade our cash for them. So instead, we trade something else: our data and our privacy.

Just as long as you know what you are giving up, and you consciously make that choice, then you are fine. But understand that whatever you know, they know, and that is the way it will be.

So here's to a better web experience: Marketers that know more about what we want than what we do, with a complete and total loss of privacy that really makes minimal difference in our lives. Heck, we share it all anyway. Don't we?

One thing is certain: On the Internet of Things, there is no privacy.

THE INTERNET IS MERELY A CHANNEL THAT "SHOULD" MIGRATE "PRIVACY" PRACTICES... BUT DOES IT?

As a data marketer, I am a firm believer in full disclosure to the consumer. This has been the practice for any one-to-one communication regardless of channel. It's the reason why loyalty programs, direct mail and even telemarketing have been strong purveyors of communication and insight.

Transitioning this to the Internet should not change the principles. In fact, the amount of information that people are creating and sharing on these social platforms should leave all of us to question how some of this information will be used.

Remember a few years back?

"The bill (SB 242) would prohibit Facebook and other social networking sites from publicizing users' addresses or phone numbers without their explicit consent."

Not surprisingly, Facebook, Google, Twitter, Skype, and Yahoo, among others banded together and denounced the bill, calling it unconstitutional and hurtful to tech companies, and said it would negatively impacting the internet economy.

Fast-forward to Fall of 2013 when stories about Prism and the NSA dominated the airwaves. Here were my thoughts at the time when these stories exploded:

The NSA, Privacy and the Blatant Realization: Nothing You Do Online is Private

I've been monitoring the events of the past week about PRISM, the NSA and the traitor/hero, Edward Snowden, former CIA, who lifted the veil and revealed to the world the questionable practices of the US Agency, practices which, in my opinion, shouldn't surprise any of us.

It wasn't the fact that US State security had been so easily and openly compromised that seemed to shock people; it was more a sudden sense of lost innocence that seemed to permeate the buzz-o-sphere.

From my friend, Julie Pippert's viewpoint, we all deserve the right to keep what we want private, private. The events of 9/11 (as justified by the US government) seemingly no longer hold our civil liberties in high regard.

 Hessie Jones shared a link via Buffer.
Thursday

"Why "I Have Nothing to Hide" Is the Wrong Way to Think About Surveillance "
g

 **Why "I Have Nothing to Hide" Is the Wrong Way to Think About Surveillance | Wired Opinion | Wired.co**
feedly.com

Many donât understand why they should be concerned about surveillance if they have nothing to hide. Itâs even less clear in

Like · Comment · Share

Shaun Larocque and Julie Pippert like this.

 Julie Pippert I don't know who in the world has nothing to hide. I have nothing *illegal* but plenty to hide and that's why I am not okay with this.
Thursday at 13:11 · Unlike · 2

 Hessie Jones Unfortunately Julie, it seems your opinion about the issue is NOT a concern for the government. They can hide behind 'national security' to justify their actions
Thursday at 13:41 via mobile · Like · 1

I had a similar conversation with Ann Marie van den Hurk, author of the just-published, Social Media Crisis Communications and she indicated, "Who is the NSA accountable to? The American people?" Apparently not.

But the NSA is accountable to the Executive Office, which granted the Agency the power to collect and analyze any and all information from the online and telecom networks.

FROM PRIVACY TO PERSONAL VIOLATION

Now, Privacy has been elevated to the point of personal violation where no stone is left unturned and everyone is suspect. Given the response from the Internet, I am observing a certain naiveté when it comes to people's understanding of how and why their information is being tracked.

Your most personal financial information: your debt, your spend patterns, your income are tracked and monitored by your financial institution and compiled by credit scoring institutions like Equifax and Trans Union to gauge your credit-worthiness and minimize risk to the bank.

While Facebook, we thought, was brought to its knees when the world watched as the FTC and Canada's Privacy Commissioner mandated clearer user disclosures and guidelines, it was, in fact, only following the lead of publishers, ad networks, and direct marketers who have been collecting online user information for years: search behaviour, clicks, purchases, site visits, content consumption, etc.

Because of my work, I crave the increased knowledge about customers and prospects. The more we know about you the more we are able to put messages and offers in front of you to increase your propensity to purchase.

Time marches on and we've seen ad evolution in retargeting capability, dynamic ads that flex with your online footprint, geography, profile and emails you write, pages you "like" etc. And the industry will continue to evolve because there are huge dollars being spent to find the receptive customer, in the right place, and target them with the right message.

Do you remember when a woman from Pennsylvania sued Google for Privacy invasion by displaying ads eerily similar to her email content? [4] Google admitted it did scan emails for malware and spam but argued that scanning content to provide relevant advertising should be an exception under the wiretap law, or as some would call The Fourth Amendment.

WE NEED TO PROGRESS

Those adamant that they own their own information, to which no one should have access whatsoever, should realize that there is a price to pay for using free services. Collecting personal information about customers is NOT new.

In the early days of direct mail and subscription-based magazines, we began to build more detailed profiles of individuals who subscribed to certain publications. When culled with transactional data, suddenly Marketers had a way to build predictive models to optimize response performance. And that was exciting.

As this article [5] highlights,

> *"It's similar to the way Amazon or eBay use databases to predict what you might want to buy next."*

Big data technologies will only grow the amount of information collected, and provide increased insights at faster rates as the world increases its usage of mobile, the web, Google Glass, mobile payments etc. We can't stop progress. The more data out there, the more demand to extract meaning from it.

Remember the CIA Facebook Program? This has made the surveillance efforts much more efficient. Yes, the government is using your data to tap into potential threats, but it would have done so, regardless, through much more laborious means if the technology hadn't been available. That's progress.

Progress also means increased cloud-based technology. Progress means convergence: Governments, corporations, small business, and Not-for-profit (NFP) will all begin to use these technologies to remain competitive and move the business forward.

And yes, that means the very marketing technology solutions used to make more informed strategic decisions about customers, will also be tools demanded by security companies, law enforcement and government.

The reality is that there is so much good that can be achieved by being able to analyze and predict outcomes from this mountain of information. But there is also a price to be paid.

THE NEED FOR CONTROLS

The economics of data need to be balanced with controls.
I found this on a website called Writingya[7]: from a purely individual perspective, where the rights of the citizen are now marginalized, the author had this to say,

> "The problem is that we have not created a privacy culture on the Internet that we can live with. We created the wrong one. What I think about is: What is intimacy without privacy? What is a democracy without privacy? Technology makes people stupid. It can blind you to what your underlying values are and need to be. Are we really willing to give away our Constitutional and civil liberties that we fought so hard for?"

The will of the people will demand more transparency. They may be unable to stop the extent to which agencies like the NSA use personal information, but the collective voice will make the government much more accountable for the safety and security of their information.

The reality of protecting the nation's security: the less people that know, the better. The more transparent the government is, the less effective are their surveillance initiatives.

But we don't want surveillance to the degree that we are effectively living in a police state. There has to be a balance between ensuring the security of the nation and protecting our civil liberties.

This post followed and drove the discussion closer to home, as consumers realized that surveillance didn't stop with government.

Data Transparency and Discretion: Has Consumer Trust Been Broken?

The cat's out of the bag. Consumers have learned what many Marketers have known for years: consumer information and behavior is being tracked and analyzed.

It's ALL true. There's nothing to deny.

But instead of understanding application of this information for business, somehow business has been lumped into the same category as the NSA: a now vilified group that's perceived as relentless in capturing user information (without regard to privacy rights).

THE PEOPLE HAVE SPOKEN

They don't trust the use of their information. Their consent or lack thereof is being undermined.

As a Marketer I have written about the value of Big Data and how it will change advertising, as we know it. I was quite excited about the possibilities of being able to gain more context into the behavior and conversations that people share online, and apply it to the current ad targeting capabilities.

One of the users sharing my post posed it in this way:

I did request a meeting to get a deeper viewpoint from Dave Cheevers. We have yet to connect. However, after hearing his viewpoint, it dawned on me just how in the dark the average consumer has been about the use of their information.

Edward Snowden, in many ways, has opened up a Pandora's Box bringing into public scrutiny what has been in play for many years. But what's he's also done is awakened the average consumer and forced them to understand the impact on their security and personal rights and freedoms.

A DATABASE MARKETER'S DREAM

As a database marketer, I was already purchasing lists and managing customer transaction records for clients.

Coming from a banking and loyalty management background, I understood these factors: the customers' predisposition to brands, their buying patterns, their customer service scores, and their purchase frequency – all these elements were integral in helping us determine the right offers and messaging initiatives to drive response.

Direct Marketing practices were strict. We followed the rules to the letter; as a customer we could communicate to you and provide to you relevant offers and messages.

However, you could opt-out of communication at any time. The information you provided to us was tied to your transaction history. It allowed us to make sure we were providing to you ONLY the offers that you would most likely respond to.

REMEMBER PERMISSION MARKETING?

When the Internet became popular in the 90's, businesses were devouring information about how marketing would migrate its way into this new connected medium.

Seth Godin stepped up and attempted to create the groundwork for making this happen. On his blog[6] he states:

> "Permission marketing is the privilege (not the right) of delivering anticipated, personal and relevant messages to people who actually want to get them. It recognizes the new power of the best consumers to ignore marketing. It realizes that treating people with respect is the best way to earn their attention."

An important note here that Direct Marketers abide by: Treat the customer like gold. Abide by their wishes. Be transparent about the use of their information. Ensure they can opt-out at any time.

> "Permission is like dating. You don't start by asking for the sale at first impression. You earn the right, over time, bit by bit."

So Marketers and consumers were able to come to acceptable terms about how the relationship was being managed. Now, consumers are demanding a whole new set of rules regarding transparency about the specific collection of information, its use, and inclusion of consumer consent.

HOW IS THE INTERNET COPING?

Has the consumer lost faith? If anything, it's nice to see the Internet has not lost its sense of humor. Check out these #NSAPickupLines [8].

> Every breath you take Every move you make Every bond you break
> Every step you take I'll be watching you #nsapickuplines
> — Stewie Griffin (@FamilyGuy_) August 25, 2013

> I'd tap that. #NSAPickUpLines
> — Sana Saeed (@SanaSaeed) August 25, 2013

> Hi there beautiful. Can I buy you a drink? And by the way Happy
> Birthday! #NSApickuplines
> — Luna (@SophiaMariaLuna) June 10, 2013

> Did you fall from heaven? Because there's no tracking data on how you
> arrived at this location. #nsapickuplines
> — Norm Wilner (@wilnervision) June 10, 2013

CONSUMERS ARE ALSO ACCOUNTABLE

The blame isn't one-sided. Consumers are increasingly aware of how much and to what extent their information is being aggregated on social networks, when they shop, when they bank online etc.

E-marketer conducted a survey[9] recently among US Smartphone users.
…The vast majority of respondents—76%—believed they [as individuals] held the most responsibility for managing their own privacy protections.

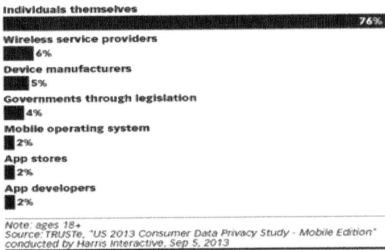

Party Most Responsible for Protecting Mobile Privacy According to US Smartphone Users, June 2013
% of respondents

Individuals themselves — 76%
Wireless service providers — 6%
Device manufacturers — 5%
Governments through legislation — 4%
Mobile operating system — 2%
App stores — 2%
App developers — 2%

Note: ages 18+
Source: TRUSTe, "US 2013 Consumer Data Privacy Study - Mobile Edition" conducted by Harris Interactive, Sep 5, 2013
163242   www.eMarketer.com

The table below reveals the instances where consumers are most concerned about their privacy.

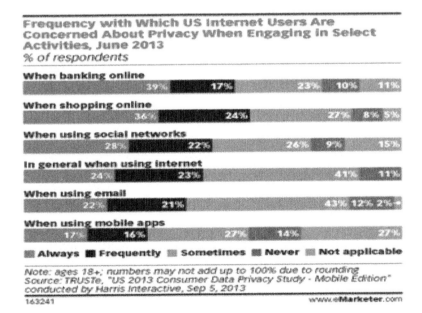

Frequency with Which US Internet Users Are Concerned About Privacy When Engaging in Select Activities, June 2013
% of respondents

	Always	Frequently	Sometimes	Never	Not applicable
When banking online	39%	17%	23%	10%	11%
When shopping online	36%	24%	27%	8%	5%
When using social networks	28%	22%	26%	9%	15%
In general when using internet	24%	23%		41%	11%
When using email	22%	21%		43%	12% 2%
When using mobile apps	17%	16%	27%	14%	27%

Note: ages 18+; numbers may not add up to 100% due to rounding
Source: TRUSTe, "US 2013 Consumer Data Privacy Study - Mobile Edition" conducted by Harris Interactive, Sep 5, 2013
163241   www.eMarketer.com

According to E-Marketer:

> *"Mobile app users are least guarded about sharing their gender information with a company—53% of respondents said they would acquiesce to such a request. Next in line was age (44%), an email address (39%) and a full name (31%). There was a sharp drop-off in the willingness of consumers to provide an app with their birth date. And nearly a quarter of respondents said they didn't want to share any information at all."*

There is an increasing reluctance to provide personal information. Consumers, understandably, are more guarded about what they disclose.

HAVE WE LOST FAITH FROM THE CONSUMER?

Consumers want more authenticity. Consumers also want more control.

I wrote a similar post from the viewpoint as a parent: Teaching Our Kids Not to Treat the Internet as a Private Diary.[10] Here I described the importance of teaching our children to be more discreet about what they share.

 **Hessie Jones**
@hessiejones

I worry about the content this generation shares and their naive belief that it won't hurt them down the road

Ironically, as a parent, I realized how damaging "too much information" was, and the havoc it could wreak down the road.

The parent and Marketer sides of me say this:

> *"I am a Marketer and these rich profiles are what we, as Marketers, crave. We want to know more about you so we can connect with you and sell you stuff. And we are willing to pay Facebook more if the information we get in return makes it easier to sell our products."*

> *"I am a mother as well so I see both sides of the coin. Big data is a huge topic these days. Everyone talks about its merits and the amount of insight we can glean from the billions of actions and post on social networks, mobile devices on a daily basis. While it has it merits there has to be controls. We need to ask the question, "Why do you need to know this?"*

FACEBOOK SEEMS TO BE MOVING BACKWARDS

When Facebook announced its new privacy policy, it seemed to subvert the authority of the FTC (and the painstaking provisions to disclose and protect the privacy of its users) and declare it had the right to collect, share, use and sell any and all content that a user uploads to its properties.

~~You can use your privacy settings to limit how your name and profile picture may be associated with commercial, sponsored, or related content (such as a brand you like) served or enhanced by us.~~ You give us permission to use your name, and profile picture, **content, and information** in connection with **commercial, sponsored, or related** ~~that~~ content **(such as a brand you like) served or enhanced by us,** ~~subject to the limits you place~~. **This means, for example, that you permit a business or other entity to pay us to display your name and/or profile picture with your content or information, without any compensation to you. If you have selected a specific audience for your content or information, we will respect your choice when we use it.**

Facebook's revision merely clarified existing policies; it didn't alter them. The FTC is concerned and is now looking into the new policy to determine if it has violated the provisions set out in the 2011 agreement.

Senator Edward Markey, Democrat of Massachusetts, took the stand [11] against Facebook declaring:

> *"This troubling shift in policy raises a number of questions about whether Facebook is improperly altering its privacy policy without proper user consent and, if the changes go into effect, the degree to which Facebook users will lose control over their personal information."*

ARE CONSUMERS READY FOR ABSOLUTE TRANSPARENCY

I found this article astounding, Will Transparency Help Big Data Face Down Its Critics? [12]

It provides an initiative by Axiom.com that allows consumers to enter their name, address and social security information in order to access a portal that reveals any and all information collected about them. But this is not one-sided. While it allows the user to opt-out of having their data used, the site also seeks to educate the consumer about the "merits of data improving people's lives." I encourage you to go to AboutTheData.com. As the homepage explains:

> *"We no longer want to receive mass marketing — getting bombarded with ads that have no relevancy to our lives — because it's intrusive and wastes our time. That's why companies want to use data about you to personalize and shape your experiences with them."*

Other companies like BlueKai [13] and Exelate [14], which sell behavioral data for online ad targeting, also have data-transparency systems. Users can visit and opt-out from being tracked.

This is a definite step-forward for the consumer and provides them with some level of control that was not open to them before. However, more companies have to come forward and trust that negotiated terms with the consumer will result in a win/win relationship. That's going to take time.

In the meantime, it is a two way street.

MARKETERS MUST ALSO BE RESPONSIBLE

Julie Bernard, the Macy's senior VP-customer strategy, spoke at a digital conference and told attendees:

"The media has spun this story so negative, and it's really a shame that people in our positions have not taken a more dominant position on speaking on the macro and micro economic benefits of delivering relevancy by responsibly using customer data."

Consumers still need to be educated on the value,

> "There's a funny consumer thing," [says Bernard]. "They're worried about our use of data, but they're pissed if I don't deliver relevance. ... How am I supposed to deliver relevance and magically deliver what they want if I don't look at the data?"

It also stands to reason that we, as Marketers, must also show restraint in what we collect and how we use the information. We have the means to track so much data on users to benefit the company's goals... but it doesn't mean we should.

Today, a company's reputation has come under increased scrutiny. Companies are more vulnerable than ever to the whims of angry customer voices, and are aware that they are being held to a much higher standard.

THE QUID PRO QUO

In my opinion, the more consumers are educated about the information that's collected about them, the more they will be inclined to share information that will further improve their customer experience. They will also be more discerning and think twice about the content they post.

For Marketers, the value of this information is to
1. Provide ONLY relevant messages to customers that keep them loyal
2. Provide customers with an experience that's second to none

If the information is not relevant to those specific goals then we should not be collecting it. Period.

Privacy is Killing the Communication Evolution

We are in an era that has seen massive shifts in how people communicate with one another, where brands have to learn how to un-sell, and instead, forge a deeper understanding with their customers. It has also been marred by some pretty significant events that have shaken consumers' trust in government and industry protecting and securing personal information.

As a Marketer, it didn't take me long to recognize this shift as it unfolded. And I have learned to evolve. Customers don't want to be sold to. Posts that joke about the demise of banners and the ensuing rise of content marketing like "You are more likely to summit Mount Everest than click on a banner ad"[14] have proven that consumers are more informed than ever before. Content is free. It's pervasive.

The Internet is a massive network organized and controlled by consumers. Taxonomy has now largely evolved into folksonomy. We have directed the path of the Internet through our behaviors, our words, and our voices–in a strengthened velocity that has instigated the rise of data-driven solutions to allow business to hear us and understand us. The 'established' institutions that once controlled what content was published where, are now vulnerable to the fickle consumer who has a wide variety of choices.

Since the news about Prism, NSA and Facebook Privacy surfaced, government and platforms have come under increasing scrutiny with respect to their aggregation of user data, use and disclosure. The Heartbleed bug was exposed in April of 2014.

Heartbleed: The Consumer has Always been Exposed

The news that took the world by storm has left the consumer and some major networks more vulnerable. What's scarier is the fact that this apparent aberration had gone undetected by the major networks/sites for some time. News of the NSA's prior knowledge of this programming error has left both consumers and industry reeling. Here's how the news unfolded[16] April 8th, 2014:

"A flaw has been discovered in one of the Internet's key security methods, potentially forcing a wide swath of websites to make changes to protect the security of consumers."

Here's the gist: Almost 2/3 of the world's websites rely on popular web encryption software known as Open SSL. SSL is an encryption technology that allows web users to protect the privacy of their information that's transmitted over the web. You'll see this in the form of a "lock" symbol or "https://" (denoting secure server) that precedes URL on your browser.

Heartbleed simplified [17]:

> *"...the SSL standard includes a heartbeat option, which allows a computer at one end of an SSL connection to send a short message to verify that the other computer is still online and get a response back. Researchers found that it's possible to send a cleverly formed, malicious heartbeat message that tricks the computer at the other end into divulging secret information. Specifically, a vulnerable computer can be tricked into transmitting the contents [in the form of passwords, security information, personal information like credit card numbers] of the server's memory, known as RAM."*

To add insult to injury, on Friday afternoon, Bloomberg[18] reported that the National Security Agency (NSA) had been aware of this "monstrous" flaw for two years prior to the announcement Monday and continued undeterred, and in fact,

...Kept it hidden from technologists and instead exploited it to hack the computers and correspondence of certain intelligence targets.

Michael Riley, journalist of Bloomberg, added,

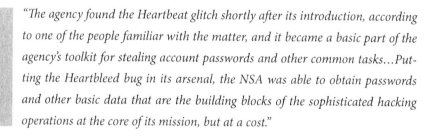

> *"The agency found the Heartbeat glitch shortly after its introduction, according to one of the people familiar with the matter, and it became a basic part of the agency's toolkit for stealing account passwords and other common tasks...Putting the Heartbleed bug in its arsenal, the NSA was able to obtain passwords and other basic data that are the building blocks of the sophisticated hacking operations at the core of its mission, but at a cost."*

"AS PER FACEBOOK: PRIVACY IS NO LONGER A SOCIAL NORM"

Remember this quote [19] from Mark Zuckerberg in 2011 when Facebook was at the heart of the Privacy discussion? Suddenly the world became aware of the extent to which the network was using the 'stuff' that we post to develop a comprehensive picture of each of us, repackage it in "informative and engaging" ways–all for the purpose of monetization. Zuck claimed that the rise of social networks meant that people no longer had an expectation of privacy.

This contentious statement, coupled with the questionable Facebook Privacy disclosure practices, including the default user settings, drew scathing remarks from Privacy practitioners everywhere. Lee Rickwood of WhatsYourTech, in his article [20] referenced Ann Cavourkian [21], Information and Privacy Commissioner of Ontario, Canada:

> *"It's all about trust...You have to engender consumer confidence. Be transparent; give your customers notice and be sensitive to the phrasing and the context."*

Fast forward to today. Facebook continues to face heavy scrutiny [22] with any minor tweak it makes to its platform:

- The controversial Sponsored Stories, which used user's likeness in ads, was finally eliminated at the end of 2013. This was amplified by the use of Rehteah Parsons' image in a dating ad [23] the young teen who took her own life, April 2013 after being sexually abused, and then bullied about the incident for a few years.
- Facebook then announced a change that would allow users to see an update to its dropdown menu: the option to select "public" or "friends" with respect to the information you share. More prominently was the option of sharing photos, which were previously deemed "publicly" available information.

- Searching for users is important to Facebook. Therefore, user name, profile photo, cover photo, gender, and networks such as your school or workplace continue to be public. Facebook justifies it as optimizing the user experience as well as "helping disambiguate you from other people in the world".
- The latter drew more noise from the marketplace when, last fall, it was announced that Facebook deleted one of its privacy settings[24] that deterred users from having the ability to block people from searching their name.
- The Facebook acquisition of "WhatsApp" messaging application provided an even richer source of intimate information based on what people say. More specifically:

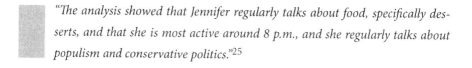

"The analysis showed that Jennifer regularly talks about food, specifically desserts, and that she is most active around 8 p.m., and she regularly talks about populism and conservative politics."[25]

And while the current WhatsApp disclosure is limited to sharing user information with third party sites to maintain the integrity of the service, the FTC is watching how the service disclosure morphs overtime.

Privacy Begins to Dictate Communication Legislation in Social Media

Compounding the FTC efforts to enforce social network privacy disclosures in the U.S., Canada recently instituted new legislation that may go down in history as a major impediment to the evolution of communication. Known as the Canadian Anti-Spam Legislation (CASL), this has been deemed as restrictive as European Privacy laws. It's one that needs to be monitored to determine its real impacts to Marketers over time.

The importance of this legislation marks the first time that communication laws are moving the definition of Commercial Electronic Messages from email to Social Media. While there is no immediate impact on US CAN-Spam laws, the FCC will be closely watching as CASL unfolds in the next few years.

The Canadian Anti-Spam Legislation (CASL): The Bane of the Canadian Communication Industry

I attended the Canadian Anti-Spam Legislation (CASL) Session in Toronto. The new legislation, which took effect July 1, 2014 had been stirring up the marketing industry, with Marketers struggling to really grasp the essence of the new law and what it means to their individual businesses.

A session titled to provoke fear and urgency had no problem drawing a massive audience.

Create Your CASL Compliance Plan to avoid the $10 million fine

DMAC & NAMMU
Tuesday, 3 June 2014 from 3:30 PM to 5:30 PM (EDT)
Toronto, ON

Here's the gist of the legislation[26]:

> "Canada's Anti-Spam Legislation (CASL), which was passed in 2010, establishes rules for sending commercial electronic messages (CEMs) as well as the installation of computer programs, and prohibits the unauthorized alteration of transmission data.
>
> The Competition Act has been amended to prohibit false or misleading representations in the sending of a CEM, whether in the content, subject line, or sender information of a message."

CASL extends beyond email. It also covers texts, SMS, Twitter, Facebook i.e. any message coming in to an electronic inbox via computer or phone that is commercial in nature.

THE COST OF NON-COMPLIANCE IS SIGNIFICANT

Visible opt-out or unsubscribe policies were part of an established norm set about when Permission Marketing[27] was introduced in the late 90's. Seth Godin wrote some best practices about the use of this-then-new-medium known as email:

Permission marketing is the privilege (not the right) of delivering anticipated, personal and relevant messages to people who actually want to get them.
It recognizes the new power of the best consumers to ignore marketing. It realizes that treating people with respect is the best way to earn their attention.

Almost 14 years later, the digital industry has evolved and the very rules that Permission Marketing established have been dismissed and exploited by "hard-core" Spammers. #CASL and the Canadian Radio and Communications Commission (CRTC) are coming to the forefront to crack down on this practice and by and large, impose significant penalties for non-compliance. Each violation can mean fines up to $1 million for individuals and up to $10 million for companies. This leaves organizations vulnerable to class action lawsuit.

At first blush, the legislation, while intended to give power back to the consumer, may also hamper business to a large degree. My friend, who has asked to remain nameless, works for a company that not only utilizes database promotions, but also evolved digital communications. Here was his take on what CASL means for this industry:

"CASL is about to send Canadian Digital Business back to the stone ages... the intent was spam...but this blunt, overreaching, overkill and unimaginative piece of legislation will impact every attempt to deliver smart and engaged digital media and neuter Canadian businesses ability to compete..."

THE RADICAL CHANGE: EXPLICIT CONSENT

OPT-IN is now the new norm. CASL specifies the following requirements for obtaining express consent:

1. The purpose of consent
2. For whom or what organization for which it's being obtained
3. Include a statement that can dismiss consent at any time i.e. unsubscribe
4. Include contact information – mailing address, telephone number, email of web address

What's important is that a party must prove (as of July 1, 2017) they've obtained consent from all individuals to whom they are communicating.

COMPILED LISTS ARE AT RISK

The biggest impact #CASL has is within compiled list industry. Rented Lists are compliant as long as the original list owner obtains user consent on behalf of the list renters. As well, the list owner must deploy emails on behalf of the list renters.

Compiled Lists that are purchased have a much rockier road ahead. This industry's death is imminent. For parties that have purchased lists, it will be imperative to obtain express consent since there is no implied relationship with the base members.

GRACE PERIOD: TRANSITION TO JULY 1, 2017

July 1, 2017 is a critical date. This means that for 3 years up until July 1, 2017 companies can leverage this transitional period to acquire explicit permission from existing business and non-business relationships.

SOCIAL MEDIA CONTINUES TO BE THE GRAY AREA

For those of us who practice within the new media space, there was less clarity defining the rules governing real time conversions and B2B social platforms like LinkedIn. Legal opinions concerning these areas were contradictory.

On one hand, a Privacy officer noted that CRTC have exempted public feeds within CASL. Only DMs (direct messages) apply. A contrary view from a Privacy lawyer noted that as long as CEMs are sent to an electronic mailbox (where Twitter can provide notifications about "public" activity), this is inclusive of #CASL.

DOES CASL IN SOCIAL MEDIA IMPLY THAT "EVERY ELECTRONIC" COMMUNICATION IN 140 CHARACTERS MUST INCLUDE A CONSENT LINK?

- I questioned Matthew Vernhout, Chief Privacy Officer and requested clarity in the following areas:
- Give the prevalence of social how does the CRTC effectively police CASL on Twitter and the millions of discussions happening every day on other social platforms?
- Conversation threads between individuals can include promotional messages, even those between friends/followers.
- Do we assume any communication on Twitter in a public feed has to contain all the consent requirements if there is future potential or promoting a message to that individual?
- While this is the plan for email, should there be another plan for Twitter and more real-time messages?
- For people who use LinkedIn and have paid for the premium service and have accepted InMail and other services as a way of networking, does this apply to CASL? Also, the premium service allows companies to promote on your LinkedIn Box. Is this compliant?

Matthew responded:

> *I can't exactly comment on how the CRTC will be enforcing things like Social Media compliance as we have yet to see any type of infractions under the legislation. At best I can hypothesize that their methods will be mostly directed by user complaints to the spam reporting center and those organizations with a large number of complaints will be reviewed by one of the CRTC's investigators. Should the CRTC find sufficient evidence of violation under CASL they will begin the process of taking action against the person/business sending the CEMs.*

Based on the three scenarios here is what I think the responses are:

- Personal Relationships (as per regulations below) have a number of exclusions under CASL for permissions and form of the message. Promotional messages between these "personal relationships" on Twitter should be able to meet these requirements for exemption from the legislation.
- CASL states that where it is impractical to include the information you may link to an external source to supply this information; i.e. a bit.ly link in an SMS message with identification and contact information being made available to the recipient. This could work on Twitter as well, and potentially making this part of the background or bio on a Twitter account could qualify for this as well. CASL is technology neutral and the rules are the same regardless of the medium being used.
- CASL has a number of B2B exemptions: each message sent via an inMessage would need to be evaluated against these exclusions. Just based on that screen shot those messages could potentially violate CASL as they are sent without and express or implied consent by the sender.

CASL NEEDS TO EVOLVE

It's clear from the updated legislation that CASL and the CRTC need to establish more clarity around the rules concerning new media. In all three cases where I have asked Privacy lawyers and Privacy officers to provide more granularity in compliance from a social media perspective, all say that they themselves don't use social media so they were unable to give solid response to the nuances of conversation and context on social networks. Without truly understanding the nuances of this medium the CRTC has written legislation without understanding the implications for Marketers.

- Does the CRTC think that organic public conversation on social networks will allow the inclusion of a "consent" link into every post?
- Can they easily enforce communications between what they deem personal relationships vs. just followers?
- If someone who receives a promotional message from a follower but does not have a personal relationship, is this a CASL violation?
- Can LinkedIn scream "exemption" because they offer a paid service that implies Opt-in for those users who have purchased subscriptions?
- While email seems cut and dry, there are still too many unanswered questions when it comes to social networks. This clearly needs to be revisited and addressed in the very near future.

If this provides some guidance, a Privacy lawyer noted: "Err on the side of empowering the recipient with the intended message".

For those that continue to have questions regarding #CASL here are some resources to reference:

Canadian Anti-Spam Legislation [30]

Innovation LLP – Interpretation of CASL[31]

The Future of the Internet is Anonymous

Right now we're in a world that sees transparency as the new form of integrity. Right now we're in a world that understands that reputation is everything.

Loyalty is somewhat fleeting as consumers, armoured with an incessant flow of knowledge from the web, have the ability to make swift judgements and decisions about individuals, companies and governments, often times to the detriment of the target.

The emergence of social media has forced companies to stop hiding from behind that veil of corporate spin and address the very things that the web has thrown at them.

Nothing is secret any longer. Even secrets that were once held secure behind invulnerable fortresses now have a strong probability of materializing.
Is transparency as a norm working? Or, are the results of transparency surfacing a new order that will create yet another tier of acceptance from the masses?

Has the rise of transparency backfired?

Brian Solis painted a great picture of our online behaviors and how they intermingle with the dynamics of the web:

> "Online, just like in the real world, actions and words speak loudly. Unlike real life though, your digital footprints are there for anyone to find on Google, social networks, and in communities. These disparate pieces are then assembled by employers, schools, friends, lovers, enemies, and anyone and everyone who wishes to learn something more about you. Whether pure, sinister or simply inquisitive, whatever the reason, today these pieces construct a semblance of you and whoever sifts through your online legacy is left to their own surmise. This is too important to leave to chance. Online is the new real world. This is your life."

I wrote earlier about No Room for Error: A Cautionary Tale of A Precarious Tweet [32] and the misstep a young lad, Chris Spiegel, made on Twitter that could potentially have prevented him from graduating with his senior class. Moreover, it could have hampered his efforts into securing college placement. One of the comments struck a chord with me.

> *"The kid made an adolescent mistake, owned up to it and learned from it. If that were the purpose of sanctions, a two-day suspension would have served the purpose. Instead, the school appears to have over reacted and is being punitive. It doesn't appear that they are interested in a true learning experience but rather in sacrificing one kid. Just plain meanness! A whole unblemished academic record appears to not matter at all. I am furious that alleged educators refuse to look at this in the content of 17 years of "good kid" slashed down in one moment over a tiny lapse in judgement."*

For kids like Chris, this incident not only made him think twice about his actions, it also suppressed any future desire of being truly himself on social media. Erratic judgements within social teach us to behave in ways that prevents us from being misjudged or attacked. Kids, who have not yet felt the wrath of social media, will learn from their peers' mistakes. They will learn discretion. Or they will learn to recede further away from transparency into a darker place where judgements are fewer and far between.

ANONYMITY IS AUTHENTICITY

I wrote this post last summer, Publishers OR Platforms? Cyberbullying and Increased Accountability by Social Networks[33], following the death of Rehteah Parsons; also following the suicide of Hannah Smith, who experienced the same torment on Ask. fm. I wrote,

> *"…The internet has evolved to an era that has given free rein to voice an opinion and use like-minded affiliations to express and further spread that opinion."*

In these cases, anonymous users kept up a stream of hateful attacks that eventually wore down both girls' defenses. Here, I referenced a polarized view of social networks via **Christopher "Moot" Pool**, founder of [4]Chan, who argued that anonymity on social was necessary:

"The cost of failure is really high when you're contributing as yourself. Those mistakes are attributed to who you are. Anonymity, in contrast, allows people to be creative, and poke and prod and try things they might not otherwise. Anonymity is authenticity. It allows you to share in a completely unvarnished, unfiltered, raw way."

And while I originally argued that anonymity was a cowardly state that allowed people to be and feel empowered by the lack of accountability, my stance has become more nuanced.

ANONYMITY IS SAFE

It becomes clear that humans, while inherently social, are discriminating of the things we disclose and to those to whom we share. As per Solis,

"We now live three lives online and will continue to do so in future; one that disappears, one that is secret, and one that sculpts our legacy."

If transparency breeds contempt, then anonymity should build acceptance.

The freedom to express opinion and judgement without feeling guarded, or without fearing others linking you to a statement is indeed liberating. And while this free rein may take the form of a soapbox lecture or criticisms (and perhaps bullying attacks) against opposing views, there is a large segment of users who want the ability to share a secret, or have a place to vent their frustrations or challenges — without the fear of reprisal.

WE ALL HAVE THIS "SECRET" LIFE AND WE SHOULD BE FIERCE IN DEMANDING PRIVACY FOR THOSE THINGS WE WANT TO KEEP HIDDEN.

Despite revelations from Snowden and the NSA that nothing on the net is private, this does not stop the wave of user adoption for applications like SnapChat, Whisper or Secret.

Launched at the tail end of 2012, it took less than 6 months for Whisper to accumulate 2 million users and a billion pageviews. Founder of Whisper, Michael Heyword said this about his vision for the app[34]:

> *"Whisper allows people to emote online in a way that won't ever be tracked to their permanent, cant-be-deleted data trail left by social media accounts... Michael Heyward designed Whisper to let people take down the facade of perfection, anonymously, and just relate to one another. "You don't have to be this brand manager," he says. "It's exhausting."*

I downloaded Whisper and my experience has been more than liberating. It has allowed me an outlet to record my hopes, desires and more importantly, my anger and not-for-public emotions. Being judged in real life or on social takes its toll. If my reputation precedes me, then I will be discriminating about what I say in places where my content and identity are linked.

Popular opinion just doesn't matter. It's irrelevant. But I want to track progress in my life: my emotions, my dark moments, my personal observations, and my milestones — all in my own digital diary.

UPDATED: *I recently removed the Whisper application following news that the US Department of Defense had been using the application to track anonymous users.*[35] *It's clear to me that even the choice to be anonymous does not give the common user any comfort of security.*

WHY SHOULDN'T USERS HAVE THE OPTION TO KEEP PART OF THEIR IDENTITIES SECRET AND SEPARATE?

It's up to the next generation.

BF Skinner laid this out succinctly when he disclosed his theories on Operant Conditioning[36],

> *The promise or possibility of rewards causes an increase in behaviour ....The removal of a desirable outcome or the application of a negative outcome can be used to decrease or prevent undesirable behaviours.*

This new medium has created is an endless, volatile loop of positive and negative reinforcement. While transparency has extreme benefits, there are just as many negative consequences that have come as a result of creating this honesty within social channels.

Society continues to send the wrong message to Millennials and the next generation, Z warning them to be more discerning and to suppress who they really are as individuals… warning them of the potential consequences should they venture down the wrong path.

How we communicate today poses tremendous issues for this younger generation. Their experiences are grounded in the fear of being vulnerable… fear of being misjudged… fear of not being accepted… fear of being punished.
…Which begs the question,

IF IT WAS ABOUT TRUST, THEN IS ALL HOPE LOST?

It's still early days, and as social media becomes more embedded in our lives, we need to move from this Wild West mentality and set the groundwork for making it work within organizations, and between government and web users.

The Heartbleed Bug won't be the last. It's inevitable that vulnerability attacks get more sophisticated, but legislating for increased government transparency needs to happen if we're all to have the freedom to keep private "what we want to keep private."

Facebook has realized that every tweak to its platform will be subject to user criticism.

When the next generation grows up, it will be up to them to shape the landscape and determine how to balance the impacts of transparency and anonymity.

So, perhaps trust is not the pivotal issue, but a balance between company and government transparency and some semblance of consumer control.

It's a long and bumpy road ahead, but we must work to reduce the communication gap between the business and the consumer.

REFERENCES

1   http://www.steamfeed.com/getting-personal-facebook-context-meets-creepy/

2   http://www.forbes.com/social-media/

3   http://www.usatoday.com/story/money/business/2013/04/21/millennials-personal-info-online/2087989/

4   http://news.yahoo.com/pa-woman-sues-google-over-182256512.html

5   http://www.huffingtonpost.com/2013/06/12/nsa-big-data_n_3423482.html

6   http://sethgodin.typepad.com/seths_blog/2008/01/permission-mark.html

7   http://writingya.blogspot.ca/2012/03/on-privacy-from-ongoing-ted-talks.html

8   http://readwrite.com/2013/09/02/nsa-pickup-lines#awesm=~oheovcJh2Czb4E

9   http://www.emarketer.com/Article/US-Web-Users-Concerned-About-Privacy-Hold-Themselves-Accountable/1010206#G5oTzrOXf9IZVYgY.99

10 http://www.huffingtonpost.ca/hessie-jones/teens-oversharing-internet_b_2923694.html

11 http://www.nytimes.com/2013/09/12/technology/personaltech/ftc-looking-into-facebook-privacy-policy.html?_r=1&

12 http://adage.com/article/dataworks/transparency-big-data-face-critics/244037/

13 http://www.bluekai.com/

14 http://exelate.com/

15 http://www.theguardian.com/media-network/media-network-blog/2013/oct/23/buzzfeed-jonathan-perelman-ad-banner

16 http://mobile.nytimes.com/blogs/bits/2014/04/08/flaw-found-in-key-method-for-protecting-data-on-the-internet/

17 http://www.vox.com/2014/4/8/5593654/heartbleed-explainer-big-new-web-security-flaw-compromise-privacy

18 http://rt.com/usa/nsa-knew-heartbleed-hacking-years-004/

19 http://www.theguardian.com/technology/2010/jan/11/facebook-privacy

20 http://whatsyourtech.ca/2011/05/09/mobile-online-privacy-by-redesign-%E2%80%93-let%E2%80%99s-start-with-the-manuals/

21 http://www.ipc.on.ca/english/Home-Page/

22 http://www.businessinsider.com/facebooks-privacy-2014-4

23 http://www.cbc.ca/news/rehtaeh-parsons-facebook-ad-a-textbook-case-of-online-photo-abuse-1.1859585

24 http://readwrite.com/2013/10/10/facebook-privacy-setting-checkup#awesm=~oBhrR4vEBEVtKk

25 http://readwrite.com/2014/04/11/facebook-privacy-controls-hand-them-over#ixzz2yjcqb9LC

26 http://www.nnovation.com/practice-expertise/canadas-anti-spam-legislation/

27 http://sethgodin.typepad.com/seths_blog/2008/01/permission-mark.html

28 http://www.nnovation.com/practice-expertise/canadas-anti-spam-legislation/

29 http://www.nnovation.com/practice-expertise/canadas-anti-spam-legislation/

30 http://www.crtc.gc.ca/eng/casl-lcap.htm

31 http://www.nnovation.com/practice-expertise/canadas-anti-spam-legislation/

32 http://www.nnovation.com/practice-expertise/canadas-anti-spam-legislation/

33 http://arcompany.co/social-networks-cyberbullying/

34 http://pando.com/2013/05/16/with-2-million-users-secrets-app-whisper-launches-on-android/

35 http://www.theguardian.com/world/2014/oct/16/-sp-revealed-whisper-app-tracking-users

36 http://psychology.about.com/od/behavioralpsychology/a/introopcond.htm

Beyond Social Listening – Changing the Game to Drive More Business

THE EVOLUTION OF SOCIAL LISTENING
by Michael Brito

All the hours you spend focusing on brand positioning doesn't matter if everyone else thinks differently about your brand. And all the media spend in the world can't change brand perception if your product doesn't deliver value to your customers, or if your customer service is non-existent.

Brands are built by having good products. They are built when brands go above and beyond when solving customer problems. They are built by passionate customers who share an emotional connection and then tell others about their experiences.

But you'll never know that these people even exist if you aren't listening.

Social listening is new. The short evolution over the last 5 – 7 years started with listening to brand sentiment (which wasn't and still isn't that accurate) and monitoring brand mentions using out-dated technologies like Nielsen Buzz Metrics.

Today, it's become much more sophisticated as technology applications are solving much more than historical reporting of a certain number. The following are 8 use cases on why you should make social listening an integral part of your business and marketing initiatives:

1. **Listen:** This one is the no-brainer. Several of the technology platforms are creating "command centers" and pride themselves on their listening capabilities. They have software that scours the Internet and captures all mentions of your brand (or any keyword) in forums, blogs, Twitter, Facebook, YouTube comments, Instagram and you name it. It then provides reports that measure share of voice, volume of mentions, sentiment, community growth, engagement metrics, etc. Just like any relationship, whether online or in real life, most of what you should do is listen.

2. **Stakeholder Engagement:** What's the point of listening if you aren't prepared to engage? Deploying social listening gives you the opportunity to find relevant conversations that are happening about your brand and allow you to add value to the conversation by participating. If you aren't prepared to add value to the community conversation, you may need to rethink your strategy or postpone it until you are ready to do so. Either way, it's wise to start with listening.

3. **Build Community:** Once you listen to the conversation and add value to it, you and your brand will become a trusted member of the community. And as Seth Godin wrote in his book, Permission Marketing over 11 years ago, you can then "ask permission" to market your products and services to them. The same holds true today. Both Facebook and Twitter spent years building their communities before they decided to monetize them and they are both doing extremely well.

4. **Foster Brand Advocacy:** Friends, fans and followers are great and it sure looks good in PowerPoint presentation when you have a lot of them. But what's next? Your goal should be to turn those friends, fans and followers of your into brand advocates. You do that by listening to your customers and then taking action.

5. **Create More Relevant Content:** Social listening can also give you the opportunity to capture trends that are happening in real-time and allow you to insert your brand into the conversation if it makes sense to do so. In this case, you wouldn't necessarily be monitoring "brand mentions" but rather topics that are trending from the people who follow your brand

in social media. While "content is king", the ability to create the right content, at the right time, in the right channel and to the right customer is where the true value is.

6. **Innovation:** Companies like Dell, GiffGaff, Lego and Starbucks rely heavily on community for innovation. They are not only "listening to the conversation" but they are taking the collective feedback from their communities and taking action by innovating their products and services. Not only does this strategy help build products that people will actually buy, but it also creates a sense of advocacy because your community will feel emotionally invested into your brand and its products.

Document Target Audiences: Social listening can also work as real-time focus groups and be used as research initiatives. Many technology platforms can extract customer data like demographics, buying and search behavior, lifestyle interests and passions; as well as give you insights into customer pain points about your products or services.

Manage Customer Support: Most social listening command centers today are manned by support agents with the sole responsibility of solving customer issues quickly and efficiently. There are several vendors in the marketplace that have this capability.

While most social listening strategies today are reactive, some innovate Marketers are using it as more of a proactive real-time marketing opportunity. We have all seen the famous Oreo tweet during the Super Bowl halftime show a few years ago. Case studies and blog posts have been written about that real-time moment. Many brands today have tried to follow suit and failed. The key to real-time marketing is to "listen" to a very targeted audience online (i.e. Millennials, IT decisions makers) and create content that is trending among this core group versus "what's trending on Twitter." Some brands certainly get lucky, like Oreo did; but most won't.

Building a social listening strategy isn't like building with Legos. There aren't sets of instructions to walk you step-by-step through the process. It's more like a puzzle and may require you to force-fit certain pieces in to make it work. Every company is different. Culture, marketing philosophies, go-to-market strategies and technology deployments are completely different and often dynamic. Whenever new leadership revolves in and out of a company, you may find yourself taking two steps back with each step forward.

> *As head of social strategy at WCG, a W2O Company, **Michael Brito** is responsible for helping clients think strategically about storytelling, social channels and paid media strategy. Previously, he was Senior Vice President of Social Strategy at Edelman Digital where he consulted for Fortune 500 companies implementing integrated content and digital marketing strategies, globally. He has worked for Silicon Valley companies like HP, Yahoo, and Intel building online communities before social media was even a thing. He is also an Adjunct Professor at San Jose State University teaching social business and also the author of Your Brand: The Next Media Company.*

IN THE BEGINNING...

In an earlier chapter we referenced a traditional company, United Bakers, that built their brand and sustained its business for many years by simply listening to their customers.

The reality is that companies operated on this notion of "See No Evil, Hear No Evil, Speak no Evil." For many years, they were able to control their movements to a positive bottom line. While they did the proper research to validate whether they were moving in the right direction, those environments were, for the most part, controlled and ultimately engineered to push the company's initiatives.

Word of Mouth existed for years but it was not significant in volume and amplification to make a company turn its head and take notice. In these restless times where social networks have given increased voice and power to individuals, companies are taking notice.

What we need is for business to be able to use the information and, as Peter Kim, formerly of Dachis Group, so wisely put it, "Be Curious, Not Furious." This allows a company to open its mind to possibilities by letting the customer "in" and evolving the business so it's always in sync with customer expectations and new opportunities.

Now, let's take a look at how one online media outlet utilized social listening and data to rapidly build community and expand their footprint.

CASE STUDY: SteamFeed - Adapting Your Plan From Social Listening Data

By Daniel Hebert, Co-founder SteamFeed

When Daniel Hebert told me his story about SteamFeed[1], how it began and how they became so successful, I knew we had to tell his story. SteamFeed is one of the best-read blogs for marketing professionals, small business and social media managers. Daniel, DJ Thistle, Co-founder and Gerry Michaels, VP of Marketing and Business Development, did it right from the beginning.

When DJ Thistle (@djthistle) and I first met online in the summer of 2012, we had no idea that SteamFeed.com would become such a success. In just over a year, we grew a website from conception to reality, from 0 contributors to over 52 featured authors, from 0 page visitors to over 70,000 unique visitors every month.

AN IDEA SPARKED FROM SOCIAL LISTENING

It came from one simple action that every single company can take: social listening. In the summer of 2012, DJ approached me with an idea for a multi-author blog. After reading countless blog posts from talented professionals, he thought that there was a better way to get all of that content together, in one place. The idea was that if we blog together as a group, we'll create a larger impact, have more visibility, and raise each other's credibility. So we came up with the initial concepts for SteamFeed, and started planning.

Then, something happened in the social-sphere. A movement started against "the social media guru." Real professionals, doing real work, were tired of reading the same crap over and over again from bloggers that had no idea how things worked in real life. We listened to the conversations and what people were saying. At the same time, a new app called "Fakers, by Status People"[2] came out that showed how many fake followers people had on Twitter. All of a sudden, screenshots and blog posts were circulating about "the gurus" buying fake followers to make themselves look more important. The social media and marketing community were in shock, and something needed to be done.

With this type of qualitative data that DJ and I gathered we completed the plan for SteamFeed, and started working on implementation.

PLANNING AND IMPLEMENTING OF SOCIAL INTELLIGENCE DATA

We started gathering blog posts, comments, tweets, etc. from social media professionals to guide our implementation of SteamFeed. What started as an idea for a multi-author blog quickly turned into a social media movement.

We decided to focus our site on Social Media, Marketing, and Tech truth. We created a vetting process for our featured contributors. We set topics and post guidelines, along with featured author agreements. And we focused our message: We called ourselves the Social Media Rebels, and we wanted to spark a revolution.

Enough with the gurus, we want the truth, from real professionals.

Equipped with these materials and our branding, we set out to recruit featured authors. By the time the site launched we had 18 real professionals, all fired-up and ready to create conversations and move the social media marketing industry forward.

REACHING TARGET AUDIENCES THROUGH SOCIAL

But with any new product (in our case, a content website) you need a receptive audience to build awareness. So, based on the qualitative data that we gathered, we went to work. DJ and I both started writing on our personal blogs, giving teasers about the launch (without giving too much detail, we wanted to keep it mysterious). We also set-up a landing page that said, "The drums are starting to bang… ¡Viva la Revolución!" It also had our logo, a graphic, and a link to register to our RSS feed for launch day.

We started engaging with the people that had tweeted negatively about social media gurus, and told them a solution was coming – most of them signed up. We kept posting every few weeks to keep the buzz going, and kept building key relationships with people who had a keen interest and need for what we were about to offer.

On launch day, we exceeded every single expectation we had set for ourselves, and ended up in Twitter jail (yup, that's a thing!) for most of the day because of the enormous amount of mentions and replies we were getting.

So what lessons can we learn from this story of an unlikely start-up that you can apply to your own business?

IMPLICATIONS FOR YOUR COMPANY

ArCompany has a great motto of "helping you turn social media intelligence into business results." I 100% agree with this, and apply it to everything I do at work, and for SteamFeed. The beauty of digital marketing is that there's so much data available, that you're already well equipped to make strategic business decisions for your company.

Integrating Social Data into Product and Marketing Planning

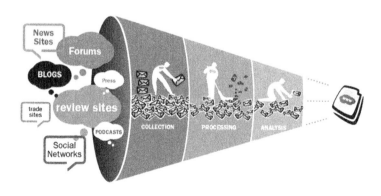

Your customers are on social media, whether your company is there or not. And guess what? They're talking about your industry, and your competitors. It's a GOLD MINE of data for you to tap into.

Social data allows you to validate products, services, and marketing campaigns before they even launch. What are your prospects complaining about? What do they want? What's the worst feature your competitor has? What's on your prospect's wish list? This data exists in the public domain; it can be found.

By using qualitative data about your prospect's wants and needs, you can guide a product roadmap, or plan a marketing campaign that will really grab your customer's attention. It will be as if you created a campaign or a product just for them. Getting validation for your plan before implementation can also save you a lot of time and money in the long-run, and increase your chances of succeeding from the start.

Have a Plan, but Be Flexible

We had a plan for a multi-author blog at SteamFeed, and we were in the process of implementing that plan when we started to see a shift in the social-sphere. Listening to social data is an on-going process, and in order to apply it properly to your organization, you need to be flexible.

Our product direction changed. Our launch campaign changed. Our branding changed... but for the better. At the same time we were organizing the launch of SteamFeed, a couple of our friends were launching very similar websites. Because of the buzz we created before and after the launch, their awareness wasn't as high as ours. And when we reviewed the performance of our website a year later compared to theirs, we out-performed them by far.

What was the difference between us, and them? We all were planning multi-author blogs in the social media marketing segment. *So why were we so successful?*

We adapted our plan to fill a need that was apparent in the market place. A need we identified from social data. And we used marketing tactics that hit consumers at an emotional level, before we launched. That's what separated us from our competitors.

CREATE AN AUDIENCE BEFORE YOU NEED IT

This is something that can apply to any start-up or company launching a new product or service. It could even apply to marketing initiatives. Take Visa's #smallenfreuden campaign[3] as an example. Before the campaign started, they had prepared buzz within social communities by using the hashtag #SmallenFreuden, and people began asking what it was. There was a lot of social conversation happening before the meaning of the hashtag or even the brand behind it was revealed. They were creating an audience before they needed it, which in the end created a lot more buzz than if they would have simply launched the campaign.

We did the same at SteamFeed – we started creating buzz within social media communities a month before we actually launched our website. There's nothing worse than launching a new blog, with nobody there to listen to what you have to say.

I did the same thing at InNetwork[4]. In October 2012, before we even had a blog and product, I created social media accounts, and started following targeted prospects.

In February, we launched our blog, and started building an email list and attracting inbounds. We didn't officially launch our SaaS product until May 2013, and we used influencers to help spread awareness to a wider audience). When we launched our product, we already had a receptive audience, a community, and people interested in learning more.

DON'T DISMISS THE POWER OF SOCIAL INTELLIGENCE

Often, when I speak with senior executives that are reluctant about social media for business, they think about Facebook and teenagers, and don't see the value for their organizations. This is because they don't understand the full potential of applying social data to their company for business results. The fact that a Product Marketer can listen to a wide-audience of targeted prospects, analyze their complaints and wishes, build a product plan that's in demand, and launch a successful product without ever having to issue a survey or ask anyone (just by listening to social intelligence data) is amazing!

There's a huge gap in the industry when it comes to understanding the tools and applications of social intelligence, and we need more organizations like ArCompany leading the way. We also need a clean-up of crappy, re-hashed content that was popular 6 years ago.

And maybe, we also need a new set of corporate speakers that have more experience in social intelligence, and real application to business results.

Social media data can be applied to much more than blogging and marketing – you just need to be creative, listen, and implement whenever it makes sense.

As per *Daniel Hebert*:

> *"It's an important lesson for any company, of any size. SteamFeed was created on a very limited budget - we didn't have the funds or anything to invest in large data solutions. But that doesn't stop you these days from doing basic social listening. Setting up free alerts, reading trending articles, listening to social queues and keywords through engagement dashboard, etc. It's a very cost-effective way of listening to qualitative data on social, and just doing that can save you a lot of hardship in the future.*

It doesn't have to be complicated or expensive to use data these days. Data doesn't have to be a luxury for large enterprises. It can be applied at any level."

The Art of Social Listening

As the Web evolves, it allows people to display their opinions more transparently. And many of those who have the most to say are speaking as customers. This is forcing companies to be more proactive in building processes and structures to actively mine customer conversation, whether it is through direct social channels or third party discussion forums, boards and social networks. This flurry of conversation is what has the potential to determine a company's demise, if it isn't properly dealt with.

Earlier (in the Power of Community), we provided a case study about Columbia House, a company going through a brand revamp: new name, new business model–all in an attempt to show the world it had changed. The new company was formed in response to its questionable customer service, pricing model and a slew of other negative customer experiences.

The bottom line? Within a short period, social media had the highest ROI compared to other direct acquisition channels. This fundamentally changed how social media was perceived within the C-suite, and management began to transform Columbia House's customer touch point processes. Most importantly, the company realized that the relationships it cultivated with its customers provided a sustainable revenue base. Eventually, these strategies would evolve into best-practices for customer retention.

What's the larger context? Here are some stats[5] related to customer retention from Customer Thermometer:

- 68% of your customers leave you because they feel you are indifferent to them
- Companies that prioritize the customer experience generate 60% higher profits than their competitors

- 43% feel less inhibited about complaining once they go online
- Satisfied customers tell 9 people how happy they are
- Dissatisfied customers tell 22 people about their bad experiences

HONESTY, TRANSPARENCY, HUMILTY

My early exposure to social media provided me an opportunity to experience first-hand the volatile nature of the online environment and its potential negative impact on companies. The lessons I've learned below have been publicized many times, but they beg repeating:

- **Humanize your brand/company:** Don't be a corporate shill. Speak with a human voice.
- **Eat some humble pie:** Take it on the chin for the company. Seek to provide solutions for the customer.
- **Be consistent:** Be the ongoing voice for your company. Your commitment is vital.
- **Expect to make mistakes along the way.** Don't expect to get it right the first time. Relationships are hard. Find the rhythm that will allow your voice to be heard and accepted.
- **Create value:** Do not sell. It's the fastest way to be shunned from the community.
- **Don't avoid issues.** Instead deal with them head on before they become bigger.
- **Don't delete comments** on your social properties because they don't align with your rules of engagement. They won't go away. You can't control the conversation so don't attempt to do so.
- **Cast your ego aside.** Responding to a non-binding statement that cedes to the other's perspective really gives nothing away except respect. Success and peace is what matters NOT who is right.
- When you are attacked, your instinct is to throttle someone because they're

wrong. Remember, the world is watching. **Your next move will determine how others perceive you.**

- **Be proactive:** Anticipate any potential customer fallout. Communicate the issue(s) and what the company is doing to remedy the situation.

It comes down to honesty, transparency and humility... all in an effort to build trust. This is, perhaps, the most difficult mindset shift in an organization.

Most companies take comfort and hide behind the art of 'spin' and obfuscation. But once a company realizes that customers can see through this, they may opt to employ a different strategy––one that is more accessible to, and accepting of, their customers.

WHO SHOULD BE DRIVING THE SOCIAL MEDIA BUS? MARKETING OR THE CONTACT CENTER?

Businesses now know that they have to adapt to the demands of social media and somehow incorporate its elements into corporate structure and operations. A major question within many companies is: who takes the lead? More and more it has to be the people who deal with customers.

The question was addressed to a distinguished panel at a Social Media Roundtable held by the CMA. The roundtable's purpose:

The emergence of social media as a prominent channel of communication amongst consumers presents significant challenges that many organizations are only just beginning to understand and address. Who should own it? How do you manage it? Where is this channel going? How do you measure ROI?

The speakers represented TD Bank, DraftFCB, ING Direct, Indigo, Sysomos and Sears.

WHO'S AT THE STEERING WHEEL?

In responding to the key question: "Who is driving the Social media bus?" All agreed that Marketing has been the driver because it has the ownership of both the brand and communication to the customer. However, as the space is evolving to social business, everyone in the organization needs to get involved.

In past years, Social Media has been tested; many never really understood its significance. Often responsibility for Social Media was relegated to the most junior people in an organization. Social Media was perceived as just another channel, and therefore it was not prioritized.

TD has seen the channel evolve into something more significant. Wendy Arnott indicated that in order to convince the Senior Executives to take notice and begin implementing changes; TD spent an entire year planning and listening:

- Understanding the pulse of the TD customer, the context of what was being said and the overriding sentiment about TD
- Creating guidelines for employees
- Defining the voice of the brand
- Setting up a strategy for the purpose of effectively engaging

MONITORING, MEASUREMENT AND ROI

Kobo VP, Mark Stevens noted that there are thousands of discussions taking place and asked: "How do you choose channels? Where do you engage and where NOT to engage? How do you measure success?"

Sysomos' Jeff Cann responded, "Figure out where people are congregating. This is where the time and energy is spent talking about your brand– where the majority of volume discussions can be found… Understand the trends of these discussion."

I was happy to hear that TD has all departments aligned: Legal, Risk, Compliance, PR, and Privacy. They continuously monitor all discussions and develop proactive policies to turn "detractors into promoters."

Laurie Dillon-Schalk of DraftFCB suggested there were still challenges in defining digital value. For social, "Work has yet to be done in determining how digital has impacted purchase. That will determine dollar investment in social media."

David Bradshaw of ING Canada reiterated, "This is a business initiative–the entire company needs to be involved".

Sears' Christopher Brockbank pointed out some major changes happening with respect to social media: "Involve the customers in the shopping experience." What this means: Customers will now have a stronger stake in defining trends, changing the shopping experience i.e. having a SAY.

Brockbank suggested the conversation was painful in the beginning. Sears approached this honestly and was willing to listen to everyone. He said this was somewhat equivalent to "admitting you're an alcoholic." What they found in the process was a large number of customers rooting for Sears to get better.

MARKETING AND CUSTOMER SERVICE ARE ALIGNED

The bulk of the discussion revealed a strong cohesion between Marketing and Operations, but there was still work to be done. David Bradshaw said the customer relationship was still evolving but roles needed to be clearly defined. Is there an overall contact point?

Laurie Dillon-Schalk noted that customers needed to spend time across different groups because each stakeholder had a different "view" of the customer. As

Brockbank shared, Social Media needs to be centred under the brand, under one banner, but the planning process would define and dictate each stakeholder role. Things that would work:

- Employ front line staff who are willing to learn, are passionate and good judges of situations
- Proper training
- KPI's (Key Performance Indicators) to measure to success
- Engagement: Be interested and be interesting
- Proper organization and a clear plan of action
- Integrating CRM (Customer Relationship Management)
- Social media guidelines for crisis team escalation
- Data gathering at all customer touch points

Do we have a ways to go? Absolutely. I take comfort in knowing that some of the biggest brands are putting their stake in the ground to lead the way and figure it out.

Customer Service: The Future Of Real Time Marketing

Sure, there have been a few tremendously opportune Real Time Marketing applications that have driven brands into a tailspin trying to figure out how to repeat, capitalize and one up.

And by a few, I mean only a few.

Take a moment and think of the game changing, real time marketing done by brands and try to name some that were really memorable. Now, take the Oreo "Dunking in the Dark"[7] tweet from the 2013 Super Bowl and remove it from your list. What's left?

Perhaps, if you are a marketing expert or an avid content connoisseur you can name more than a few great real time marketing campaigns, but for the vast majority, the channel is still in its infancy and for the most parts brands are still fumbling to make it work for their business. Begging the question:

What is the most "real time" opportunity for marketing?

What if I was to suggest that the best opportunity isn't a form of marketing at all? Well, that is what I am going to do because I believe, bar none, that the best opportunity for brands looking to capitalize on real time marketing is for them to implement real time customer service.

EXPLORING REAL TIME CUSTOMER SERVICE IN THE DIGITAL ECONOMY

Did you know that 67% of consumers expect a same day response to their social media service requests?[9] Of that group, 42% expect a response in one hour, and 32% within 30 minutes. Meaning nearly 1/3 of consumers expect to hear from their favorite brands within just 30 minutes.

In a world where consumers are driving technology, we have entered a realm where their expectations demand responsiveness.

While the debate may rage as to whether or not the customer is always right, we all understand that the customer is always the customer. If we want to keep them buying and advocating for our brands, then we need to provide a good customer experience.[10] And although some of their on demand customer service expectations via social media may be unrealistic… brands will have to adapt.

One of the key phrases being used for the new business paradigm is Peer-to-Peer (P2P); this is the idea that B2B and B2C are becoming less relevant[11] as our expectations are being set by our universal experiences.

A simple example is that we tend to look at our best customer experiences across all of our interactions with businesses, whether professionally for our company or individually, as a consumer[12]. In short, a great experience with a Starbucks barista may make us rethink how we engage with a manufacturer or consulting service.

This is an excellent reason for businesses of all types to think about service as a real time marketing opportunity.

HOW BUSINESS CAN IMPLEMENT REAL TIME CUSTOMER SERVICE TO DRIVE IMPROVED CUSTOMER EXPERIENCE?

We have entered a world where people will recommend brands based on good customer experiences; isn't it time that we start looking at customer service more like a marketing channel?

Did you know that 95% of consumers will take action on a bad customer experience[13] and 82% of consumers will eventually defect for the same reason? It is true!

What is even more staggering is that only a fraction of the number of people that defect for customer service reasons defect for product performance reasons. Meaning, it is time to get serious about responsiveness.

Here are a few ways that businesses can get started with real time customer service.

- **Create The Channels:** Make sure that your customers know all the ways they can reach you. Beyond just traditional phone and email, make real time channels like Twitter and Facebook accessible for customers to express their needs (and pay compliments).
- **Set The Expectations:** While real time to some extent means to the second, when it comes to service it can be "within a few minutes" and still be seen as real time. If you are going to offer real time service via social channels make sure customers know what to expect in terms of response. (Hint: it should be really fast!)

- **Watch the Channels:** Having a special Twitter handle for service requests is a great idea, however if no one is watching the channel it can become a terrible disaster. Make sure you have a plan for social listening to any locations where you are committing to real time response. In fact, the fall- out for a company proclaiming real time service that doesn't perform would probably be exponentially bad. Can you imagine?

- **Respond Thoughtfully:** Just responding is good. It makes everyone happy to know they are being listened to; however real time customer service works best when those on the other end of the line can actually help. Make sure you put people on the other end of real time service channels that can jump in and do more than just put the customers in queue.

For most businesses, the most real time opportunity to be more responsive and get closer to your customers may just be in how you serve them.

Social channels provide a great opportunity to improve customer experience and be more prepared to fix the little issues that can lead to defection. Fast companies will see and act on this trend immediately. After all, every business interaction that takes place is between people, so shouldn't this impact how we listen and respond online? Of course it does. Just watch, Tweet and see!

P2P Shifts The B2B Customer Experience Landscape

Business Is Human, First and Foremost

If I were to ask you what every business transaction in the world had in common, what would you tell me?

Before you suggest that such an idea is crazy, would you agree that, in every single business transaction, in there is a buyer and seller, and while the buyer and seller may be an entity, at the root of the transaction are people?

Simply put, every transaction in the world that takes place involves people. This is the very premise of P2P (Peer to Peer/Person to Person), because in the end whether a transaction is B2B or B2C, it is really P2P.

Behind this very idea lies a substantial shift that every business, especially B2B's, need to think about as a part of their customer experience strategy[14.]

VISUALIZING HIGH IMPACT CUSTOMER EXPERIENCE

When we are asked to draw on examples of great customer experience, where do most of our memorable experiences come from? While I can't speak for everyone, most of my best customer experiences come from B2C experiences.

Maybe this has to do with the fact that customer experience is looked at more closely when we are spending our own money, or maybe it is because as individuals we engage in many service focused activities like dining out, travel and entertainment. Why do you think this is?

Let me ask you to visualize the last time you received remarkable customer experience. Not just a forgettable, slightly better than mediocre experience, but the kind that is so good that you feel compelled to tell anyone that will listen.

What was it that set this particular experience apart for you? If I had to guess, it was almost always an interaction between yourself and another person, right?

Can you seriously tell me that you have had a truly memorable customer experience where you didn't have to interact with a person even once?

Here is why I don't think you can have a memorable customer experience without dealing with another human being: because those types of experiences fall directly in the bucket of Above Average to Good. Take for instance shopping online. If you go online, buy the product and it arrives when it is supposed to, that isn't great or memorable, but rather what you expected. Am I right?

WHEN THE PERSON MAKES THE CUSTOMER EXPERIENCE GREAT

After much indecisiveness I finally made the decision to buy an iMac for Christmas.

Being that I am fairly savvy with the technology and I was already an Apple user, I went to the Apple Store online, picked out the machine I wanted, the accessories I wanted, and I submitted the order. It would be ready for pick up in 3 days.

Great, in 3 days I would be able to pick up my machine, and then I'll be really happy. Still, waiting 3 days for the gift I bought myself was a bit much.

24 hours later my phone rings and it was the Apple Store letting me know that my computer was ready for pick up.

Wow! I was thrilled; I only had to wait one day when I was expecting to wait three. I jumped into my car and off I went to Apple to pick up my new laptop.

When I arrived, my computer was all ready and the "Genius" that set me up handed me his card and said, call me if you have any issues with the setup. I laughed thinking…

1. It is an Apple, so there will be no problems.
2. This guy isn't going to help me; I didn't pay for the "Custom Setup."
3. There are a thousand people (seemingly) in this store. He won't even remember me.

Sure enough the store employee detected my snark; he grabbed the card and jotted down his Cell Phone and stated, "Seriously, if you need my help just call."

The setup went perfectly so I had no need to call; however, when I finished the set up I decided to give him a call just to thank him for the offer. When I called, he picked the phone up (as he said he would); he remembered me and immediately asked how he could help. I told him I didn't need help, but wanted to thank him for going the extra mile.

So even though shopping online was simple and intuitive and the install went flawlessly, what do you think it was that made the customer experience great?

It was the store employee that went just a little bit further to help, and it made all the difference in the world.

With this in mind, let me ask you another question:

DOES YOUR EXPERIENCE AT DAIRY QUEEN IMPACT YOUR SERVICE EXPECTATIONS IN B2B?

Okay, before you ask why Dairy Queen, I chose them randomly to serve as an example. In actuality, the example could be Dairy Queen, Midas, Starbucks or any other place you have a human interaction, just like my Apple experience above.

The important take away from the question is, do you ever consider great online or in person shopping experiences that you have B2C when you are looking at B2B? For a long time B2B has been a bit of a vacuum where service has been allowed to be delivered at its own pace.

Same day call-backs and quick resolutions were often luxuries, and many B2B buyers just dealt with these slower responses.

Today this is changing.

GREAT CUSTOMER EXPERIENCE NEEDS TO BE A FOCUS OF EVERY BUSINESS

Did you know that, on average, only 12% of a company's marketing budget is spent on Customer Retention, while more than 55% goes to new customer acquisition?

Perhaps this seems obvious to you, but when you consider that the probability of selling "more" to a current customer is 60-70%, whereas selling to a new customer is only 5-20%, there may be enough information there to make pause.

Considering that not only are your current customers perhaps your best source of new revenue, but in the end, they are often your best chance of growing your business via word of mouth.

Think about this: 90% of buyers online trust a reference that comes from their personal/professional network. Do you think that your current customers know a few more people you could sell to?

Chances are the answer is yes, but the question that businesses need to ask themselves is "why aren't we getting these recommendations (or more of them)?"

With all of these numbers in mind, you can't ignore how important it is to keep your current customers happy, and to do so you have to lead with customer experience.

And if the numbers aren't enough to drive you to focus more on customer experience then take a minute and think back to the customer experiences that were most memorable to you.

B2B's have to recognize that it is experiences just like the one that caught your attention that are setting the bar for customer experience in every business. If the person behind the counter at Dairy Queen can go the extra mile, or the "Genius" at the Apple Store can do just a little more to make my experience great, then B2B's large and small can take notice and put better customer experience as a top priority item.

If your business has been avoiding putting more structured focus on your customer experience strategy, you are not alone. Only about 20% of businesses have a well-defined customer experience strategy; however the vast majority of the rest (73%) are at various stages of creating and implementing one.

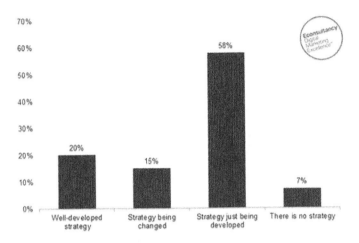

No matter where you are with your customer experience, two things are for sure.

1. You need to have one.
2. Every customer experience must be considered a benchmark.

Remember, every transaction in the world ultimately takes place between two humans. Keep that in mind when deciding how you want to create great customer experiences for those that drive your business.

CUSTOMER STRATEGIES EVOLVE AS A RESULT...

It's clear that companies are moving ahead, slowly, but surely. Listening has become a mainstay and it's clear that where this has traditionally benefitted marketing, the value of customer-led opinion has already begun to transform how Operations and Marketing function collectively. The importance of this data is driving further customer strategies that now make it more important than ever to cater to this always-on customer. In the coming chapters, it'll be clearer as this will begin to impact how organizations change.

REFERENCES:

1   http://www.steamfeed.com/

2   http://fakers.statuspeople.com/

3   http://www.marketingmag.ca/brands/visa-reveals-its-the-brand-behind-smallenfreuden-78554

4   http://innetwork.net/

5   http://www.slideshare.net/custthermometer/22-customer-retention-stats

6   http://www.the-cma.org/education-events/social-media-roundtable

7   https://twitter.com/Oreo/status/298246571718483968

8   http://millennialceo.com/social-media/real-time-marketing-businesses-size/

9   http://www.convinceandconvert.com/social-media-research/42-percent-of-consumers-complaining-in-social-media-expect-60-minute-response-time/

10 http://millennialceo.com/customer-service/5-tips-create-unparalleled-customer-experiences/

11 http://millennialceo.com/customer-service/p2p-shifts-b2b-customer-experience-landscape/

12 http://millennialceo.com/customer-service/p2p-shifts-b2b-customer-experience-landscape/

13 https://www.zendesk.com/blog/customer-experience-is-more-important-than-advertising

14 http://millennialceo.com/customer-service/leaders-enable-customer-experience/

True Influence: Why Business Must Pay Attention

INFLUENCE MARKETING
by Sam Fiorella

The study of influence in marketing is not new. In fact, Dale Carnegie first published How to Win Friends and Influence People in 1936 and it is still one of the top selling business books of all time. Daniel Edelman, founder of Edelman Public Relations, turned theory into practice when he pioneered the use of celebrity spokespeople in 1966 to influence brand awareness. In 1984 Dr. Robert Cialdini elaborated on the science of what makes people say "yes" based on three years of research experimenting with sales techniques in various businesses.

Fast forward to modern times and, thanks to the growing popularity of – and access to – social media, influence marketing has once again become a central strategy and tactic in the Marketer's tool kit, yet not without some controversy. The dominance of social media as the primary engagement interface among peers has seen tools like PeerIndex and Klout emerge to identify people who are influential in online conversations and sell access to those people for marketing purposes. However, within three years of those tools becoming popular among Marketers, they been proven to be mostly ineffective in identifying people or conversations that directly influence a purchase decision – the one goal every business strives for.

That failure does not diminish the importance of what those companies tried to accomplish or the role of influence marketing as a critical sales and marketing strategy for business. These tools highlighted the opportunity present in the increasing volume of online conversations and the power of the wisdom of crowds. Studies that show people trust the opinion and comments of their peers – whether they know those peers or not – over those written and shared by brands or their spokespeople.

As the devices that access the Internet and Social Media increase – from computers to smart phones to tablets to wearable devices – the power of peer commentary grows. And with that change, the ability to influence has moved from being an art to a science. New platforms such as Appinions and Traackr have emerged to provide a more scientific listing and analysis of who creates the opinions that sway conversations and who affects purchase decisions.

Along with my co-author Danny Brown, I conducted my own study of this modern phenomenon, which was published in Influence Marketing: How to Create, Manage, and Measure Brand Influencers in 2013. We discovered that the larger social communities grew and the more conversations that were added to those groups, greater influence was being exerted through smaller subsets of people with more clearly defined relationships, than through people with a larger, more generic following.

One of the famous case studies that demonstrates this shift comes from Telenor Group, a Norwegian telecommunications company that conducted a study to determine how people choose which brand of smart phone they purchase. The study concluded that if one of their customer's friends had an iPhone, the customer was two times more likely to purchase an iPhone; if two of their friends had an iPhone, the customer was fourteen times more likely to purchase an iPhone.

Despite the recommendation of tech journals and bloggers, catchy marketing campaigns or clever native advertising efforts, what drives purchase decisions – as opposed to brand awareness – is the recommendation of people closest to the end consumer.

And therein lies the modern challenge of influence marketing: What drives brand awareness and what drives actual purchase decisions?

Moving forward, understanding the life cycle of a consumer and what factors affect those decisions, from brand awareness to the act of purchasing, will become the baseline for effective influence marketing and how it's measured.

Social technologies have opened a Pandora's Box of social engagement that cannot be closed. What was unleashed has created an environment that has solidified the importance of influence on the purchase decisions of consumers in both B2B and B2C sectors, as well among non-profit organizations. Ironically, the larger our social graphs become, the more important one-to-one conversations are. Influence marketing is no longer a cyclical footnote; it's a permanent fixture in the marketing mix.

Sam Fiorella is a Managing Partner and CMO at Sensei Marketing Inc., a Toronto-based customer experience consultancy. A serial entrepreneur, Sam is also the co-author of Influence Marketing: How to Create, Manage, and Measure Brand Influencers in Social Media Marketing, Partner/CMO at Thirty750s.com, Professor of Marketing at Seneca College and an Adjunct Professor at Rutgers.

The Age of The Brand Influencer

WE AREN'T INFLUENCED BY ADS, BUT WE ARE INFLUENCED BY PEOPLE. SPENDING WILL FOLLOW.

If there is one thing that I have learned in my career, it's that the money always follows the trends.

This can be good when the trend is linear, and it can be quite lousy when a trend is short lived. (Think Pet Rock)

One thing is for certain is that people, by in large, are not influenced by advertisements. In fact, there isn't a single "True" advertising medium that is trusted at a rate of greater than 50%.[1]

In a social world we are influenced by our trusted network at a rate of near 90%, and that alone speaks volumes for where things are heading. While content marketing is not new, in the past year it has hit the radar of just about every CMO with a pulse.

Content is far more trusted than ads, with retail sites, brand sites and blogs being the 3 most influential content vehicles; brands are going to look at ways to move budget dollars from lesser performing vehicles like advertising to better performing methods, like blogging, video and infographics.

Currently, brands are seeing the greatest results in building trust and community through their content efforts; however more of their budget still goes towards advertising.

To be precise, in 2013 nearly 50% of brands' Social Marketing Spend[2] went to Facebook Advertising and less than 10% went to Influencer Outreach and Blogging; Meaning that brands spent 5x as much on Facebook ads as they did on creating

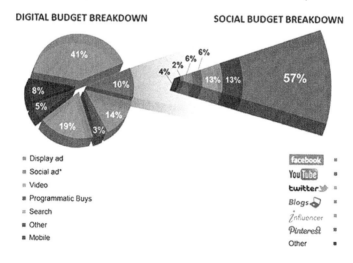

DIGITAL BUDGET BREAKDOWN   SOCIAL BUDGET BREAKDOWN

- Display ad
- Social ad*
- Video
- Programmatic Buys
- Search
- Other
- Mobile

- facebook
- YouTube
- twitter
- Blogs
- Influencer
- Pinterest
- Other

owned content and driving earned media.

Think about that: What are you more likely to trust and engage with? A Facebook Ad or a Blog Post written by someone influential about the product or service?

What is even crazier is that these out of proportion spends on advertising came after a 40% increase in what companies budgeted for Social Media in 2013.

I believe this is leading us to a seismic shift in how brands will do business.

With Facebook making it harder for brands to be seen (even paid brands), and the fact that sound, "Owned and Earned" strategies will lead readers to brand-owned sites, companies that want to drive influence are going to have to focus on their influencer outreach.

To accomplish this, brands are going to need to seek out thought leaders and content creators that influence buying behavior in their respective industries.

WHO ARE THESE THOUGHT LEADERS?

While the terms 'thought leader' and 'content creator' sound sophisticated, what I'm really talking about here are bloggers; those who write and publish content to the web, most often on their own sites or on a multitude of their own sites.

While brands are enamored with vehicles like Facebook and Twitter to cultivate followers and drive brand engagement, the most influential people are merely using Social Channels to drive readers back to their sites (86%).

This means that those that can influence their brand's success aren't well represented where the brands are looking for them, making it harder for brands to find influencers that can support their marketing initiatives.

DRIVING INFLUENCE THAT PAYS OFF BIG

While each brand's goals for marketing IS a little bit different, I think it is safe to say that all brands have a goal to drive positive brand sentiment.

This positive feeling toward a brand moves buyers' confidence levels in making brand purchases higher as they see people they trust supporting a certain product or service.

For many companies that know their target audience, this makes influencer marketing even more valuable. This is because 54% of consumers believe a small, highly engaged community is far more influential than a larger, less loyal community. In fact, only 12% believe a larger community is more influential. [3]

This data point is incredibly important and in actuality is very good news for brands looking to "Buy Influence."

In short, brands need to seek out influencers who can drive and create very small yet loyal communities to advocate for their brand.

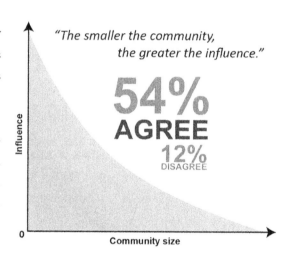

With so many people being separated through social channels by only 1 or 2 degrees, a small yet highly loyal group can reach far and be much more influential than a large army of wishy-washy folks who like a brand on Facebook or follow a brand on Twitter.

With buyers being influenced at far greater rates by people within their networks, brands are trying to figure out how to get closer to the influencer.

Again, for each product and service the influencer may vary, but the data does not lie. People will buy from brands they trust and the trust comes directly from content generated by the brand's intentional and unintentional community.

Influence will be the great brand equalizer, begging the question… how will your brand use influence and outreach to turn those new to your brand into enthusiasts, and those that know your brand into ambassadors? First, brands must be paying attention to how they approach influence marketing and moreover, with whom they work.

BRANDS: CHOOSE INFLUENCERS AND ADVOCATES WISELY

There has been a lot of talk in 2014 about how influence marketing is going to make the leap into the mainstream this year.

Given the state of content shock that consumers are in, the idea of finding individuals who can move the needle for a brand makes a lot of sense.

In a world where we are exposed to thousands of advertisements daily, yet we don't trust a single source of advertising at a rate of even 50%[4], earning and maintaining the attention AND trust of consumers is imperative for the long-term health of a brand.

In reality what it comes down is that brands need to earn trust, and they need to do it quickly. Knowing that consumers will trust a referral from their personal network[5] at a rate of 90%, and that they find that referral online more than 81% of the time, what better way to expedite trust than to pay content creators to blog, tweet and share their strong sentiment for a brand?

It is like shooting fish in a barrel, yes?

Not so fast. While the idea of finding influencers to support your brand seems easy—and more and more brands are doing it each day—I want to caution brands looking to use this tactic.

There may be more to influence than meets the eye.

FINDING THE RIGHT INFLUENCERS
IS MORE THAN METRICS

I had the opportunity to attend the Social Intelligence Summit in Las Vegas. One of the speakers was *Penny Baldwin*, CMO at McAfee. Her standout moment was when she said:

> *"80% of the Internet's Impressions are driven by just 6% of its users."*

Score one for influence, but with this statistic another challenge for brands is born: Who are the right influencers for their brand?

Many brands are turning to data to figure out whom they should bring on to their influence team. They look at metrics like followers on Twitter, likes on Facebook or Alexa Rank of their blog. All of these numbers have some meaning, but not necessarily as much as one might think.

This is where brands must do their homework and figure out how connected these supposed influencers are to their community, and whether or not they can move the needle for the specific brand in need.

To figure out whether an influencer can move content and drive improved brand sentiment, brands need to go beyond the raw data to determine what they are trying to do. Is it better to find an influencer who can connect the brand to 20 or 30 really meaningful decision makers, or are 10,000 page views more important even if the vast majority aren't really potential buyers?

The 30 meaningful relationships can mean millions of dollars in revenue (product dependent); whereas 10,000 page views will do nothing more than impress people that probably don't care.

If you consider what your per-customer acquisition cost is versus what the typical investment looks like for a brand-influence campaign, I suggest brands seek out the influencers who can make a handful of meaningful connections over broad reach any day of the week.

BUYING INFLUENCE VS. EARNING TRUST

While brands can buy influence, brand influencers cannot.

Much like the premise of brands buying reach, influencers can do the same through a number of tactics; not all of them lead to highly engaged communities. Brands looking to build advocacy through influence campaigns need to steer away from the temptation of reach and instead turn their attention to what the numbers mean.

If brands seek to use influence campaigns to build trust, then those chosen as brand influencers must have the ability to deliver meaningful content that drives brand sentiment within their community upwards. Having an engaged audience is the only way to do this. Reach means nothing if nobody is listening.

We have legitimately reached the point where consumers have run out of time to consume content, making it more important than ever for brands to focus on quality as a means to separate them from the pack. [6]

Influence marketing is undoubtedly a way to earn and keep more eyeballs where brands want them; however this can only be done if the influencers can transfer the trust they have built with their community to the brands they choose to support.

Influence marketing will work for brands that understand the connection between their target audience and the influencer, and focus on working only with those that can strengthen that connection not only for the short run, but also sustainably into the future.

A Listless: Misguided Brands Must Stop Sponsoring Schmucks

It is without a doubt that influence marketing has reached a tipping point, with good reason.

People are doing more and more searching online for articles and information[7] to help them make purchasing decisions. This goes from diapers to digital, and it is rooted in the trust that we as consumers have in other ordinary people as opposed to "Big Brands" and their deep pockets trying to manipulate us through clever ads and catch phrases.

In short, we trust other people[8] ... brands... not so much.[9]

So, the perfect marriage is when we get ordinary people to write about our experiences as they relate to a product, brand or industry. This is reflected in the rise of brands as media companies. [10] Smart brands started doing this years ago, and other (less smart) brands are following suit.

Pardon my snark about the less smart brands, but sadly the innovation of sponsored content from influencers[11] is old news. On a more positive note, when done well it works. However, this is more the exception than the rule.

This is primarily because brands obsess about the wrong things, and too often the agencies they hire proliferate this because they are equally clueless.

RAW METRICS ARE A WEAK INDICATION OF INFLUENCE

While every brand has its reasons (hopefully) for engaging in influencer marketing, the idea that an A-list blogger with large follower counts, page likes, and page views will make a strong brand advocate is misguided.

I tell this to brands I work with everyday:

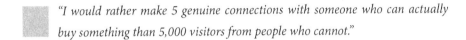

> *"I would rather make 5 genuine connections with someone who can actually buy something than 5,000 visitors from people who cannot."*

For all intents and purposes, these meaningless visits are just window shoppers. [12]

They come into your store with no intention to buy, and, in many cases, with no ability nor interest.

The real key is in the influencer's ability to connect to a specific audience [13] and drive buyer sentiment among a small yet focused audience of people who are potential clients.

I refer to this group as Micro-Influencers [14] and for the most part this is the group that brands need to be pursuing.

CONNECTING TO THE RIGHT PEOPLE, THAT ISN'T IDEAL, IT IS THE DEAL

I know it is difficult for a Marketer to identify the people who connect to their ideal customers. That is precisely why BS metrics like Klout,[15] Follower Count and page views become key indicators, but just because the easy way is what is accepted as best practice, doesn't make it right.

The other day an agency executive told me that a brand came to them looking to engage in an influencer program. They wanted A-listers with 30k unique visitors a month (minimum). He proceeded to tell me how he laughed at them.

I was hoping what would come next would be a story about how he educated them on the fact that 30k visits doesn't matter as much as these influencers moving the needle for a small group who become more loyal to the brand [16] as a by-product of the campaign.

Sadly, I heard the opposite. The agency executive proceeded to tell me that 30k isn't an A-Lister, but rather 100k plus.

After I finished throwing up in my mouth a little bit I caught my breath, and changed topics because there was no hope to find common ground here, but what I can say with absolute confidence is:

30k or 120k I don't give a +K or a K(rap). If I'm a marketing executive for a brand I want my content connecting with buyers. And other than the old law of averages for door-to-door sales people, I have seen almost no correlation between great volumes of eyeballs and brand conversions, especially as the products and services grow in complexity.

FOCUS ON THE RIGHT INFLUENCERS AND THE RIGHT AUDIENCE

If I were a brand working on an influence campaign, I would take a step back and seek out content creators that are relatable, create interesting and useful content and show real subject matter expertise.

For instance, if I were selling a data center solution I would look not just for those that write about technology but those that are immersed in cloud, data center and tech disruption. While this much narrower audience may yield a much smaller number of page views, the audience that is reading this content is almost certainly a group of real prospects.

On the other hand, the generic tech writer with a massive audience may be the obvious choice, but often these generalists are too superficial (content not personality) to really connect with those that are most sought after.

Again, it is about the audience. While the CIO may be a target for any tech focused marketing campaign, often times with emerging technology where great expertise is required, these folks depend on consultants and highly skilled members of their teams to make recommendations. They are the target for which the content should be focused, because they are the ones influencing the person who can sign the purchase order.

Isn't that the whole purpose? Creating brand sponsored content to influence buyer behavior?

FOR GOODNESS SAKES, STOP THE PAGEVIEW PORN…

Perhaps for no other reason than brands being completely misguided by unicorns, Bigfoot sightings in Yellowstone and the idea that page views and Impressions translate to revenue…

If that was truly the case then the best brands in the world should put banner ads on Porn Sites. Because those get far more page views than any A-List blogger on the planet.

But as you may have surmised by now, the numbers by themselves don't mean that much.

At some point brands in the influence marketing game will realize that hiring people who get a lot of page views but don't influence the right people end up being extremely expensive ambassadors who don't move sentiment. Nor do they create revenue, and therefore they are nothing but an overpaid waste of money.

So what can brands interested in smarter influence marketing do to get more for their investments in influence? How about they get their heads out of their asses and start hiring people who actually connect to customers[16] and remove it from the obsession that is A-List bloggers? And when hiring an agency, if they try to tell you to just hire A-Listers, go ahead and fire them now. If you're skittish about it, call me and I'll do it for you.

Nothing against the A-List, I guess. These professional "Thought Leaders" (whatever that means) and pundits alike are tremendous for putting eyeballs on stuff. Their thought leadership often extends to the brilliance of 5 years ago as they regurgitate, perhaps eloquently, the messages of the past and the innovation of what is obvious to those who most need it. And to their credit they have built solid readerships, which should count for something.

But if I were betting my job or my relationship with a brand on an influence marketing campaign I would turn my attention elsewhere, toward people who can help me build trust with consumers, improve knowledge and sentiment, and perhaps most importantly sell something to someone.

That being said, what about those influencers who are right for brands and verticals? What should they consider when deciding about brand partnerships?

Influencers: Be Cautious When Choosing Your Brand Associations

Building influence online and offline is hard work.

At the core of becoming influential is the ability to earn trust within your community. This trust becomes the catalyst for getting things done.

This trust is displayed by CEOs, leading businesses, educators guiding students to higher levels of enlightenment – and is even shown from time to time by political leaders who momentarily remember why they are in office and choose to serve for the betterment of the people.

When it comes to brands looking to drive their marketing through influence, a similar trust is required. For those who have put in the effort to build a meaningful bond with their community, they know how much time and effort the nurturing process can take.

BECOMING A HUMAN BILLBOARD

As a brand influencer one of your most valuable assets is your ability to make meaningful connections between a consumer and a brand. However, this ability is rooted in your neutrality, and the second you associate yourself with a brand, your position as neutral can turn hazy in light of your relationship with that brand.

From the moment people start to question the intent of your message, the hard-earned trust you built becomes compromised; when the trust vacates, influence follows.

Every day I see social-media pros using their online influence to hock the next gizmo or gadget. Brands like Nokia, Microsoft and others regularly send their new products to "influencers" in exchange for a blog, link or social media post. If you have any of these supposed influencers in your network, you immediately recognize this kind of activity when you see it. The question is, does it make you feel differently about the product or the brand? In my experience, the answer is no.

REAL INFLUENCE IS ADVOCACY, ALIGN CAREFULLY

To make influence programs work, brands need advocates, not influence. Better yet, they need influencers who are advocates. In a recent study [17] by Forrester it was found that consumers trust influencers (defined as bloggers, pundits and celebrities) at a rate of only 18%. On the other hand, consumers trust "Brand Advocates" (defined as satisfied customers) at a rate of 92% [18] which is at the same trust level as a friend or family member.

This small difference in labeling terminology between influencer and advocate may very well be the difference between an influence campaign that flourishes, and one that flounders.

However, as noted above, it goes beyond just terminology as perception moves into the equation.

If people perceive that a person truly loves a brand then they will likely see them as more of an advocate. Conversely, if they believe that the person is working with a product strictly for the financial benefit, the message is weakened by more than five times, as the advocacy shifts back to the less trusted influencer.

While some may believe that you can "fake" advocacy, most often the truth will surface in time. For instance, Alicia Keys would never use a Blackberry by choice, and for the more experienced members of our audience, Michael Jordan most likely didn't really love his Chevy Blazer.

THE ROLE OF TRANSPARENCY FOR PAID ADVOCATES

For those who seek to use their influence to make financial gains by helping companies grow, it is important that they align with companies they truly believe in. While this may limit their potential gains to some extent, the maintained integrity will pay off by providing real results for brands, and transparency to their community.

This also means that when you are paid to advocate for a brand, you are open and honest about it.

Most brands will require that hired influencers provide a disclaimer so readers know you are compensated.

Brands that are doing influence marketing well will often provide the disclosure but also seek to allow their influencers to deliver an unfiltered voice, meaning that even though they are paying for a person to associate with the brand, they aren't dictating what you are sharing, rather they are seeking to do the following:

- Build reader sentiment through connecting them to quality content (paid).
- Come to their site (owned).
- Keep the reader on their site where they convert them to the next level of the buyer's journey (earned).

In the end, influencers must seek to connect to brands with the long term in mind. Their goals are to create awareness, build trust and improve their community's sentiment toward a brand.

The moment a community sees intent as anything other than to educate and support their well being, the hard earned influence that an individual earned is weakened, which is precisely why influencers need to be very cautious in choosing brands with which to align.

Another area that has become hotly contested in the influence space is the role of PR. With many brands wanting to dip their toe in the influence marketing game, they have turned to their agencies and communications teams to move the needle. But influence marketing isn't the same as PR, well not really.

PR: The Missing Piece of the Influence Equation

As the world turns and brand journalism elevates to the forefront of the content overload experience known as the internet, the desire for increased visibility and placement has become the Holy Grail for Communications and PR.

For the longest time the role of PR for brands was to pitch stories to media and their journalists with the goal of getting coveted earned media exposure.

Brands love to say, "We don't pay for Media, we are Comms/PR."
Of course they are paying the person doing the job of pitching the story, so it is kind of ironic, but nonetheless they are right when they say they don't pay for the exposure they seek to get.

This must be because the coverage they can bring their outlets is so monumental that those being pitched couldn't say no, or so they would like to think.

INFLUENCE MARKETING AND THE NEW PR PITCH

At the top of this chapter, we discussed the emerging trend of the online influencer. This demographic is comprised of writers, forward thinkers, and occasionally (and often the most compelling type) the successful, experienced industry practitioner.

With the growing market visibility many online influencers have, brands have become increasingly excited to work with these people. While occasionally (and more often) in a paid capacity, many companies still love to pitch these people to contribute content for free in exchange for the publicity that it brings.

This pitch is comprised of a communications person reaching out to a successful blogger or other influencer and asking them to write an article in exchange for them posting it on their site, and occasionally driving a link back to the influencer's site. While sometimes lucrative, this practice is becoming increasingly suspect as brands struggle to drive meaningful metrics to their sites.

SIDEBAR: IMPRESSIONS MAY BE A METRIC, BUT IT'S A DUMB ONE

Before I go any further, these pitches for free content often are rooted in a commitment of high Impression numbers. Throughout this book, we've cautioned about the reliance on the "Impression" metric.

You'll hear something like, "Your post will receive 1,000,000 Impressions on our site."

Just ask them how many people read the blog and to skip impression numbers because those numbers rarely mean anything. All that matters is who clicks, reads and takes action on the content.

But I digress…

PR NEEDS TO JUST SHUT UP AND PITCH STORIES TO THE RIGHT PLACES

Sure it is easy for a PR professional to ask for content from influencers, or even offer their "Free Content" to sites in exchange for certain exposure, but most brands need something more.

Corporate PR and their agencies need to put a little effort into their PR pitches and start finding creative ways to get their content placed on sites that are going to drive meaningful exposure to the brand, and to those who create the story.

Sure there may be cases where a niche product story fits great on one blog or another, but as a whole, big brands need their story to be told to a big enough audience to actually move their "Brand Story" forward. This means going back to the roots of PR and building relationships with outlets that can really help a company and not just placing fodder on a bunch of blogs.

AND IF YOU WANT TO WORK WITH INFLUENCERS…

For brands that still believe influencers are the way to go, it is important that they realize the expectation of taking someone's valuable time and getting something for free is a big mistake. In the world of social and digital influence, reciprocity is a core value, meaning that you have to give to get.

If the PR efforts by the brand can genuinely help both the influencer and the brand, then this is where there is a real opportunity to connect. For instance, if you ask a well-respected writer to generate content for your company, then make an effort to place it on a site that gets more visibility for that person. That is what makes it a win. But just to place it on some brand owned site that gets read by a handful of people is a waste of that person's time (and yours). In these cases, even if you get them to do it, you'll lose their support after one post when they see that and realize you wasted their time.

In short, if exposure is what you offer, then make sure you go and get it. Give influencers metrics that matter and recognize that relationships work when all parties benefit. In the old model, reporters needed stories; PR had them. The reporters get to break the story first; PR gets the credit for placement with their client, and it's a win-win.

Now, because the sphere of influence has widened immeasurably and anyone can pitch or write, the reciprocity model is disrupted and more complex.

The good news is there's still room for all parties to exist and thrive, but only if we adapt.

In a day where many of the most influential writers aren't "Ad Sponsored," their time and allegiance is how they drive income.

But for goodness sake, quit short-circuiting the work that is most needed by brands from their PR teams. Find and connect your brand to places that will drive greater amounts of the right exposure, and if you don't want to do that, then maybe it is time to recognize you are in the wrong field?

CAN BRANDS BUY REAL INFLUENCE?

Digital influence is real. No question about it. However, as quickly as I posted about the shift in brand influence I was hit between the eyes with a dose of reality that I couldn't ignore.

My Facebook notification went off and I saw Olivier Blanchard, "The Brand Builder", tagged me in a post.[19] Olivier (whom you heard from earlier in our ROI chapter) is one of the most authentic people I know on the web so I always like when my content grabs his attention. Additionally, he is well regarded for his thoughts on influence, which you should read if you haven't already.

This time however was different. It wasn't a quick share or a "Hey, check this out." It was more of a "Hey, buyer beware…I'm sharing this, but only partially because I like it. Mostly because it is missing something really important."
What was it missing?

The answer is very simple; my article was missing the incredibly important context that most people who proclaim to be influential aren't influencers at all.

Here is what Olivier had to say…

Olivier Blanchard via Daniel Newman

about an hour ago ·

For the record, I am not a fan of the "brand influencer" movement. (Too easily gamed, wrong metrics, still focused on reach more than actual impact, not genuine, and so on.) Welcome to 'The Emperor's New Clothes: Digital Marketing Edition, Season 9.' It isn't all bullshit, but 90% of it is. There IS a way to do this right. Unfortunately, you won't see a whole lot of companies and agencies taking the time to leverage mavens and the communities they belong to properly.

Translation: would-be social media gurus who got on the speaking circuit too late are already recycling themselves as 'brand influencers.' So brace yourselves for the deluge of pseudo Twitter celebrities trying to boost their "personal brands" and Klout scores to get on that train of bullshit, unapologetic shilling and easy money. "OMG, this Kentucky whiskey is the best thing ever! I really really really mean it."

If it isn't genuine, it doesn't work. It's as simple as that. How does bribing your friends to like you more sound?

See, the problem with a) not understanding how influence actually works, b) being desperate for a new mouse trap with which to score spend from clients without really giving a crap about the community or the client, c) focusing on gimmicks and "the next thing in social" instead of just coming up with creative and smart campaigns, and d) misunderstanding the relationship between metrics and what they actually measure (deliberately or not), is that you end up adopting strategies improperly and for all the wrong reasons.

The result: consumers will end up figuring out that your "brand influencers" are posers, that the content they create for your brand (which they expected to be genuine) isn't genuine at all, and once all that influencer money has changed hands, the one left holding the bag is the brand. (Enjoy earning people's trust again once you've bribed a bunch of douchebag bloggers into shilling your wares.) Cynicism is a tough residue to scrape off.

Having said that, the data in this post is pretty interesting, and I kind of dig Daniel Newman, so it's worth a read. With any luck, you'll be one of ten or twenty companies this year who will actually do this properly. ☺ Good luck.

THE MORAL? CONTEXT CANNOT BE IGNORED WITH INFLUENCE MARKETING

In short, what Olivier said that is so important for brands considering influence marketing is that brands cannot think that influence can be bought by employing a few bloggers, but rather influence is driven through genuine connections.

I couldn't agree more, and I felt it was really important to communicate this to all who read the last post and to any brands considering campaigns with online influencers.

Further, what Olivier alludes to is how important it is to find influencers that are deeply entrenched with a brand or as he refers to the "Micro Influencer." This type of influencer will drive a very small number of people; however whether it is 10, 20 or 50, the micro influencer will lead to real conversions.

That is another salient point that Marketers cannot ignore in their selection of influencers.

My response to Olivier's post:

 Daniel Newman Olivier first thanks for sharing this (even if you aren't a fan of the concept) You make some really salient points in this post. I want to go on the record by saying I agree with you that influence isn't merely a line item that you put in your amazon shopping cart. It can most definitely be gamed and brands that don't do their diligence will pay the ultimate price. Building community takes time and effort, you can't just ask some "influential" people to tweet and boom you have arrived. However, I believe that brands that are smart, choose wisely and look for not only people willing to take their money, but rather influential people who are passionate about their brand, the effort can go a long way. I won't put my name on anything that I don't believe in, regardless of the money (nobody has offered enough to test my will power yet, lol). Anyhow, I love the insight as always, Olivier. Hopefully you and the others on this thread will continue to educate on the thin line that separates influence and manipulation. Cheers!

about an hour ago · Like · 👍 2

THE MORAL OF THE (INFLUENCE) STORY

The interwebs (a nickname I have affectionately given the internet and social media) have become chuck full of "wannabe" influencers and people who will swindle brands for money for perceived influence. However, real influence is much more organic.

Paid or not, the type of influence brands are looking for comes from real people connecting to real people on an emotional level. That type of connection is where brand advocates are born. Money alone will rarely (if ever) build the type of influence most brands seek.

For influence to work there has to be more than just paid content; there has to be a deeper connection. For brands looking to build an influence campaign, this need for deeper connections cannot be ignored.

Building an influential brand, like everything in life worth doing, takes commitment. Brands that get it right will reap the reward. However, I won't be the least bit surprised to find many brands will cut corners and learn this lesson the hard (expensive) way.

In a few short years, influence, itself, has evolved. Previously, where we have covered the traditional definitions of 'influence' in media and industry and identified "online celebrities" that can help move the needle, we also introduced the notion of micro-influence that opens the doors to a concept that may be more sustainable as we tap into niche networks. This is also where influence technology introduced has the ability to scale in much higher proportions.

Who Are Micro Influencers and Do We Need Them?

Earlier in the chapter I alluded to the idea of micro-influence. Here we explore it just a bit further. But first ask yourself this question.

Is your brand seeking to get on the influence bandwagon? [20]

Has the growth of Klout, Kred, PeerIndex, and Traackr got your head spinning trying to figure out who the right folks are to accelerate brand awareness and lead generation or conversions?

You are not alone. If you were, these platforms wouldn't be growing in popularity.

The main problem with these platforms is that there is no proof that they actually work.

While brands think they are seeking out digital influencers, in reality they are not. What brands are really seeking are micro influencers, many of whom use digital as their platform.

So…what is the difference between a Macro Influencer and a Micro Influencer?

The answer is fairly nuanced; so let me use an example:

Many brands looking to quickly grow awareness and mass appeal turn to a macro influencer, typically a celebrity, to promote their product.

For example, Nikon wanted to sell more digital cameras, so they hired Ashton Kutcher to do an advertising campaign, and I'm sure all us older folks remember Gatorade's "Be Like Mike" campaign.

Michael Jordan had virtually every kid on the planet drinking Gatorade before, during and after games. We all wanted to be like Mike, even though to this date we aren't sure that Gatorade is a great hydration source, especially for younger athletes.

While all campaigns vary in their success (note my first example vs. the second), many campaigns like this appeal to the masses because the chosen celebrities (macro influencers) have the kind of clout required to help sell a product.
Fast forward to 2014 when the Internet, specifically blogs and social media, are full of influential people. These people have substantial followings and are often well known for something specific like marketing, leadership, or even parenting. These people, by-and-large, are micro influencers.

The difference in micro and macro influencers is that what appears to be a large audience/community for a micro influencer is in all actuality, very small. Trust me.

Put any of these so-called "Social Media Gurus" in a Cadillac Commercial and see what happens. You would see a whole lot of nothing, because even though these "gurus" are to varying degrees influential, they cannot compare in scale to macro influencers.

Perhaps the biggest difference between the macro influencer (celebrity) and the micro influencer is that the micro influencer needs to be squarely placed within their community (center of influence) to make an impact. However, when done correctly, their impact can be significant.

BUYERS BEWARE: INFLUENCE APPLICATIONS ARE FLAWED

Earlier I talked about some of the platforms that are focused on identifying influencers like Klout and Peer Index.

At the highest level these platforms have value for brands, especially those looking for some baseline data on digital influence (which you should be).

Having said that, there are millions of holes that can be punched in all of their services.[21] For the most part they use algorithms that look at things like Likes, Retweets and +1's on social media as a way to determine influence.

Don't get me wrong, moving content via social is important for content marketing and SEO, but it doesn't tell the whole story. For instance, Klout (or any of the others) can't connect its API to self-hosted blogs. However, they can connect and measure influence for people using Blogger, Tumbler and BlogSpot.

I want you to think about that for a minute. How many highly acclaimed bloggers use those free blogging platforms? I'll tell you: very few. Most are using self-hosted WordPress sites or something similar. What this means is that influence scores don't consider the traffic that some of these writers generate when scoring. Instead they just look at social signals, which again, don't tell the entire story.

FINDING BOTH PRECISION AND ACCURACY WITH MICRO INFLUENCERS

In the connected world, it seems like everyone knows everyone. This must be why so many brands take the shotgun approach to building their networks. They collect Likes, Followers and web traffic with no real idea of why. The assumption is more must be better.

However in the digital age "more" is irrelevant.[22] For most brands, especially those that do not have a product for the masses (B2B's or Niche Products), it is important that they aim to employ micro influencers that can be both precise and accurate.

The two words (precision/accuracy), while seemingly synonymous in actuality, are not.

If you think about aiming at a target that is your ideal audience, then hitting the bulls-eye would be "accurate." If you were to hit the same spot consistently, then you are precise.

The idea is to be both precise and accurate by driving an influential voice consistently to your target audience.

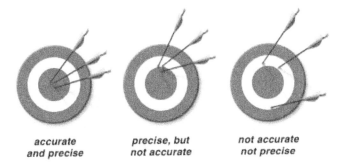

| accurate | precise, but | not accurate |
| and precise | not accurate | not precise |

FIND THE RIGHT MICROINFLUENCER
FOR YOUR BRAND

Micro influencers are a great way for brands to grow awareness and community through influence campaigns. However, finding the right person(s) is the key to the campaign's success. A great way to start is to understand what your brand is really trying to accomplish with an influence campaign.

Some questions you may want to ask yourself are:

- Do we know our target audience (you should)?
- What platforms are we planning to utilize?
- Have we considered what the ideal outcomes are?

Seek out potential candidates to work with your brand only after you have answered these questions. While I know many Marketers are infatuated with metrics, make sure that you don't obsess about the wrong ones. What I mean by this is to look beyond Followers, Likes and Klout scores and make sure the micro influencers you are looking to engage can actually help your brand accomplish its goals.

Remember, numbers only tell part of the influence story. [23]

While every company is different, if your company sells enterprise software, then make sure you find someone that influences the tech community with a knack for B2B. A successful micro influence campaign may only yield 25 real opportunities based on the micro influencer's ability to garner interest from a small, accurate and precise group of IT leaders and CIO's. Although 25 may seem small, what would a B2B software company invest to get 25 CIO's interested in their product? A lot I imagine, but not just any person can get those CIO's going. The right micro influencer can.

A company with a more mainstream product may want someone who is highly influential with food, gadgets, pets or babies depending on the specifics of the product. Nevertheless the key to micro influence is the right influencer aligning with the right product.

The great news is that micro influence can work for many brands of varying shapes and sizes so long as they focus on the right metrics and an accurate target audience.

So when it is time for your brand to partner with influencers, how do you capture their interest? Furthermore, must influence be bought? The answer may surprise you, but you will have to go a little further to get to the bottom of this interesting and hotly-debated topic.

WHY BRANDS SHOULD PAY FOR INFLUENCERS

In the evolving space of influence, there's one debate that's getting hotter by the minute – whether brands should pay influencers for their content, ideas and participation. And while paying for influence, as I've noted above, can still yield perceptions that are suspect, the game is changing.

In an age where consumers' content consumption has almost reached the brink of saturation, finding individuals who are considered influential when it comes to consumer decisions can make a world of difference for brands. More than any advertising, consumers trust real people. And, it goes without saying that brands can capitalize on this human side of influencer marketing to capture and maintain the interests of consumers on a long-term basis. All is hunky-dory until we start talking about what influencers get in return for all those laurels they shower upon brands.

 "Time is the most valuable thing a man can spend"
- `Theophrastus

ROLE OF AN INFLUENCER IN A BRAND'S SUCCESS AND WHY THEY SHOULD BE PAID

Brands and influencers share a symbiotic relationship. While brands get to spread their story to hundreds and thousands of people, for most influencers their blog is a means of connecting and informing consumers to help them build their personal reputations as well as their businesses.

Writers, forward thinkers, industry mavens – they write about brands, products, solutions, and services through which they influence people's perception of these things. It's their way of earning loyal followers and growing their business. They don't (usually) seek to advertise as a monetization strategy, which makes them different from the rest of the typical media. Therefore, when brands ask influencers to write, speak or attend events on their behalf, payment should be considered not as a means of buying loyalty, but as a fair exchange for taking someone's time and leveraging their ideas to build your own business.

WHAT PRS DO AND WHAT THEY SHOULD DO INSTEAD

In many instances, the old school PR machine believes that these online influencers should be providing their brand support for free. Remember how we talked about this? After all, aren't they going to be even more influential because of the reputation of the brand courting them? Won't they get lots of exposure and reach and Impressions as a result of whatever it is the brand wants them to do? Well, for the record, Impressions mean nothing. We'll continue to emphasize this. Certainly not to someone who's experience in the online space like bloggers and influencers. What really matters is how many clicks a particular piece of content receives, how many people are reading it, and how many of them are actually taking action as a result. In reality, this is a rarity.

Public Relations and their agencies need to give up on this utterly slack attitude, both for the benefit of the brand and the influencers. They need to find means to garner better and more meaningful attention. They should resort to their PR basics of building relationships with media that can spread the brand's story far and wide – that's the whole point of it, isn't it?

VIRTUES OF RECIPROCITY

You give some to get some – that's how the world moves. Expecting to use someone's time and influence to your advantage for free is big mistake, downright selfish, and it can be exponentially more beneficial to a brand and to their PR team if they rethink their strategies here with regard to influencer marketing.[24] Instead, they should focus on choosing their influencers wisely, compensating them fairly and building long-term relationships with them.

If there's someone who can help both the influencer and the brand benefit from the allegiance, it's PR. They should try to place the influencer content in places where visibility is high. This serves both purposes – first, increasing the reach of the brand story to a wider audience, and secondly, giving the influencer a more meaningful platform where his/her voice can be heard by hundreds of interested audience. This is a win-win relationship that brands should be trying to build with their influencers.

Perhaps the last great challenge for brands is to find the perfect marriage between micro-influence, industry specific influencers and the data/tools that measure what may not be immediately visible to the naked eye. As Sam Fiorella mentioned at the beginning of the chapter, there are a few technologies that are taking an entirely different approach to find relevant audiences– an approach that is in alignment with our current views on influence. One of those is a platform called Tellagence.

Tellagence Challenges Business to Focus on Relationships

Influence technologies, Klout, Peer Index, Traacker, as mentioned above, have emerged with less than significant use cases to justify their value. Klout, itself, has been subject to increasing scrutiny in the past few years because their flawed definition and metrics that correlate with individual influence.

I met *Matt Hixson* and was intrigued by the approach Tellagence was using to tackle the influencer problem. Below is my interview with *Matt Hixson*, CEO and *Nitin Mayande*, Chief Scientist of Tellagence:

In this rapidly evolving space, influence has provided Marketers a way to hasten the spread of messages. The number of followers or fans was a primary metric to identify those with the most leverage to gain audience attention. And that seems not to be changing. Even a known current influence index has changed algorithms to appease its critics.

> *NM: Tellagence's value is the ability to create networks of meaningful, inter-active relationships based on context to predict where -- and how far -- your messages will travel. Most services analyze one-to-one relationships; dotted line connections and the potential reach that a single, seemingly highly influential individual or celebrity can have based on a qualitatively high -- but quantita-tively imprecise -- number of followers. This formula banks on one-directional broadcasting power, but cannot foresee who will engage or who will forward the message beyond the initial sphere of followers to individuals who actually care.*

MH: This is the gap that Tellagence fills: Tellagence instead points organizations to a network of relationships that care, and will move content forward exponentially, thus providing more impactful reach that is boundless, lasting and effective.

What is Tellagence? How is it different than what is currently out there today?

NM: While many companies focus on more generic elements for social media monitoring and engagement -- such as targeting individuals with high follower numbers or celebrity status -- Tellagence's science identifies and develops deep, common-interest-driven relationships to give brands more meaningful and exponential reach.

MH: By meaningful, we mean absorbed. Acted upon. Shared. Content that is broadcast to a wide audience without consideration for whether that audience actually cares is wasteful. Identifying key gatekeepers and engaged advocates is the key to generating meaningful, efficient and effective campaigns.

To achieve this, Tellagence marries human behavioral science with high-computative predictive modeling to consider the affects of elements such as decision making, increases or decreases in strength of relationships and network roles. The company's first product, Tellagence for Twitter, captures the context of conversations and makes predictions by considering the ever-changing dynamics happening within a network.

Let's go back to the beginning. How did this come about? Where was the inspiration to start this journey?

NM: In 2005 I became a PhD student in Engineering and Technology Management at Portland State University and was simultaneously employed with Intel. During my time at Intel, I was challenged to identify how things go viral on social networks by my manager, Bill Pearson. It was during this time that

I decided to leverage my student research to better understand the elements of online communities, the affects they have on relationships, and the changes that occur.

My research ultimately revealed there are gaps in the current methodologies of analysis that cannot be directly applied to online networks.

Fast-forward four years to 2009, where I met Matt Hixson, then a Business Unit Director at Tripwire. Matt was a pioneer in social marketing strategy for the company, and was searching for a way to predict the reach of brand messages and their measurable impact on social marketing efforts.

I presented my research to Matt, and we recognized the opportunity that our findings could mean in the age of evolving mass social communications technologies like Twitter.

From this encounter, Matt and I built on my science and his experience to create Tellagence in 2011.

Some time ago, Ev Williams seemed to back peddle somewhat and indicated that the new "dream" metric is Retweet (RT). He indicated that the number of followers doesn't accurately measure the message distribution. RTs reveal how many people actually saw your Tweet. Do you agree?

MH: It does not define how many people saw your Tweet, also known as Impressions. It defines how many people engage with your product and proactively pass it along which promotes additional engagement with your brand and message. It is an element of defining strength of relationships, which, at its highest level, is called advocacy.

With the wealth of data being collected within rapidly growing datasets, traditional relational database tools do not have the capacity, or functionality, to adapt as

quickly. Marketers are now looking to evolving technologies to extract meaning and enhance decision-making. How does Tellagence position itself in this world of big data?

> NM: *Traditional relational databases are adept at handling data that is structured, but fail in one key function: They are insufficient at managing and measuring high volumes of "unstructured" data. The hard truth is that today, 90% of data is unstructured.*
>
> *Therefore, with the rise of big data, technology's emphasis must change from structured data to unstructured data.*
>
> MH: *Context -- meaning topical, relational and timing data -- represent "unstructured" data. Tellagence not only focuses its computational power on the high volume of the big data, but also focuses on the breadth and scope of big data to emphasize context.*

How do you think the game is going to change in the next few years? While traditional marketing methods have a seemingly limited shelf life, there are no real signs of impending death. How quickly do you see technologies (such as yours) being adopted?

> NM: *Offline relationships will continue to evolve as people continue to build social relationships on top of technology that also continues to evolve. It is important to realize that the models built in the 60's -- which are shockingly the same ones we use today -- are not sufficient are relevant for measuring or managing today's online and digital relationships.*
>
> *These models are dated and reliant on archaic technology. So, as relationships and their channels evolve, so too must the science by which it is measured and managed. Change in our understanding of online + offline relationships must happen in step with changes in technology.*

MH: This said, we are seeing a very strong reaction from the market to the analysis, measurement, forecasting and engagement solution what we are offering with Tellagence. There are many tools that give you analytics about transactions, re-tweets and people's "influencer" scores, but they are still not solving the business problems people have today.

Social media is still built on collecting old data points based on old models and building a generalized model of how it all fits together. We want to change that by basing a system on the collection and understanding of ALL data points -- structured and unstructured -- and building a strategic model of how it looks now, and again tomorrow and the next day...

Where do you two see yourselves in the next 10 years?

MH: In 10 years I will be seeing my first daughter graduate from high school. I hope to do that knowing that Tellagence has made a huge impact on the world. I may be working on similar problems or completely new ones. It is hard to tell what will come in 10 years but I'm looking forward to the challenges.

NM: For me the next 10 years are going to be very interesting. I believe that social networks are in their infancy and there is a lot of work that still needs to be done for their metamorphosis from mere "technology" into a viable economic and infrastructural system (like the internet or roadways). I see myself - and Tellagence - playing a very disruptive role at the forefront of this inevitable change.

The future of Influence changes the game for brands seeking sustainable alternatives to traditional advertising and PR outreach. And while macro-influence has been the ticket to develop awareness and credibility, it's clear that you can't possibly scale social if you don't take the time to build relationships. It has to be methodical and transparent. In the new world, this is what's going to put businesses ahead of the competition.

REFERENCES:

1   http://millennialceo.com/innovation/rules-return-trust/

2   http://technorati.com/report/2013-dir/executive-summary/

3   http://technorati.com/report/2013-dir/consumer-behavior/

4   https://econsultancy.com/blog/4175-online-consumers-trust-real-people-not-companies

5   https://econsultancy.com/blog/4175-online-consumers-trust-real-people-not-companies

6   http://millennialceo.com/social-media/2014-age-brand-influencer/

7   http://millennialceo.com/leadership/keys-understanding-consumer/

8   http://millennialceo.com/leadership/keys-understanding-consumer/

9   http://millennialceo.com/guest-blog/brands-treat-trust-gold-steveolenski/

10   http://millennialceo.com/branding/rise-brands-media-companies/

11   http://millennialceo.com/guest-blog/build-owned-media-influencers-danielghebert/

12   http://millennialceo.com/social-media/b2b-marketing-measure-matters/

13   http://millennialceo.com/social-media/5-steps-build-trust-content-marketing/

14   http://millennialceo.com/social-media/5-steps-build-trust-content-marketing/

15   http://millennialceo.com/social-media/gaming-influence-walking-fine-line/

16   http://www.forbes.com/sites/onmarketing/2014/02/11/brands-choose-influencers-and-advocates-wisely/

17   http://millennialceo.com/social-media/brands-buy-real-influence/

18   http://www.zuberance.com/downloads/brandAdvocateInsights.pdf

19   http://thebrandbuilder.wordpress.com/2011/02/22/digital-influence-recalibrated-part-1-klouts-measurement-spectrum/

20   http://millennialceo.com/social-media/2014-age-brand-influencer/

21   http://www.jureklepic.com/2012/05/16/clout-vs-klout-or-the-real-meaning-of-social-influence/

22   http://millennialceo.com/social-media/b2b-marketing-measure-matters/

23   http://millennialceo.com/social-media/brands-buy-real-influence/

24   http://millennialceo.com/influence-2/brands-choose-influencers-wisely/

Where Search and Social Collide: Consumer Behavior and Propensities Intermingle

THE TACTICS OF SEO MAY CHANGE BUT THE CORE REMAINS THE SAME by Sean McGinnis

Over the last 12 years, I have watched many trends come and go in the search engine optimization space. Some of those changes have been dramatic and abrupt (universal search results), while others have evolved over time (personalized search results). Some new trends have spun off into their very own specialization areas (local search).

To be sure, SEO has changed dramatically over that time. The tools we have access to today are very different (and much improved) from the tools of yesteryear. I would also argue that the overall level of understanding of search has improved over time. The entire SEO industry operates in a more open and transparent environment than it ever has. There is more reporting, more experimenting, more authoritative studies conducted to prove or disprove theories than ever before.

Moreover, Google has done a much better job over the last half decade of stomping out bad SEO behavior with the various Penguin and Panda updates. A strong focus on quality has created a shift in SEO mind-set among many practitioners. The "well, they are doing it so we need to do it too" mindset has yielded (in many respects) to a risk-averse "do no harm" approach to SEO.

Despite these changes: better tools, more openness and transparency into specific ranking factors, and radical changes to the ways search engine result pages (SERPs) look and act, the core of SEO stubbornly remains the same.

The Future of SEO is Determined by its Past

The most interesting thing about SEO is not the way in which SEO has changed, but rather, the way it has remained the same.

The core of SEO has stayed largely unchanged since its inception. Even more importantly, it is likely to never change. Ever.

So if you want to know what specific tactics to pursue, what tweaks to make to your site, to its structure and to your specific activities tomorrow or next year, you need to stay focused on the essential things Google is looking for.

Every day, Google search results answer millions and millions of questions – and it does that by asking two questions of its own millions and millions of times. Every time a user types a query into Google's search engine, the algorithm performs many calculations all in an effort to answer the following two questions:

3. Out of all the pages in our index, which pages are relevant for this search result?
4. Out of all the pages in our index that are relevant for this search result, which pages are authoritative?

Boiled down to its essence, this is the crux of what Google's search engine does millions of times a day.

Relevance and authority. Authority and relevance. These are Google's stock-in-trade.

Historically, the quest for relevance was best answered by specific tactics and signals related to on-page optimization efforts. These include things like ensuring your key phrase is included in the title tag, within the main content and in header tags (or content that is otherwise highlighted – like bolded).

To illustrate this point, imagine a site devoted to things all about dogs. The site is filled with blog posts and products related to dogs: god beds, dog tags, dog behavior, dog barking, dog psychology, dog breeds etc. No sane person would ever build a web site with thousands of pages about dogs and wonder why they did not rank for phrases about cats, pianos or laptops. Why? Because that site is not relevant for those search queries!

If the realm of relevance is historically rooted on on-page optimization, the quest to demonstrate authority is typically focused on off-page optimization. One of the main ways Google divides authority is to mine data related to the quantity, quality and anchor text of links pointing to a page. To be sure, there are many more signals than these (thematic depth of our example above for example – a site with thousands of pages ONLY about dogs might be interpreted as more authoritative than a site with 100s pages each on dogs, cats, horses, lamas and emus.)

If you view your SEO efforts through this simplified lens, it provides a great deal of clarity. No longer will you wonder whether one specific tactic or another will be more or less effective at "improving rank." Instead, focus your efforts on making your site more relevant for the phrases that are important for your business and on building more authority the specific tactics will take care of themselves.

Relevancy and authority. Authority and relevancy. Be sure to make them your stock-in-trade, and your web site will perform in ways you never thought possible.

 Sean McGinnis is Director of Marketing at Sears Holdings Corp. where he leads the marketing team at Sears Parts Direct. Sean also consults with clients on a variety of integrated digital marketing topics, where he brings over 15 years of experience to every client engagement.

Search vs. Social: Early on it was a Bout to Knock Each Other Out

It wasn't that long ago that Search ruled the roost. While the market for display advertising was peaking about 5 years ago, the Pay Per Click Ad market began to command more advertising budgets. At the same time, the emphasis on organic search ranking to augment search results provided Marketers with a more sustainable strategy for traffic generation and retention.

When social became mainstay and infiltrated the web, it commanded increasing consumer attention. It became apparent that the two channels, search and social, were beginning to converge.

SEARCH VS SOCIAL

It has been a knockdown drag-out fight between Search and Social over the last few years— the Internet was changing. Search and Social continue to be locked in a fierce duel for exposure, traffic and, ultimately, revenue. Who would win? Could the two co-exist or would there be only one victor?

SEARCH AND SOCIAL: TWO PEAS IN A POD

The early days of Search saw the growth of Word of Mouth, which was previously an offline medium. A typical search medium was a directory. In those days - it was a company called Overture that dominated, not Google. Yahoo!'s purchase of Overture [1] in 2003 was a clear indication of how competitive the market was becoming. Unfortunately for the latter, this acquisition would prove to be a bust. Google's domination quickly became apparent and Bing and Yahoo! sadly watched from the sidelines.

Then came Social Media where people were moving away from corporate sites (including portals), and slowly away from advertising. First we had email, then IM, and then these networks where you could establish a profile and connect to friends.

The Web became increasingly complex because we moved away from research to consumption, then to connection. Search became the authority for finding the best information on the Web; Social became the hangout space. Relevance became the word of the day as the beginnings of social content became integrated into the search algorithm. The interconnectedness between the two became readily apparent.

When Ratings and Review sites emerged, suddenly users had places to go to help them in their decision-making process. Peer recommendations made their decisions easier because there was an inherent trust already there. However, where the user was in the purchase decision funnel determined the extent to which he/she went to the respective networks or to Search. Once the user was further down the funnel, the higher the likelihood they would use Search.

An industry colleague, Laurie Dillon-Schalk provided me with a strong comparison of online search behavior and social discussion about "Black Friday. " It was clear that "Search" behavior veered towards the interrogative: "What is Black Friday?" "When is Black Friday?" while "Social" discussion centered on deal sharing. Laurie emphasized the importance of forums, which were underrated social spaces that didn't typically get indexed by Search, but represented strong niche influences in purchase behavior. Strong forum players like Red Flag Deals have represented feeder sites for the rest of the deal sites.

Google seems to be a strong adversary to the two biggest social networks, Facebook and Twitter. While Facebook continues to maintain its walled garden, Twitter gladly acquiesces to the search giant's indexing algorithm. Does relevance get thrown out the door and does the user lose out?

Throw in another wrench: When Google introduced G+ it was favoring its own property, regardless of relevance, and making us all question the integrity of its search algorithm. Google was becoming evil.

Google runs the search algorithm, and 'search' has become essential. They arbitrarily make the decision to change the "black box code" without having to inform anybody. If the Panda update[2] was any indication of how many legitimate businesses lost traffic as a result, it can be argued that Search needs some form of regulation. If users go to Google as a trusted source, then it has to be accountable for displaying results that are relevant, positive, and legitimate, right?

I would argue Google, these days, is a company accountable only to its shareholders. There's a reason it will not disclose the contents of its search algorithm. Regulating the giant may cause more harm than good, and potentially stifle the growth of the Search economy.

Across the field, if Facebook and Twitter are pulling away from Google, do they feel they can operate autonomously? Twitter Search is known, for the most part, to the engaged Twitter community. Many users claim it is their source for breaking news. Search is not as quick to provide this information when it is critical. If Facebook can make search work, it will help pave the way for social search. "Kicking Bing to the Curb"[3] clearly is the first step in this endeavor. But given the fragmentation of the existing social networks, only web wide search can provide the holistic view of information that the user seeks.

Fast forward: Social enables more favorable search results....

SEO IN THE PAST

Take everything you have ever heard about SEO and chuck it!

Well maybe you don't have to go that far, but here is the thing:
If you are looking to build a site that Google loves, that shows up on the first page every time someone searches for your product or services, then you need to realize the rules have changed a little bit.

In the past search was impacted by one thing more than anything else -- Link Building. It was Link Building efforts that held SEO and PPC Marketers' focus because it was about the quantity, and more importantly, the quality of links that drove page rank up, and therefore position, in a Google Search.

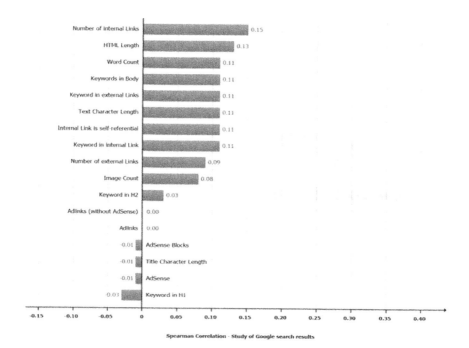

Spearman Correlation - Study of Google search results

After Link Building, SEO was heavily focused on formatting. SEO experts turned their attention to using the right keywords in the header tags (H2, H3) and then splatter the keywords throughout the content and using italics, bold, and underline to further improve search rank.

Link Building is still very important[4], but other factors have become more pertinent, and B2B Marketers need to take notice.

SEO TODAY: QUALITY CONTENT, SOCIALLY AUTHORITATIVE

One of the first questions clients ask about SEO is "How do we drive SEO to be found on Google?"

While the traditional SEO items I mention above are important, I usually take clients down a different route. This route covers two areas: focusing on their content strategy and marketing efforts as well as their social media, curating and sharing strategy.

SEO AND THE ROLE OF CONTENT

First question: Do you have a blog [5] and do you keep it up to date with quality content driven to answer your prospective clients' most important questions [6] about the solutions you offer?

If the answer is no, then we are starting on the ground floor.

Even the most optimized B2B site offering simply static products and services will have a difficult time growing and sustaining traffic.

Wondering just how important content is? Check out this Search metrics visual aid[7] showing the content factors driving search:

In short, to improve in almost all of these areas you need more high quality content. [8]

SEO AND THE ROLE OF SOCIAL MEDIA SIGNALS

The second question I ask is: How does your organization use social media?
Are you consistently sharing the content you create across the platforms?
Do you curate and share other useful content to build trust and relationships with
potential clients interested in similar subject matter?

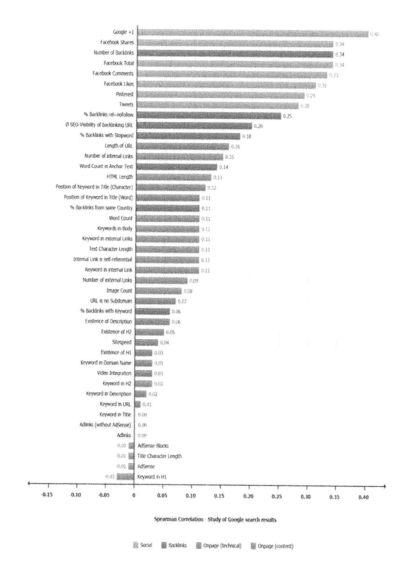

Spearman Correlation - Study of Google search results

Social   Backlinks   Onpage (technical)   Onpage (content)

Is your brand engaged and having conversations with readers in your target audience?

The purpose of these questions is to find out one thing: Is the brand social and do they have an engaged community of any sort that shares content?

Here is a less known secret of SEO that most B2B's are failing to realize: Social sharing is a huge driver of SEO! Looking for proof? Check out this second study from Searchmetrics. [9]

Notice anything here?

Seven of the top 8 factors driving SEO are social sharing related and not traditional SEO drivers whatsoever!

Want SEO? Drive Content, Get Social

Companies are asking, "How do we improve SEO?" The answer is simpler than you may think.

The challenge for business is that, unlike in the past where the building process was

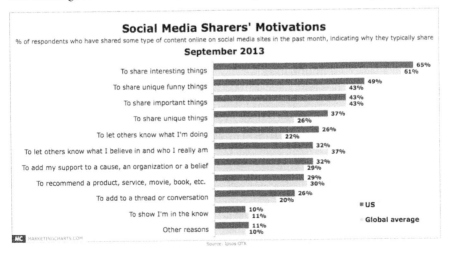

Social Media Sharers' Motivations

% of respondents who have shared some type of content online on social media sites in the past month, indicating why they typically share

September 2013

	US	Global average
To share interesting things	65%	61%
To share unique funny things	49%	43%
To share important things	43%	43%
To share unique things	37%	26%
To let others know what I'm doing	26%	22%
To let others know what I believe in and who I really am	32%	37%
To add my support to a cause, an organization or a belief	32%	29%
To recommend a product, service, movie, book, etc.	29%	30%
To add to a thread or conversation	26%	20%
To show I'm in the know	10%	11%
Other reasons	11%	10%

MARKETINGCHARTS.COM

Source: Ipsos OTX

more about following steps, grabbing backlinks and properly formatting content, the rules have changed.

If you want better SEO, then you need to be creating more content and driving it through social channels. [10] It really is that simple.

Looking to better understand what drives social sharing? Check out this great graphic [11] from Marketing Charts.

As we begin to see the increasing connectedness between Search and Social, the role of content becomes an important vehicle to tap into user needs, and enable that important connection with the business. It's hard to believe, but a well planned marriage between content and SEO may even change the way businesses handle relationship selling.

Content is the New Sales Call

When Google came out with their Zero Moment of Truth[12] reports, there were a lot of highly compelling data points that made CEOs, CMOs and sales heads stop and reconsider almost everything they were doing, at least as it pertains to marketing.

For those less familiar with the Zero Moment of Truth (ZMOT), it can best be defined as "the invisible moment by which a consumer makes a decision about a brand." It can occur on their mobile device, while chatting on a social network, or when they search for information.

- Some of the highlight reel data points of the ZMOT study were:
- 84% of buyers engage in Zero Moment Activities (Online Information/ Education)
- 10.4 Pieces of Information in the Buyer's Journey Prior to Purchase

The ZMOT isn't a new discussion point. In fact it has been written about thousands of times from many different perspectives, but for businesses that are slow to adopt or that still think digital and social are fads, the takeaways are becoming more and more important.

When a Forrester Study [13]showed that on average customers are 70%+ through the sales cycle prior to engaging a vendor, they were announcing a shift of massive proportion that affects nearly every business. The more complex your product and service, the more this number should resonate, because what this study is saying is that people want to do their own research.

No longer are we in the days of consumers (B2B or B2C) picking up the phone or calling their trusted advisor to gain more insights or information on what they were looking for. We have taken on that role ourselves, and that is why we seek to do everything from diagnosing our physical ailments to procuring major business software packages without a single vendor meeting.

While a blanket statement that every business must replace their sales efforts with content would be irresponsible, that fact is something business cannot ignore. I implore business leaders to ask this question:

If not from us, then where are our customers getting their information?

For companies that are not creating low touch, easily accessible content in the form of blogs, articles, white papers, infographics, videos and more – how are they providing the 1:1 marketing experience that entices, educates and engages customers to move along the buyer's journey 13 with their brand?

Chances are that prospective buyers are garnering their insights somewhere, and many times those resources become the new trusted advisor, the sales person of the past and the influencer of the future. This, in turn, means companies that are waiting for the phone to ring, those without a proactive sales force, may be missing out on a significant opportunity by ignoring the invisible portion of the buying process.

DATA THAT CAN'T BE IGNORED

There has been a shift from 1:1 Marketing that took place between a sales rep and a buyer. Even brands that still see this as a viable channel must realize that clients are more informed than ever, and it is the boundless volume of content that is creating information parity. At the very least this shift realigns the sales professional's role from informer and educator to creator and innovator.

If nothing else, brands must recognize that by the time the prospect has landed at their door, the process has long been underway. The companies that "get it" will recognize and prescribe content as a means to be more involved and engaged in educating the consumer, and creating those zero moments of truth. Those that don't "get it" will be left on the outside looking in.

These days, the prescription is valuable content. However, in order to establish true value, Marketers must have exposure to, and understand, audience needs, and have context into the type of information that truly resonates.

The Future of Marketing Will Be Semantic: Shifting Search

Let's take a journey back about 3-5 years in the world of online search. Imagine that it's a Friday night and you are trying to determine where to have dinner. It isn't a typical night out, but a nice night out. You've lined up a sitter for the kids and you are eager for adult social time.

You are a suburban Chicago family, but tonight, you are heading into the city.

Where do you go? Perhaps you want to get a nice steak and a good bottle of wine? Let's go online and search it out?

"Chicago Steak Restaurant" or

"Steak Chicago" or

"Chicago Best Steak" or

"Great Steak Chicago Downtown"

Now, we look at the above "Search Phrases" and we ask ourselves, is this the right way to find what we are looking for?

Perhaps more importantly, is this the best phrase to enter to get the search result we are looking for?

THE EARLY DAYS OF THE WEB WERE ABOUT SEO

In the early days of the web, and more specifically of search, your findings in a given Internet search had little to do with your searches.

Rather, the outcomes had to do with the sites that were specifically developed to be found when you entered certain search phrases.

Consider the example above about the steak house. Why would someone type a search query like "Chicago Restaurants Steak?"

Wouldn't it make more sense to type, "I'm looking for a great steakhouse in Chicago?

I think the answer is obvious: Of course it makes more sense to type the question as you are thinking it, but a couple of years ago the results would have been unusable.

In the earlier days of the web, it was about search engine optimization, keywords, easy-to-spider menus and footers, and other "tricks" to help the search engine find your site more successfully.

For the SEO professional that knew what they were doing, it was easy for them to have a steakhouse in Milwaukee yet win your "Chicago Restaurant Steak" query by just setting up the page correctly.

Great for the restaurant in Milwaukee, sort of, but for the couple just looking for a night out? Totally useless! Well, at least if they were hoping to solve their restaurant decision by using a Google search.

FAST FORWARD TO THE MODERN WEB

So here is the thing: when search engines were first developed, it was really about making the Internet more manageable.

Now with Petabytes of data being created [14] on a daily basis, much of which is unstructured, highly disorganized data, the complexity by which we search is becoming more complicated.

But not because what we are asking is more complicated, but because the search engines have more information to filter through in order to find us the results that we are looking for.

Let's move this from Date Night to Business 101: if you are a business and you have a product or service to sell, chances are you are online. If not, I'm afraid for you. Businesses today have taken their web presence from where it was a few years ago, which was likely an "Online Brochure," to some type of second generation website that incorporates trends such as social media, content marketing[15], and of course search engine optimization.

The reason we as business owners do all of this [16] isn't because we love technology, but rather, because we know that people are doing more and more of their research about what they want to buy, online. This behavior isn't going to change anytime soon. In fact, it is going to proliferate faster than most of us could ever imagine.

THE FUTURE OF SEARCH IS SEMANTIC

Why are we really online?

We have reached a point where business, social, intelligence and emotion are all intertwined online.

While our business presence and our personal presence may have great disparity, our existences are largely captured online, and the way we interact with the web is intermingling with how we market our businesses online.

In essence, we have reached the point where the web is no longer about filtering search results; rather it is complex, emotional and intelligent.

Today the web is being filtered in a new way, we are asking more questions.

In a world where our queries are more than "Thing, Location" we need to be able to get answers that tell us not just who, what, when, where and how, but why.

This is the semantic web, where search results are driven by more than just how keywords are stacked on a page, or even by how many inbound links you have, but rather, how socially engaged your site is, and by how well you contextually provide relevant information to match a search query.

I'm by no means here to challenge the likes of Matt Cutts, or the team at Search Engine Watch [17] as to the mechanics of SEO for the modern web. When it comes to that part of Internet, there are many, many great minds that know more than me.

I believe that even in an age of semantic search where social and context are the guides to search results, all sites can benefit from the proper use of best SEO practices. However, having said that, I believe in the future the web will be entirely about connecting consumers with better information and ideas from the most relevant sources by allowing them to converse with the web the same way they do with people. The only difference is that results can be drawn from across the Internet rather than just those sitting with you across the table.

The Future of Marketing Is Semantic: Uncovering the Meaning Of Your Search

So the search of yesteryear is gone; no more keyword only focused searches, well at least not if you want the very best results.

For a minute let's forget the big words here. Contextual, semantic…after a while they all start to sound a bit like an MBA dissertation and less like a critical marketing topic. However, do not, for a minute, kid yourself or allow the buzzwords to distract you from the seismic shift that is taking place.

Let's choose a new word: Conversation.

LET'S HAVE A CONVERSATION WITH A SEARCH ENGINE

In the future, and even today, the most qualified and successful searches are going to be driven by conversations.

When Google Hummingbird [18] was launched, Google used the idea of conversation rather than keyword as one of the biggest evolutions of the new algorithm. Rather than thinking of search in terms of the keywords given, Google can now look for meaning behind the words that you enter in your search query.

Previously, I talked about a couple searching for a dining experience and how rather than plugging in words like "Steakhouse" or "Chicago," they would today look to plug in "Where can we get a great steak in Chicago?"

Before search had the capability of better understanding the meaning behind search, if you were to enter that entire phrase, the search engine wouldn't know whether you meant a restaurant or a grocery store. Furthermore, it would have very little data to qualify what makes a steak great. It would have used spiders and other white hat SEO practices to find sites that have the words Chicago and Steak in them.

With Hummingbird, and more importantly, the advances in semantic search, the search engine is now able to understand the nuances of what you are searching for. For instance, it could likely discern that you are looking to go out for a steak rather than finding a store that sells them. Furthermore, it can determine outcomes that take into consideration your exact location to better filter results, rather than just giving you a list of all the steakhouses in Chicago. (Remember this from last chapter?)

In addition, the semantic web has the potential to integrate your query with your referent network. Since we are widely influenced by others' opinions online, why not incorporate social into the search results to further "conversationalize" the web?

MARRYING SOCIAL SEARCH AND SEMANTIC SEARCH

Now that Search has evolved and we can more or less ask questions to our search engine much like we would another person, doesn't it make sense that the evolution of the web is to incorporate social results into semantic search?

Let's revisit the Steakhouse example one more time. When I ask conversationally for the best places to get a great steak in Chicago, the way semantic search works is to look for meaning beyond just the keywords. As mentioned above, it will strive to better understand what I'm really asking and not just analyze the individual words.

By overlaying Social Search into the equation, the web can work to extract meaning from my query, but also look for people within my social networks from Google+, Facebook and others to help. Ideally, it will come from those I am closest to, those who are most influential on certain topics [19] or those within certain communities. Furthermore, social search can poll sites such as Yelp, Trip Advisor and other review sites where user generated content is providing supporting data for my query.

Say the first result following my query is Gibson's Steakhouse in Chicago. Chances are that if the establishment has a great product, people will be talking about it on the web. Rather than just seeing the results that my query created, now I can quickly and easily see what others are saying about it both on the review sites and perhaps, more importantly, people who I am connected to socially.

Some may say that local search has been doing this for some time, and there is a certain amount of truth to that; the biggest difference is that local search is generally a process done as more of a "drill down," where you start with an overarching subject matter, and you pick a location and local data comes up to specify the locations, hours, and reviews.

Furthermore, local never really tied influence marketing or social input into the equation. A review on Yelp may be helpful and specific, but if a close friend or relative has an opinion about the restaurant, it would likely be more influential on the potential consumer.

The Future of Marketing Is Semantic, Conversational and Social

As we can see, the web is changing directionally, from keyword to conversation; the evolution is being used to better understand what the buyer wants.

As Marketers, this will continue to impact our content marketing, social media, traditional print and communication channels. As we seek to create and keep customers in a world where the buyer has the Internet at their disposal, we need to consider not just what information we have out there, but how we are making it accessible through the marriage of paid, owned and earned channels in a digital world gone semantic.

THE FUTURE OF MARKETING IS SEMANTIC: SEARCH PREDICTS THE FUTURE

It's becoming eerily apparent that the Internet knows a lot about us. Due to our lust for free applications, and our complete oversight of the privacy we relinquish for access, there are cookies and bots that have endless insights about what we are interested in.

Don't believe me? Recall your past few conversations online and then look at the ads that appear on your Facebook page.

However, this is the result of big brother and big data, not some type of ESP that the Internet has about our needs wants and desires.

The internet is getting smarter, and this growing intelligence and insights is populating a new kind of semantic web that is providing more than the most relevant results for people searching, but also some key data to Marketers that may just tell us about intent.

Movie fans out there may remember the movie Minority Report. In this, Tom Cruise, feature film the star would go out and stop crimes before they happened, as intelligence reached a point where it could see a crime that was about to be committed. At the time the concept seemed pretty far-fetched, but really this type of intelligence is very similar to how the semantic web may be able to tell you who your next big customer may be.

Marketers, what if you didn't have to wonder where future business was coming from? What if the Internet could tell you through the application of insights supported by data visualization?

Well, this future isn't so far away. Let me explain further.

THE SEMANTIC WEB IS CREATING
CLARITY ON INTENT

By its very definition the idea of "Semantic" is to find meaning and/or intent behind someone's words. But as of today, through knowledge graphs, socially validated search and modified SEO, most of the intent for what is being searched for today.

Revisiting (just one more time) the example of the "Chicago Steak," search understood that the person searching wanted to go out for steak in downtown Chicago at a high quality restaurant, even though very few of those words were actually keyed into the search.

AN EXAMPLE ON FUTURE PURCHASE INTENT

This same ability to extract meaning from search could be a powerful tool for Marketers to better understand what a consumer may intend to do. The question comes down to how Marketers can collect, sort and utilize this to connect with a consumer at exactly the right time to drive a purchase their way.

One of my favorite examples of a transaction that can take place almost entirely online is the purchase of a car.

What may have been driven early on by a disdain for slimy car salesmen, has evolved into a consumer driven purchase experience that puts the buyers at the controls when it comes to gathering information critical to their purchase.

For a Marketer, by the time the buyer shows up at the dealership it may be too late to drive the purchase one way or another. But through the potential of the semantic web, this could be possible.

If a Marketer could acquire information on a buyer, who was searching for information, pricing and reviews on three different car models, they could gather that they have an interested buyer who is undecided as to which of the three they will buy.

The time spent researching shows clear intent that the shopper is interested in purchasing one of these cars. Now that the intent is clear, their next clicks on features or lease options could tell more about the vehicle they want and how they may be looking to pay for it.

Using other semantic cues like social data from public posts, data visualization could isolate the buyers geographically. The responses could be graphed to better understand how their network may have influenced them,[20] providing the Marketer with a clear picture of just how interested is the buyer.

Knowing that the buyer is looking for a lease and a certain type of car with a specific subset of features, a Marketer could target that consumer acutely by packaging the entire deal based upon their intent. If delivered at just the right time the Marketer could steer them to one particular model over another by using the intent data that was provided by the consumer.

SEMANTIC WEB MEANS BETTER UNDERSTANDING FOR MARKETERS

In the end it is going to be the marriage of Big Data, Semantic Search and User Generated Content that will tell the story of intent for consumers. The web is smarter, but mostly because we constantly use tools that allow data to extract meaning. For consumers, this leads to better content being driven our way; for Marketers it is a goldmine for understanding current behavior and how that may lead to a purchase in the near future.

This trend is in motion and irreversible. The Marketers that maximize it first will cash in by taking the benefits of mass customization and driving it into a 1:1 marketing experience.

As intent algorithms become more pervasive in search, social platforms like Facebook are also cultivating more sophisticated algorithms to understand the strength of context at a more granular level.

Semantics, as per above, is a form of natural language that allows platforms to become more in-tune with the needs of the customer. As this next article attests, evolution in developing deeper and more real-time understanding of users on social platforms will present some challenges as consumers become more aware of this. Coupled with the increasing demands of privacy, the power of data in its ability contextualize our online behavior has reached a point where we, as users, question if there is any line between our privacy and the content (ads) being presented to us. I'm sure you have your suspicions, but let's explore this just a little bit further.

Getting Too Personal on Facebook: Where Context Meets Creepy

I was intrigued when I saw *Dan Sullivan's* post on Facebook. Dan is the Founder of Crowdly, a platform I call the anti-Facebook on Facebook. Its premise is to encourage brands to identify and engage with their strongest advocates without the need for advertising.

I emailed *Dan* to understand the context of his post. Here's how he responded,

> *"We really spend a significant amount of time engineering and measuring what causes a brand post to succeed or not, particularly looking at early engagement, subsequent engagement, second level engagement once shared, all kinds of story bump drivers, and how those contribute to the individual experience.*

> *…We don't dig in as deeply on personal, non-brand related posts, but Facebook definitely has a correlating but somewhat different algorithm for what friend posts you see at all, and with what frequency. Last number I saw, about 20% of your friends will be reached by your post, skewing heavily to a core group that you most frequently interact with (and have most overlap with)."*

Dan Sullivan
11 August at 16:15 · Boston, MA, United States ·

Hello all my friends, happy to announce some very big news! I've accepted a position trying to make Facebook believe this is a really important post about my life! I'm incredibly excited to begin this small experiment into how Facebook engine understands and gives priority to certain language and increases visibility to all of you as a result. Really appreciate all of your support! Yay!

Unlike · Comment · Share · Buffer

You and 68 others like this.

3 shares

Dan Sullivan Thanks everyone for your support in this huge imaginary announcement!
11 August at 16:25 · Like · 4

Serena Antone I'm so confused, but interested...
11 August at 16:26 · Like · 3

Jared Chung Should we like this post or just allow it to be promoted on its own?
11 August at 16:26 · Like · 2

Dan Sullivan Go ahead and like. Primarily interested into how visible it is on friend's feeds based on FB's interpretation of important language, so liking is my best indication of who actually saw. I think the high priority words plus some relevant level of engagement are the two factors at work here. LMK if it gets top posted or if you see it a bunch.
11 August at 16:28 · Edited · Unlike · 1

Caitlin S Hey Top post in my feed
11 August at 16:37 · Like · 1

James McPherson I make lots of money working from home just five minutes a day!
11 August at 16:40 · Like · 2

Matthew Thistle Does this mean I'm taking over as CEO?
11 August at 16:40 · Like · 3

For personal posts, Facebook is now purportedly parsing language in those posts to determine if they seem to be high value, which is why every engagement, new baby, new job, pregnancy post rockets to the top of your news feed from someone you went to high school with.

For this particular post, Dan was inspired by the article, "Tricking Facebook's Algorithm,"[21] and he proceeded to follow a similar, method creating a post on Facebook using "high impact words" and "important life events." The result:

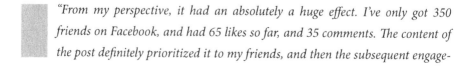

"From my perspective, it had an absolutely a huge effect. I've only got 350 friends on Facebook, and had 65 likes so far, and 35 comments. The content of the post definitely prioritized it to my friends, and then the subsequent engage-

ment as they played along further impacted it. By comparison, a high quality photo of my son high fiving the president received 73 likes (which this one is likely to pass). And when I announced my wife was pregnant with our twins on my birthday, I received 52 comments."

I continue to follow the evolution of data intelligence and the degree to which algorithms have become increasingly sophisticated to surface meaning more accurately, and at a much faster rate. Given these advances it's important to understand:

- How the world's biggest social network is evolving its intelligence
- How can it be applied and
- What this ultimately mean for brands and Facebook users

SEMANTIC IS THE NEW BLACK

As we've alluded to above, the idea of "Semantic" is to find meaning and or intent in someone's words. But as of today through knowledge graphs, socially validated search and modified SEO, most of the intent is to bring clarity as to what is being searched for today.

To ensure that the user experience is meaningful, Semantic algorithms are applied so that the intended search query better matches the results. Beyond "keywords," this establishes a deeper mathematical understanding of language that's more accurate and scalable.

For Facebook, its investment earlier this year in Vicarious FCP [22] is telling. I found this fascinating:

"Vicarious has an ambitious goal: Replicating the neocortex, the part of the brain that sees, controls the body, understands language and does math. Translate the neocortex into computer code and "you have a computer that thinks

like a person," says Vicarious co-founder Scott Phoenix. "Except it doesn't have to eat or sleep."

Enabling technology to solve the world's problems [I'm simplifying]: "cure disease, find cheaper renewable energy sources," let alone replicate the human thought process, sets a precedent for truly displacing the value of the human mind.

But I digress.

While that's the panacea, today, just being able to scale human intent is leaps and bounds ahead of simple keyword queries, provides Facebook the ability to data-mine a goldmine of perceptions, behaviors and interactions with the potential to predict outcomes.

Sullivan indicated that Facebook is building deeper profiles of individuals – the type and frequency of interactions, the type of individuals users engage with, and the type of content that seems to resonate – nuanced insights that are invaluable.

KEEPING BRANDS ON FACEBOOK

Here's the reality: The Newsfeed is NOT getting less cluttered. Advertisers continue to complain about the increasing cost. According to Sullivan, only 5% of content on the newsfeed comes from brands. Marketers were up in arms when it was reported, earlier this year, that brand Edgerank was on a steep decline. [23] Enabling better reach of users on Facebook continues to be a challenge for the social giant.

Today, this is how Facebook determines post success: posting an update on a Facebook Page will go out to a test audience of your users. Based on the types and level of interaction, Facebook will determine organic reach. This will give an indication, not only of the value of the post, but also the quality of your audience. The latter is a different matter entirely and deserves a separate chapter.

Now, if Facebook were to provide the semantic capabilities that allowed brands to score their posts before they were published, this would help solve the newsfeed problem. However, it also opens the doors to gaming. As per Crowdly's experiment, while packing a post with " highly emotional" terms and milestone-type content may increase fan engagement, in the end it makes the brand appear highly suspect and disingenuous.

WHAT ABOUT THE USER?

The user experience needs to be the priority. Zuckerberg knows this. How often have the ads on your page been uncannily relevant to you? I regularly have the same conversation with friends who are served up dating ads, knowing the "type" of men for whom they're predisposed; weight solutions; depression help. Dan and I agree: There is a fine line between context and creepy.

And here's the thing: Relevance doesn't translate into demand. While we both agree that privacy is a moving goal post, users on Facebook have little patience for content that encourages them to publicize the things they want to remain secret.

Artificial intelligence has a long way to go in discerning relevance from true user value. As Sullivan noted, "Use the data to find context at a human level." Once it advances to truly mimic human discretion, we will see significant impacts on user behavior.

Where it all leads….

At least both Search and Social can come to an agreement: user value is paramount to building relationships and ultimately, conversion.

I see a world where Marketers will begin to have access to deeper user profiles that include search intent history, transactional history, tiered customer value, a more granular understanding of individual propensities, and micro-influencers within a multitude of industry categories.

For Marketers, this presents endless possibilities for advanced targeting, especially as we evolve to more real-time marketing. As we'll see in the next chapter, this also provides inherent benefits to CRM, the products and services and the business at large.

And as the media industry has been forced to adapt, so will business.

REFERENCES:

1   http://searchenginewatch.com/sew/news/2067396/yahoo-to-buy-overture

2   http://en.wikipedia.org/wiki/Google_Panda

3   http://techcrunch.com/2014/12/13/facebook-dumps-bing-will-introduce-its-own-search-tool/

4   http://moz.com/beginners-guide-to-seo/growing-popularity-and-links

5   http://broadsuite.com/return-on-content-marketing-where-your-focus-should-go-b2b/

6   http://broadsuite.com/return-on-content-marketing-where-your-focus-should-go-b2b/

7   http://www.searchmetrics.com/knowledge-base/ranking-factors-us-2013/

8   http://broadsuite.com/which-more-important-content-frequency-or-quality/

9   http://www.searchmetrics.com/knowledge-base/ranking-factors-us-2013/

10 http://broadsuite.com/how-to-build-a-content-sharing-culture/

11 http://www.marketingcharts.com/

12 https://www.thinkwithgoogle.com/collections/zero-moment-truth.html

13 http://blogs.forrester.com/lori_wizdo/12-10-04-buyer_behavior_helps_b2b_marketers_guide_the_buyers_journey14 http://leaderswest.com/2013/09/04/infographic-companies-with-a-blog-get-55-more-traffic/

15 http://www.forbes.com/sites/danielnewman/2014/07/01/big-data-roi-making-

better-decisions-that-drive-community-retention-and-revenue/

16 http://www.forbes.com/sites/danielnewman/2014/07/15/what-is-next-for-content-marketing/

17 http://millennialceo.com/leadership/seo-simplified-todays-business-leader/

18 http://searchenginewatch.com/

19 http://searchengineland.com/google-hummingbird-172816

20 http://www.forbes.com/sites/danielnewman/2014/04/10/the-role-of-influence-in-the-new-buyers-journey/

21 http://www.theatlantic.com/technology/archive/2014/08/tricking-facebooks-algorithm/375801/

22 http://blogs.wsj.com/digits/2014/03/21/zuckerberg-musk-invest-in-artificial-intelligence-company-vicarious/

23 http://techcrunch.com/2014/04/03/the-filtered-feed-problem/

It's Inevitable: All Roads Lead to Social Business

SOCIAL BUSINESS IS ROUTED IN CONVERSATION, NOT PLATFORMS

We have given our lives to social media, no doubt there. In fact, for many social media is omnipresent. No matter what we do – eat at our favorite restaurant, take the kids skating, watch a movie, go grocery shopping, or hop next door to the coffee shop – we are routinely sharing our experiences, either with words or images or both, and we are literally documenting our lives and our experiences through social media channels and interaction.

We Tweet, we Instagram and we upload to Facebook– all in the hopes of communicating and interacting with our friends, family, and peers. We smile less, we "smiley" more; we appreciate less often than we "like" or "share"; we don't talk as much as we "tweet" and we would rather ask life questions on Quora than ask our parents and friends those questions in life outside of our screen. Marketers have been taking note and a whole new business type has branched off from there – social business.

So often, the first question asked by businesses getting into social media is which social channels do they need to be on? Should they be on Twitter or do they even need to bother with Instagram? For businesses wishing to be social, the first thing they need to recognize is the importance of being where their audience is. You might have a dedicated team managing your social media profiles, planning your campaigns, or handling all of your social media activities. But, if you're not interacting, forget about your plans for social business, because you're shouting at a wall.

If you wish to build a successful social business, you have to break the wall. Get your employees to participate genuinely in your social media initiatives. Make them your brand's voice and let them interact in their own social circles. Your social media efforts seem more human, and this human touch is what people want, need, and look for.

PEOPLE ARE TALKING, BUT ARE YOU LISTENING?

We witness a dichotomy when it comes to social media use. People (and brands) hop from one social media channel to another at a dizzying speed, rarely taking time out to monitor and listen to what is being said. That's one category of social media users. The other? They religiously plant their social media teams on every imaginable social media channel, and they post, share, tweet, pin, stumble, hashtag and so on at the speed of light, without giving a hoot about involvement or interaction.

The travesty is easy to see. Whether you are hopping or planted, you may never get your social media spotlight or your goldmine of customer intelligence without listening as well. If your business wants to focus on connecting and building closer relationships, then it is less about what you share on social media and more about how the things that you are sharing are driving meaningful conversations.

Most of the time, the best results come from the simplest actions. It rings true for social media as well. But, remember by "simple" I don't mean "easy". It takes persistent effort to hone your business' listening ear and make social media your market analysis tool. But, trust me, the efforts are well worth it.

SET FOOT ON THE RIGHT PLATFORM, BUT PAY MORE ATTENTION TO CONVERSATION.

Instead of trying out fancy new tricks, or getting yourself registered on every new social platform that makes an appearance, restrict your activities to two or three channels and invest time in reading through discussions, listening to user-generated content, and understanding current interests. You can even ask your audience to show you, making social media an even better tool for gaining customer insights. You no longer have to guess, when you can directly ask your audience about their choices via quizzes, polls, and discussions.

Make social listening the foundation of your social business. Stop resting on the laurels of 'likes' and 'shares' and start listening. You will be headed for a successful social media presence, built by learning your customers' preferences and customizing your products and services around what you hear from them.

In a world where people want to make connections with brands through the people that represent them, the goal of social media has to be about starting and maintaining conversations and connection through active listening. The platform you use is up to you (and your community)!

In this final chapter we will show you why all roads lead to social business, but first, let's take a quick journey through the past decade and some of the events that have been instrumental in creating an entirely new way for business to communicate; not only with clients and customers, but with the world.

The Future of Business: How We Got Here and Why It Will Radically Change Everything as We Know it

Unless you're burying your head in the sand, you understand that the world as we know it is changing. Things we've come to rely on as standards are no longer working. Economic, global, technological and consumption events have and are making business rethink the tried and true. Business does not live in a vacuum. These days, the customer voice, and employee actions – both enabled by technology – radically shift the power away from the business and much more into the hands of the consumer.

Below are some of these fundamental shifts that will change business forever.

AN UNSTABLE WORLD ECONOMY

2008 revealed to the world that no business or government, no matter how powerful or seemingly stable, was immune to the Financial Crisis. Major market sectors, that seemed to have been unbreakable, were breaking. The contagion that first began with the financial downturn of the housing market from the questionable subprime mortgage practices, quickly spiraled into the financial sector domestically and abroad. This, in turn, delivered its blows to industries like the auto sector, which relied heavily on the credit industry. The likes of General Motors, Chrysler and Ford plus the largest insurance Giant AIG, among others were vulnerable.

Powerhouse financial institutions like Freddie Mac, Fannie Mae and Lehman Brothers were devastated. This not only put the financial industry in disarray, it created a destructive path abroad as markets like Japan and, China and many other once-fiscally strong nations were in a recession by the end of 2008. In the last 6 years, we witnessed the European economy begin its own decline. The term, "austerity" became the prevailing defense in Europe as economies in Ireland and Greece, among others were forced into a period of rationalization – one they didn't see coming, hence were seriously unprepared for.

This domino effect quickly translated into negative impacts on pensions, education, healthcare and employment.

For the first time since the Great Depression the US felt a significant the impact. With the highest debt load in its history, the most powerful nation on earth was, itself, left powerless.

RESULTING BUSINESS IMPACTS

Global rationalization has brought with it a new mindset. Spending cuts across government and organizations has created a new mindset: business must be more accountable. Resource constraints and squeezed budgets have, more than ever, challenged business to allocate expenditure in areas that derive the most business value.

Marketers no longer have the luxury of free-flowing budgets. Marketing is no longer a cost-center. We are more accountable than ever to the bottom line. As we've stated throughout this book, the KPIs that we previously peddled to prove the value of our efforts, have now been displaced with Return on Business Investment. This will not change anytime soon. Impressions, clicks, cost per acquisition, and web traffic will have less relevance going forward unless they have strong attribution to the business objectives.

THE BALANCE OF POWER HAS SHIFTED

Technology has splintered communications, which has changed from a one-way to a two-way channel. It's radically changed the communications dynamics. Technology is enabling the market to evolve at a pace much faster than a company's ability to adapt. Up until just over a decade ago, the voice of the consumer was but a whisper. Now it's being heard loud and clear.

Conversation has evolved consumer behavior. Technology has enabled abundant sharing of opinions and recommendations. This has now become a primary source of influence for many consumers. Connected, communicating customers and employees have more choices, and more amplified voices, than ever before. They have more knowledge than ever before. The strength of the collective voice and the speed at which this information travels has transferred power from the business squarely to the hands of the consumer.

Real time discussions are having more impact on business and have motivated business to transform to maximize effective communication. Netflix has been one of the few companies that has capitalized on the value of peer communication and influence, and continues to reap the benefits today.

Other examples of this power shift that have forced businesses to take notice include:

EMPLOYEES HAVE NO LOYALTY

Employees, angered and frustrated at company decisions once felt powerless. Now employees who cannot impact changes internally can take their messages to their own networks and allow the media and world, at large, to be judge, jury and executioner.

I was at Yahoo! at the time the infamous Peanut Butter Manifesto[1] memo was leaked to the press. Brad Garlinghouse, Sr. VP of Yahoo! wrote a memo to the Executive team expressing his frustration at the current state: "lack of focus....lack of vision... lack of accountability and ownership." This memo was one of the first to reveal the fact that the individual employee was no longer afraid. While the company made attempts to find its perpetrators, it eventually came to the realization that it would be unable to deter similar events in the future.

As the RBC Outsourcing[2] scandal has proven, the larger they are, the harder they fall. At a time when one of Canada's largest banks had laid off employees in the IT division, information leaked about those impacted employees having to train their replacements – outsourced temporary foreign workers. The leaked story gained steam rapidly on social media as a Boycott RBC Facebook Page, quickly built up an enraged audience. The scandal also came at a time when RBC was disclosing its more-than-fruitful quarterly earnings.

COMPANIES ARE MAKING MISTAKES

There are countless examples of company faux pas in social media:

While the nation wrestled with the aftermath of a shooting in Colorado[3] that left 12 people dead, a Twitter account for the National Rifle Association had this to say:

In Toronto, in the aftermath of a snowstorm, the City of Vaughan Twitter[4] account erroneously posted,

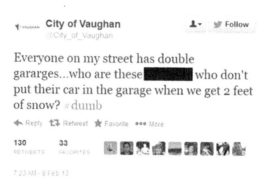

Many of these incidences increase a company's vulnerability. The resulting impacts on reputation have been difficult to manage. As Dell, United and Dominos Pizza can attest, the business requires a significant reality check to mitigate future disasters.

SOCIAL DATA BEGINS TO SURFACE CONTEXT
AND ENABLE SENSOR TECHNOLOGY

This Online dialogue has drastically increased the well of data and information. The individual becomes the product as behaviors and events continue to feed this data well at an alarming rate. Aggregated and analyzed, businesses now have at their disposal, a deeper understanding of their customers – profiles that extend beyond demographics to behavioral, influence and preference propensities. Making sense of the real-time nature of this data will force business to rethink and alter process to properly manage its influx. It's this information that has the ability to radically inform and provide more power in business decision-making.

What's more, the Internet of Things that introduced wearable technology and more sensor-type applications for business and environment has already begun surfacing context that allows innovations in these areas:

- Smart Parking - to find free parking spaces within specific locations;
- e-Health - to predict the movement of ailments and potential epidemics across geographies;
- Smart Environment - to detect CO_2 emissions, and water quality;
- Retail efficiency: channel optimization, and inventory management

Now we are able to collect data everywhere from our environment, infrastructures, businesses and even ourselves, and this huge amount of information is generating a new ecosystem of business opportunities around its storage, analysis and accessibility.

THE ADVENT OF MASS CUSTOMIZATION

If the above hasn't made it clear, the strength of the consumer voice has made business rethink their approach by moving away from product as a core business function. Instead, customer experience has forced its way to the front of the line.

Dave Gray alluded to this in his book, "The Connected Company",[5]

"Product saturation/abundance was born in an age of mass production and mass communication. These days, the opposite is true. Enter Mass Customization that has given rise to increased customer service."

We are moving to an increasingly niche economy - with more fragmentation than ever before. Everybody has shoes; everyone has a TV. Now, it's about taking those mass goods and creating more personalized products to suit individual customer needs. This custom-made process can be delivered with low unit costs that are traditionally associated with mass production.

Take, for example, Nike ID, which allows the consumer to design his/her own shoe. In other cases, customers can purchase a product that has been customized to meet his/her exact needs, for example the color of his/her car, his own drawing on a T-shirt, or even creating a pair of customized sneakers.

From a company perspective, mass customization has been defined as [6]

"...The ability to provide customers with whatever they want, whenever they want it, wherever they want it and however they want it."

This poses a significant competitive advantage in the future. The iPhone is the most practical example of mass customization. While the base product has limited options for the user, the ability to customize the phone via applications creates an inherent user value that now distinguishes it from user to user.

THE FUTURE OF BUSINESS IS HERE

It's clear that what we're experiencing is by no means a trend. The economy will continue to struggle. Pundits are already forecasting the next financial downturn, and it's safe to say that stability will not be a foregone conclusion. Technology will advance to continue to enable peer-to-peer discussion and influence consumer-to-business collaboration more than ever before. However, it also has the potential to displace human capital.

Big Banks & Social: To Be or Not to Be?

Before we jump into this section we wanted to take a moment to share why we chose the banking industry, and why we believe it relates to the broader markets. As one of the most highly regulated industries, the slowest to evolve AND one that is fiercely data driven, we felt that many verticals and business lines could identify with banking's issues. As an industry rooted in 1:1 Marketing, banks would naturally evolve to this newly-formed customer-centric environment. Ironically, this is not the case.

No less than 8 years ago, I found myself happily taking a detour from the banking industry. I decided to flee a dinosaur that was slow to change. It had all the best intentions of tapping into emerging technology – however, riddled with red tape, regulation, and rigid policy, this old and established institution had a hard time keeping pace.

In this day and age where tremendous changes in digital emerge…

> *The financial industry, which you'd think has the wherewithal to adapt to and capitalize on the pummeling volumes of unstructured data may, in fact, be the slowest to jump on the bandwagon.*

Here we discuss some of the in facets of banking that challenge its steps towards embracing big data and becoming a social business.

BANK TO THE CUSTOMER:
"WHAT HAVE YOU DONE FOR ME LATELY?"

In marketing, we fed on data results to help us define our market. We relied on clustering to allow us to segment groups with like traits and rank their value to determine the value to the company. Back then (and even today), the "value" of a customer was based purely on how much that customer was contributing to the company's bottom line.

When I entered the credit card industry, the opportunity to learn more about the customer got me excited. All customers were given a value. The value of a customer was based on the following factors: frequency of credit card transactions, the number of products–credit card or otherwise; their ability to pay off outstanding balances, and even total debt to the bank.

As a customer, the more debt you carried, the more the bank loved you. We knew everything about the customer: purchase history, credit score, complaint history etc. We used this information to sell them more stuff. The problem is we didn't see their value from a bank perspective. Our view was much narrower and tied to the division with which we were accountable: credit cards.

So, not only did we score customers based on what they did for the bank's revenues, we also created a very narrow view of who our customers were. This was hardly Customer Relationship Management (CRM) at its finest. That picture has radically changed today:

> *Value, today, is a two-way street. Customers now have more control and more information. Banks are required to listen and know more about their customers in order to drive stronger, more sustainable, and therefore more profitable relationships.*

…. Which leads me to the next point:

IN BANKING, THE PRODUCT RULES

It's pretty ironic that in an environment where data is a primary element to communicate to customers, rarely do we look at the customer and their overall value to the bank. Products, or as banks would say–Lines of Business (LOBs), are their own kingdoms.

While there is process and oversight in ensuring over-communication to any one customer is mitigated, there is little effort for LOBs to further collaborate with each other.

Mortgages define their customers differently from Lending and from Credit Card Services. Now, as a bank customer the messages I receive from one bank are fragmented; many voices communicating separate messages through different mediums.

> *Minimal communication between departments typically has resulted in duplicated messages to the customer, and an apparent inefficiency. The right hand rarely knew what the left hand was doing.*

This is the reason why today each division maps its own course for social media, resulting in varying tools and technology, and fragmented social accounts and programs.

ATTEMPTS TO DEFINE THE BUSINESS BY "CUSTOMER" ARE FUTILE

Banks don't typically put the customer at the center of the equation. That's not how they're structured. My VP was a maverick. She made an attempt to undo this siloed thinking within the LOB and create a litmus test for the rest of the bank. Whereas marketing was structured by card product first, an initiative was launched to revamp the department based on customer value.

We would have a holistic view of the customer, all transactions, frequency, purchases, products, revenue potential, and customer satisfaction. While this was being defined, a core team helped define the functional impacts and impending changes that were required.

Along the way some critical insights began to surface:

- The practices previously used by one product were not consistently adopted by another group.
- Subsequently, successes realized in one group were not consistently shared with the other products.
- The central data team struggled to re-organize customer data to accommodate the new value system that was being implemented.
- The customer call center needed more than just minor process tweaks to properly service customers based on the new configuration.
- While Credit Cards was making a move towards recognizing and re-evaluating the customer as a core focus, the rest of the LOBs continued with the status quo.

It was clear that it would take much more "dismantling" of process and structure in order to deliver on a customer centric environment. The attempt of ONE department to do the right thing also meant that the entire bank structure needed to change … and that would mean serious upheaval in the process.

> *The reality was that the bank environment did not reward performance based on customer retention. It rewarded performance based on product revenue.*

In order to accommodate a customer-driven strategy, it demanded a bank-wide cultural shift. Unless the mechanisms were already in place: performance, structure and process were revised to support the new strategy, the initiative would fail.

Suffice it to say, Credit Cards had no choice but to revert to the original structure. Today, the demands of the social customer require banks to be ready to restructure their systems and processes. This is, by no means, an easy task.

A single customer could potentially have data residing within multiple systems and databases. The integration of all that information into one customer record will require disparate systems technology systems (in most cases, legacy databases) to interoperate in real time. This is imperative in order to seamlessly integrate offerings across markets and LOBs.

COMPLIANCE: THE ELEPHANT IN THE ROOM

Compliance mandates much of the bank process and policy. It encompasses regulation, product disclosure, data integrity, security, and privacy.

Banking is bound by regulation.

Here are the facts: In social media, customers will expect the bank to be more responsive and deal with their concerns, regardless of product. This will mean four things:

1. Frontline staff will need to be armed with more information plus a single view of the customer in order to effectively manage requests and issues.
2. Interactions will need to elicit more rapid response resolution, which will require frontline staff be given more authority to make decisions.
3. Governance needs to be established consistently across all channels and LOBs so there is firm-wide guidance and access.
4. Bank-only data will need some interoperability with social data to build a more holistic picture of the customer to support all touch points. This will be, by far, the biggest endeavor once the institution commits to a customer-centric environment

According to the Social Banker Report:

> *"Beyond integrating thousands of data points in real time, the shift to a CRM system will also demand rigorous controls, streamlined processes and effective governance frameworks to ensure that data is being properly managed and secured."[7]*

ING Direct in Canada integrated the Facebook API (application programming interface) into their technology environment (becoming…the first bank to deploy this functionality globally).

According to a colleague who worked in the technology side of a major bank, the Holy Grail is having the one "key" that validates the match between the customer bank record and the social accounts, while minimizing risk exposure of the customer data. This is a critical step in beginning to build the CRM framework to support all customer touch points.

Privacy concerns will become more apparent as banks begin to take advantage of mobile behavior, conversation, influential relationships and increased psychographic information to better inform relevant offers and communication. Regulation will evolve in tandem.

SOCIAL BANKS ARE INEVITABLE…
THE QUESTION IS WHEN?

For banks to become truly social it will take a cultural shift, an executive mandate, massive systems restructuring, decentralization of decision-making and empowerment at the edges. Banks are now in the process of figuring this out. TD has already made the move to bring in firm-wide collaboration and communication solutions. Most banks are beginning to expand the definition of "social" beyond customer service and communications.

However, until there is an urgency to make these changes, I suspect that old habits will die hard. The rise of big data has seen some early signs of significant promise for organizations, but as I have said, big data is really only as good as the organizations willingness to invest in putting meaning behind the data. This further reiterates the need for social business because data alone is only part of the equation. The remainder will be solved when companies begin to leverage the power of connectedness throughout all levels of their business ecosystem. Many businesses think they are already heading down the road to social, and some truly are, but many are missing the mark so let's dive into where businesses have gone wrong when attempting to be social and then try to put you on the course to a more meaningful social business strategy.

Why Your Social Business May Not be Social After All

There is a lot of buzz out there around the concept of a social business.[8] Do you know the type of company that embraces new media? It's the company that nurtures a culture of sharing ideas, conversing and evangelizing for your brand through informing and inspiring readers rather than promoting and pistol-whipping them into submission with your corporate propaganda.

Heck yes, the concept makes so much sense. And the data supports it emphatically. People have never enjoyed being sold to, but most people are like-minded in the fact that they like to learn, share and feel a part of something. Furthermore, in a world where there are new rules and new KPI's for connecting consumers and brands [9] there is a great need for change. Social business, in principle, holds the keys to both achieving these new KPI's as well as meeting the engagement requirements of employees and consumers (which in actuality are one and the same).

Lately however, I have seen a disturbing trend, and as much as I would like to say this trend is taking place in a vacuum, my observations are that it is snowballing. What is it you ask? It is the rise of the "Pretend Social Business."

WHAT IN THE WORLD IS A PRETEND SOCIAL BUSINESS?

If you hadn't asked, I would have posed the question myself. The "Pretend Social Business" constitutes of companies that merely participate in a portion of what makes a business social yet proclaim to embrace the concept in entirety.

The worst perpetrators of this trend are those that continuously preach social business but are merely littering social outlets with their content – even if the content is well intended and useful. The companies that do this will push their teams to share the content; however when someone stops to like or respond to the content the sharers are no place to be found. It's like a cold call salesman that leaves messages, receives a call back and then doesn't talk to the prospect. WHAT?

Other pretend social businesses find themselves creating and sharing content at the enterprise level (large or small) but do almost nothing to ensure that their employees and communities are spreading the good word, or even aware of what is being shared. These companies have social silos that aren't taking the value of a social business from end to end but rather just going through the motions. These are also companies that are likely to deem Social Business a waste of time after a short span of trying it proclaiming things like, "It doesn't work" or "It isn't possible".

Of course it isn't possible if you don't lube the engine. Just shot-gunning content out without the support of your closest stakeholders is ridiculous.

SOCIAL BUSINESS NEEDS TO BE FIXED BECAUSE IT'S A REFLECTION OF THE BUYER'S JOURNEY

Social business isn't a good idea; it is a necessity in almost any industry. In a recent article I discussed the evolution of social selling from Innovation to being "The Way." [10] In short, the reason Social Selling has become the way is because people buy online. They tend to start and finish their journey online using content and influence as their guide. With this in mind, doing "Part" of the work of a social business is like doing part of the customer experience process.

Consider the customer experience for your business. If clients and prospects tend to use content and social media as a means for better understanding your industry, available solutions and buying options, then why wouldn't you help take them through the entire process digitally by considering all of the parts?

- **Brand Awareness:** Companies can build awareness and connections to their brand through the sharing of ideas and content in social communities. In the earliest phases of the buyer's journey it helps to share content with the intent to educate and inspire. It's imperative to stay away from strong brand oriented content and focusing more on what you want the market to know about; the problems that your business solves.

- **Brand Affinity:** If you want to build a community around your brand you have to give them the ability to feel more connected to your brand. If you are only sharing then you may be a source of information, but you will rarely gain their loyalty. If you think about the best teachers or business partners you ever had, there was a give and take relationship. This consisted of sharing, conversing and learning together – a two-way interaction. Affinity is built through continued conversation and engagement that can take place between a consumer and a brand. If employees are just dropping links, that isn't social business; it's like putting flyers on the windshield.

- **Purchase:** The final stage and the goal that underpins most social businesses is to sell something to someone. Yes, it is revenue that allows us to exist. All of the goodwill, education and sharing needs to generate revenue or it's a waste of time. But social businesses see the purchase phase as the start of the generation of customer experience. Social becomes a way for customers to stay more connected to the brand– to learn about changes and better ways to leverage products and services purchased. And these days, it's also a way to get support when something goes wrong. A social business takes social from the very first introduction to the customer through to the customer life cycle.

- **Quit Fooling Yourself. Social Business Is Hard:** Social business is more than a mindset. It is a top down, bottom up cultural phenomenon [11] that takes a combination of passionate people and well thought out procedures. Much like old sales territories and paid media campaigns, social business needs to be thought out and implemented, but one thing that can't happen is allowing it to be ignored.

Sure, part of the solution is better than none, but if you are fooling yourself into thinking a half-hearted effort into social and content is enough to sustain the buyer of the future then you sadly mistaken. People don't want to buy products from a company that does things half way, so I guess it is time to grab your ball and carry it across the finish.

A CRASH COURSE IN WHAT A SOCIAL BUSINESS SHOULD LOOK LIKE

Ok, so I may have said that many of today's proclaimed social businesses, aren't social and I stand by that assertion 100%. Having said that, the quest for social business isn't unattainable, but it does take work to achieve.

Before I jump into the constructs for a successful social business, let's just take a quick crash course as to why a business wants to be social.

Believe it or not, the hype behind social media is only a minute reason for businesses to get social. Instead it comes down to a different set of values that today's businesses need to have.

1. **Connectedness:** In a world where we are plugged in around the clock, people and brands (comprised of people) have a desire to be more consistently connected.
2. **Collaborative:** Beyond just the connection, how do brands and their stakeholders communicate in ways that drive more productivity and

greater levels of customer satisfaction?

3. **Measurable:** In a data driven world, almost anything can be measured. Social businesses are measuring their activities with the goal of being able to most efficiently put their resources to use.

4. **Customer Centric:** A pillar of any great business, social businesses leverage the channel to drive great customer experience. This is created by vehemently striving for numbers 1-3.

The rise of social business was really proliferated by a changing breed of consumer. Social media itself is merely a channel, but in a technology driven world we are more connected to everything all of the time. This has created a mindset of consumers with greater expectations for quality and expediency from the brands with which they associate.

SO HOW DOES ONE BECOME (AND MEASURE) A SOCIAL BUSINESS?

It is one thing to theorize about social, it is another thing to suggest why a business isn't social. Perhaps the hardest thing to do is really pin down the blueprint for creating a social business. More simply put, what must a company do that wants to be social? Both Maddie Grant and Jamie Notter, co-authors of Humanize have identified some key elements for this transition:

*   **Cultural Transformation:** First and foremost, companies that are serious about becoming social businesses have a top down, bottom up cultural shift taking place. The perils of social as a way to connect, collaborate, measure and deliver greater levels of customer satisfaction are seen as valuable across the organization. While social success can start in factions of an organization, until the entire organization is on board you aren't a social business, but rather a business that does some social activities.

- **Increased Accountability and Empowerment:** When a business is truly being social they are putting a larger portion (ALL) of the organization in front of the world and letting them have a voice on behalf of the company. Regardless of any disclaimers that social media users may make (i.e. Opinions are my own), we all know that each and every thought that comes from an employee in some way shape or form represents the whole organization. With the increased voice of the majority comes increased accountability. Employees who are part of a social business culture are acutely aware of the power they wield and the need to use that power wisely.

  Furthermore, the smartest social businesses allow their employees to utilize social as a channel to create happier customers, which we know requires a certain level of empowerment.

- **Brand Advocates:** Employees within social businesses recognize that they are key stakeholders in supporting and keeping customers happy. This includes listening and jumping into situations across all channels (social or non) to keep customers from churning. Along with their more empowered state as brand advocates, employees are not only aware of their risks of being a brand advocate, but they also accept it and see it as increased responsibility and participation in the company's success. Internal branding now becomes paramount in developing a productive, loyal culture that's inclusive. The Guide to Internal Branding by Nina MacLaverty and Hugh Oddie identifies key strategies that allow businesses to focus on its most important advocates.

- **An Increasingly Matrix Organization:** While all organizational hierarchies vary, social businesses within a "flatter" structure have strong dotted line connections that encourage more interaction between employees, departments and the different ranks within an organization. Remember, immediacy means more instantaneous response to customers, which mean the decisions makers need to be accessible. Tall organizations with heavy bureaucracy cannot make quick decisions and they are missing one of the major keys to being a social business.

- **Measuring Social Business:** Across the spectrum of connect, collaborate, measure and customer focus, a social business needs to analyze their activities using data driven methods to determine the success of their program.

Just going through the motions of sharing and even engaging doesn't make a social business. Again, that is just a business that does social activities.

To be a social business it is cultural. It means more engaged, accountable and empowered employees that genuinely care about their brand and have the ability to quickly reach the right person(s) in their organization to accomplish whatever must be done. The goal is to create, sustain and build satisfied customers who become the most influential purveyors of your message across the spectrum of communication channels.

Now that there is more clarity on how Social Business has evolved as a business imperative, it's time to explore the organizational impacts. Who owns social media and how does it connect customer service, public relations, marketing and just about every other facet of the organization? Should it be owned by any of them, or is social business a pure overlay? What is the responsibility of external agencies versus internal marketing teams? What should be the balance? One thing is becoming more and more evident: Social Business needs to be less about being controlled and more about being taught and proliferated as part of a strategy so employees can utilize it to deliver better communication inside and outside of an organization.

Convergence: Merging Disciplines Between PR and Marketing

Here is a classic definition of Public Relations: [12]

 "PR is the practice of managing the spread of information between an individual or an organization and the public. Public relations may include an orga-

nization or individual gaining exposure to their audiences using topics of public interest and news items that do not require direct payment.

The aim of public relations by a company often is to persuade the public, investors, partners, employees, and other stakeholders to maintain a certain point of view about, its leadership, products, or of political decisions."

The classic definition of the role of Marketing: [13]

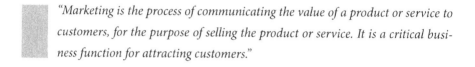

"Marketing is the process of communicating the value of a product or service to customers, for the purpose of selling the product or service. It is a critical business function for attracting customers."

WHERE THE TWO WORLDS CONVERGE

The customer and the prospect now live in this one existence area called "Social Media." There is a clear divide even within Marketing. Retention and Acquisition Marketers used different channels, different lists and different messages. PR always sat outside of this function because the role of PR rarely involved impacts from a customer level.

For the most part, all three channels coexisted but "never the twain shall meet." That is until now.

WHO CLAIMS SOCIAL MEDIA?

I have PR friends who claim that Social and PR belong together. After all, if PR has always been tasked with managing a company's reputation, then social media should be a natural part of what they do.

I respectfully disagree. Before social media the voice of the consumer was but a whisper, rarely heard or listened to. By and large, the reputation of a company was developed and managed by the company itself. It was shaped based on relationships with media, and damage was mitigated also based on these relationships. The consumer had little say or had little bearing, unlike today.

Now, that same consumer is the prospect… the customer… and the reputation catalyst. Whether we like it or not these roles are converging in a big way. The question is how to evolve each of our roles and how to play nice in the sandbox.

HOW WILL THE ROLES EVOLVE?

In today's reality, you will need a combination of PR and Marketing to stay on top of the conversation, and be ready to develop compelling content to engage and build advocacy. This article, "Real-Time Social Media Creative Marketing and PR" depicts this nicely:[14]

The Bridge, a "holistic engagement network" combines the disciplines in a symbiotic way:

> *"…the Bridge pairs mainstream and digital media experts with creative specialists like copywriters, digital designers and video producers to uncover storytelling opportunities in real time, deliver critical business insights, engage influencers and customers and create the content that shapes news and conversations."*

I love the same approach that /newsrooms has evolved to break out from a traditional media news channel to make available a service that gives brands their own "CNN" for a day. /newsrooms[15] a content and continuous marketing network launched by Sabaa Quao and Chris Hogg, runs the constant brand coverage that only the resources of a news organization can provide.

"CNN and The New York Times were built for news, /newsrooms was designed for brands. Brands need content. Brands want coverage. And brands demand conversion."

"Imagine content cut up into pieces and distributed to the right audiences at the right time on the right platforms. Continuously. Every day, without stopping. We can do that. We can also create that content in real-time, at live events, with coverage in almost every major city worldwide."

PERHAPS A NEW MANDATE AND SHARED RESPONSIBILITY

The abundance of conversations has created a new reality. Listening is now table stakes. Real-time response is the expectation. Content carries more credibility than advertising. Storytelling's approach is proving to be an effective draw to appeal to consumers. Real-time marketing, driven by strong creative executions, is now the standard. Optimizing, measurement, and tracking need to accompany the validation for this new medium. There doesn't seem to be clear line drawn between the two functions.

If anything, as this space evolves, the respective strengths of PR and Marketing will need to work together to tackle the increasing consumer demands and expectations that continue to challenge this space.

Digital Agencies Have Reached An Inflection Point: Agencies Must Get Faster, More Responsive and Increase Differentiation

The death of the digital agency has perhaps been announced prematurely, but where there is smoke there is fire, and if you are in the business of serving up brands with the traditional full suite of agency services, you may be on a short leash.

If the business were to defect, where would it go? In a recent study by the association of national advertisers, 60% of Fortune 500 companies are considering moving away from some, if not all, of their traditional agencies in favor of bringing it in house.

While there is much speculation as to the cause of these companies considering such a monumental shift away from agencies, I actually think the desire to shift may be rooted in something quite simple.

Most Agencies Really Aren't Digital

Having spent the past few years working with a wide variety of marketing, communications and public relations firms, I have been able to observe how most agencies have made the migration to digital.

While there are exceptions to every rule, as a whole, many agencies' digital strategies seem to be nothing more than penning the word digital on their various collateral and then passing it off as a strategy.

I could just imagine an agency in their planning for the migration…

> *"Okay, let's keep doing everything the same except once we do it let's Tweet about it…Oh and put it on Facebook too!"*

In reality, the ability to successfully provide a company a full complement of digital services reaches far beyond just including core terminology such as SEO, social media and content marketing in a proposal. To be successful, agencies need to understand the entire eco-system that is digital. Furthermore, they must have the proper talent in-house to deliver a strategy that will succeed and the execution required to yield results.

The rapid evolution of the digital space creates so much downward pressure on agencies that even hiring the right talent to fill the gaps is becoming increasingly difficult. Consider this: a student just leaving college now with a degree in marketing will not be up to speed on the shifts that are taking place on almost a daily basis in the digital marketing realm.

Think SEO for example. If you spent the past 4 years studying SEO you would have had to re-learn many of the best practices on almost a yearly basis as Google continued to update its approach to Search. With the Hummingbird update, Google threw out everything that SEO experts had been preaching, as social signals became the largest influencers of search rank.

This is a little bit like the shift that computer science saw in the last 10 years. I regularly engage with agencies that claim to be "digital" that are surprised when I tell them about changes like those made upon the release of Hummingbird. If you are the brains and the brawn behind a brand, this is completely unacceptable.

INFLECTION POINT: TIME TO WALK THE WALK

I think the reason that agencies were able to get away with a half-assed approach to digital for so long was rooted in the slow speed by which many larger companies move. While they may have seen the digital revolution coming, they were hardly ready to embrace it. In fact, their budget that had been copied and pasted from the year before still had earmarks for traditional advertising, print marketing, Public Relations and Marketing. I suppose the best course of action was not to rock the boat.

So when the agencies came around and said "We've gone digital," the brands were sufficiently impressed by taking their strategy and publishing it online. Better than nothing, right?

In the past 3 or 4 years, digital penetration has become too great for even big brands to table any longer. They are now looking for more innovative, faster and more specialized work from their agencies. They are looking for their agencies to guide them from publishing traditional marketing online to a point where they are driving meaningful social engagement. This entails building relationships with online influencers and embracing the shift toward brands acting as media outlets.

If you consider the fact that more than 80% of people start their information searches online, digital marketing is imperative, and just checking the boxes is no longer good enough.

Perhaps the biggest challenge I see as it pertains to the success or failure of agencies trying to make the digital migration is a lack of intimate knowledge as to how successful online marketing works. Many of the account leads within agencies have no real experience building relationships in the digital sphere. And while it may not seem like a requirement, how the heck are agencies supposed to help brands develop meaningful relationships with their audience if those in charge of the effort have never done it themselves?

With digital marketing being so dependent on human-to-human engagement, perhaps the biggest need for brands are agencies whose account leadership have the hands-on experience of building a meaningful digital community.

This isn't to suggest that they need to all be widely published authors or the most followed people on social networks, but to some extent they need to show an ability to build relationships, move content and drive some sort of meaningful conversion.

THE FUTURE FOR AGENCIES LIES IN THE SPEED AND DIFFERENTIATION

For the most part, the companies that need agency support the most are those that require creativity and execution to happen in short order. Large companies are filled with bureaucracy, and they can rarely be opportunistic because of their endless mass of red tape.

Agencies that truly wish to be full service in the digital economy are going to need to show the ability to change and adapt at breakneck speed to the shifts in social media, SEO and content marketing. They will need to show proficiency in utilizing all the tools on all of the platforms to bring the brands they represent closer to the consumer.

In essence, their digital experience must align closely with the customer journey.

I asked *Kevin Green*, a former agency executive from Racepoint Global, and current marketing executive at Dell if he believed that the agency had reached an inflection point with a relative expectation of being met with contention. Instead he said this:

> *"From my perspective, large organizations are bringing digital in-house because of the rapidly increasing importance on the customer experience. Agencies are slow and they don't fully understand every consumer touch point like an internal team would. CVS just pulled all of their digital work in house. Why would this happen? In short, because they are a complex retail/healthcare organization and the vision for the brand requires complete dedication and immersion not only in the brand, but the business objectives. Agencies have struggled with being true business consultants and living and breathing the customer journey. As a result, I expect to see consultant firms like McKinsey and Boston Consulting Group start acquiring the talent needed to provide end-to-end solutions."*

The good news is that the end isn't here for agencies. In fact I think it is really just the beginning. However, one thing is certain: the way it has been done is no longer good enough. Agencies must evolve in order for brands to continue using them significant part of their strategy. For those that put their money where their mouth is and start building organizations that can truly walk the walk, the potential is almost unlimited; being found, seen and heard online will only get harder as information continues to be generated at an unprecedented pace forcing marketers inside and out of organizations to constantly be on their game if they want to stay relevant.

10 Things Marketers Need to Know to Remain Relevant

Marketing has been one organizational function that has succumbed to tremendous pressure to evolve in the last decade. It's turned both ad agencies and companies on their ears, furiously attempting to learn and adapt, while desperately hanging on to what they already know. The evolution for agencies is clear, but the Marketer in the client organization has to also keep in step and stay ahead of the curve.

Perhaps it's time to let go. If there ever was a time to accept change, it's now. I've witnessed an incredible evolution in the digital space by way of technology and targeting. I've also witnessed rapid changes in consumer consumption and the increasing fragmentation of media. Adapting and learning has been integral in helping me evolve with the market demand.

Consumers and technology have changed the game for Marketers. As a result, Marketers are slowly becoming obsolete. At the start of this book, I referenced an archaic view about the death of traditional marketing:

> "I, along with many of my colleagues, came from an era where the Marketer and the business controlled everything:
> ◊   we built the better mousetraps
> ◊   we "assumed" who bought our product

♢ we catered the messaging to those whom we assumed would buy

♢ we came to rely on pervasive channels to get our message heard

♢ we relied on research that assumed "statistical significance and validity", and was, many times, subject to "groupthink" … all this to prove that we knew how to build markets for products…and not the other way around."

These very same colleagues are becoming obsolete. They have NOT evolved with the times. They've hung their hats on traditional measures, and traditional mediums.

They are used to taking 4 months for traditional target group research and 2 months for strategic planning. They are not used to performance accountability and switching tactics on the fly. They ARE used to throwing something on the wall and hoping that it sticks.

We are witnessing the old-dog-new-trick syndrome.

This article recently appeared in AdAge: [16]

> *"CMOs Are Preparing for Digital to Grow to 75% of Marketing Budgets… But almost half are worried about managing this change"*

Daniel Hebert, Co-founder of Steamfeed posted this article on LinkedIn and noted:

> *"This is great, but are we ready for the change? My gut says no. There's a huge gap in skills required to make digital marketing effective. How will CMOs get talent ready for the budget shift?"*

… to which someone named **Kevin Hardy**, replied,

> *"…a big portion tend to fear the digital side. For a number of differing reasons they tend to shy away from the things they don't understand. They tend to*

"rebel" for lack of a better word, when asked to change up what they have been doing everyday for X number of years. Leaving one's comfort zone is not the easiest thing for many people to do. One MUST leave their comfort zone. One must push himself to learn and to tackle new things head on. They only way for true growth (personal or professional) is to go right after the skill gap & close that gap to as close to zero as possible..."

Becoming obsolete is a reality in today's fast-moving environment. Yes, today's Marketer needs to leave their comfort zone and venture into an environment that does not want to sit still. Luckily, it doesn't necessarily mean abandoning the principles they've learned along the way. It just means evolving their thinking and applying these same principles to the new mediums.

If you've taken anything away from this book so far, here is a summary of these lessons:

1. **Data is the new norm:** The promise of big data brings with it enormous benefits that can now inform customer preferences and propensities, identify relevant prospects in real-time, and distill meaning from reams of information where it impacts competitive or brand reputation. The opportunities to target more granularly beyond just "company"-collected transactions provides opportunities to find the right customer, at the right time, in the right channels, with the right message. The need for strong data analysts to compile this information across multiple platforms and mediums will be an essential component to effectively target for acquisition; improve retention rates and optimize for real-time performance.

2. **Agility is imperative:** Gone are the days of relying on historical data. These days, any data point longer than 30 days is too old and therefore, irrelevant. Gone are the days when media plans or strategies are "baked." No longer are we required to sit and wait for results. With data becoming more embedded in our daily work, Marketers must

work towards a more agile environment. This means becoming more data responsive to an increasingly fragmented and splintered market, and having the structures and processes to change tactics on the fly.

3. **Value is the new currency:** One of the hardest lessons for Marketers to learn is to refrain from leading with overt company or product messages. "Leading with value" has become a difficult principle to adopt, after years of "me-me-me" communications. Declining performance of digital ad units means Marketers must rethink content from the position of the customer. The rise of editorial as an essential function within marketing will be necessary to instill this new discipline.

4. **Customer convergence has arrived:** All mediums are converging. Appointment TV is dead. The customer dictates the content they want to consume, across multiple mediums and platforms, at the times they want it. On-demand mediums will challenge the Marketer as consumers move swiftly between tablets to smartphone to television. The new ways of targeting customers across multiple-platforms now allows the Marketer more long-tail opportunities that will augment and support traditional mass targeting.

5. **Customer experience mandates an always-on presence:** A more informed customer expects an optimal experience that "allows them to shop and receive their purchases where they want, when they want and how they want." This means providing the 'continuous experience' across brands, devices and format: mobile Internet devices, computers, brick-and-mortar, television, radio, direct mail, catalog etc. Today's Marketer is channel-agnostic and is aware of sites, platforms and channels the customer is researching, eliciting recommendations, price-comparing and ultimately, buying.

6. **Sustainability, not campaigns:** The value of social media as an open channel, two-way conversation provides brands with the ability to not only build relationships, but benefit from the effort and commitment to nurture

customer relationships through these channels. Word of Mouth and
Advocacy are strong indicators of brands doing it right.
The value of organic traffic that results from content value,
social consistency and customer-commitment, will surpass
the more costly campaign-driven ad-buys and promotions.

7. **Social cannot be outsourced:** Agencies will never be able to build
    effective community management services. This function needs to live
    within the organization. Customer relationships with brands cannot be
    fostered via surrogate means, and then adopted into the organization.
    Only employees within the organization, with the proper knowledge and
    solutions, can effectively troubleshoot customer complaints and provide
    the right responses in the expected timeframe. An emerging discipline in
    community /customer relationship management will be critical to gauge
    the pulse of the community and to bridge the gap with the organization.

8. **Context is key:** Google has gone beyond keyword and now tries to extract
    real meaning from what people search or speak about. Semantic algorithms
    go one step further and now give Marketers the tools to truly understand
    what people need and want. This will help predict and define areas where the
    brand can connect and provide value to customers. The best explanation of
    this was from Matt Hixson of Tellagence: It's here he writes, "Relationships
    are formed, often over a period of time, around a context. Think about your
    relationships. You may have interacted with me over time about startups
    or social analytics. The more we interact the more we start to trust each
    other about the subject. If one day I start giving you parenting advice you're
    probably going to look at me like I'm nuts. You don't know if I have kids or if
    I'm a good parent or bad parent. We may form a relationship within multiple
    contexts but our relationship and level of trust changes from topic to topic."

9. **Customer-centric needs to be the standard:** As digital grows up, the
    areas mentioned above will move companies to start to shift in ways

that puts the needs of the customers at the center of the organization. One-to-one marketing will become a reality as data allows us to truly customize experiences for each customer. Retention will get increasingly difficult as mediums and platforms rise and fall with the nomadic consumer. Facebook and Twitter will become less standard platforms. Where pundits have prophesied the death of marketing, a more responsive, dynamic and collaborative organization will take its place.

10. **A dynamic organization is a social organization:** The result of these changes will inevitably move away from marketing and become embedded in all parts of the organization. A responsive, dynamic organization means that PR, HR, Product development, Inventory Management, Operations will need seamless communication channels to properly receive and disseminate information in and outside the company to stakeholders and customers. The future CMO will become more operations-minded, but will rely on the collective organization to function effectively.

Marketing is no longer a discipline with best practices and tried and true techniques. As long as technology exists, and media evolves, consumers will continue to find new ways to connect and consume information. What's clear is that these days our traditional definition of longevity is short-lived. Not only does the Marketer need to morph with the times, the organization and its employees do as well.

Social Business Requires Social Employees

Do you want to know the fastest way to have your business' social media and content marketing strategies go south? Create a department for social media and have the planning, execution and metrics live there. In essence, build a social media silo and have them handle all of the company's social profiles and activity without outside involvement.

Now, do you want to know the most important component to building a successful social business? Build an organization that educates and inspires its employees to participate in its social initiatives.

The nuance between success and failure may seem pretty small, but the difference is far different than it may first appear.

LEARNING SOCIAL BUSINESS FROM SOME OF THE BEST:

Companies like Nike, IBM and Comcast immediately come to mind as companies doing powerful things with social media. At Nike, they focus on making engagement easy by having branded support sites throughout social media. This way, customers with an issue can get through to the right channel and get help immediately. Many brands have followed this philosophy by creating multiple handles and pages for support needs versus brand promotion.

As a B2B with global brand recognition, IBM empowers its more than 434,000 employees worldwide by encouraging them to participate in social media through the sharing of knowledge and advocacy throughout their trusted and ever expanding social networks.

In the B2C technology space, customers can become incredibly frustrated when things aren't working the way they are supposed to.

Comcast is changing the landscape of service immediacy by helping connect customers to a better service experience through social media platforms like Twitter. The people they employ to man their Twitter service are both capable of fixing problems and highly responsive.

There are two major takeaways from the above examples:
1. What these big companies do can be done by companies of any size. (Responsiveness, Empowered Employees, Easy Interaction)
2. Not all large companies do this well.

Even Big Companies Need Some Basic Direction for Building Social Businesses:

I had been working with a client who has more than 10,000 employees worldwide. Struggling to understand how to move the needle, this highly sales oriented organization seeks to improve the reach, and more importantly, engagement between their content and social media efforts and their customers.

As I sat across the table from the head of the company's social business, I asked him, *"What sort of understanding does your average employee have of the company's social business initiatives?"*

It was in that instant I saw a light bulb go off. What was funny was that nothing I said was particularly provocative. Really, it was common sense.

Here we were, trying to understand how to move the needle with the company's social media efforts, and right at our fingertips there are ten thousand potential advocates. Was this particular business a unique circumstance, or were they the rule? While I would like to think it was the former, in my experience, far too many companies big and small that are trying to expand their social reach are missing their greatest advocacy opportunity: their own employees.

THE STRONGEST ADVOCATES FOR THE BUSINESS: YOUR EMPLOYEES

Whether your business has 10,000 or 10 employees, ask yourself these questions:

- Do your employees understand your organization's goals to be a social business?
- Furthermore, do they understand the value of social media? Are they fa-

miliar with the mechanics of social media, and how they can use it to share the company message, educate customers and maybe even sell more?

When you consider you have a team of potential advocates at your disposal to share the company's content and ideas and you aren't leveraging them, it should make you shake your head and ask: Why?

Of course this lack of effective social engagement may go back to those questions I asked above:

If your company has thousands of employees, how does social media education disseminate throughout the organization? Should the company offer formal training or is there a certain expectation of fluency and competency amongst employees?

At one time not everyone knew how to use email. Obviously that has changed, and the expectations have changed with it. Go tell your boss you can't send an update to your client today because you don't know how to use email. See how that one goes over.

Having said that, social media isn't nearly that mature and there are still so many unknowns for even experienced users. These unknowns require the need for companies to have social media policies and guidelines that help users understand what is tolerated and what is not. These same guidelines should also serve as a means to better understand what is expected from an organization's employees.

At Dell, they empower social employees through the offering of social media certifications. In addition, they have social media champions programs to get more employees involved with events plus social media mentor programs to help less familiar employees become more fluent in social.

Notwithstanding, advocates for social business will run into those in their organization that don't believe in the power of social, and others who express concerns about the company's risk profile of allowing too much social activity.

However, I would be far more concerned about missing revenue than someone tweeting the wrong thing. Chances are there will be more poorly done social media in a company that doesn't advocate its use than in a company that does.

HOW EMPOWERING EMPLOYEES TO BE SOCIAL CAN DRIVE SOCIAL BUSINESS

Put the logistics aside for a moment, as there are endless mountains of books that can tell you and your employees how to do social media. Now, ask yourself the following question: What is more effective: having one or two social media advocates in our company begging the outside world to engage, Like and share our message OR having the majority of your employees contributing to the company's social presence?

If the answer isn't obvious, then I will be the first to say, "I probably cannot help you." However, the answer is obvious. Building an organization that empowers employees to be social is a tremendous way to extend the reach of the company's message. And, yes, the training and education need to be a part of it, but missing this opportunity is a mistake that brands can't make.

Businesses that focus their employees on being social where their customers are move fast, reach farther and connect more successfully with their customers. These businesses are social businesses, comprised of social employees.

1   http://www.wsj.com/articles/SB116379821933826657

2   http://www.huffingtonpost.ca/news/boycott-rbc/

3   http://www.usnews.com/news/articles/2012/07/20/colorado-theater-shooting-read-the-tweets-from-victims-survivors-tweets-from-victims-survivors-at-denver-shooting

4   http://toronto.ctvnews.ca/city-of-vaughan-ont-issues-apology-after-inappropriate-tweet-1.1148630

5   http://www.getstart.pt/files/The_Connected_Company.pdf

6   http://en.wikipedia.org/wiki/Mass_customization

7   http://www.kpmg.com/Ca/en/IssuesAndInsights/ArticlesPublications/social-banker/Documents/TheSocialBanker-v8-WebAccessible.pdf

8   http://www.forbes.com/sites/danielnewman/2014/08/26/social-listening-enables-social-business/

9   http://www.forbes.com/sites/danielnewman/2014/06/24/beyond-sales-the-business-kpis-of-marketing-roi/

10 http://www.forbes.com/sites/danielnewman/2014/09/03/selling-is-social-forget-the-buzz-it-is-just-the-way/

11 http://millennialceo.com/social-media/dotted-line-required-social-business-success/

12 http://mashable.com/category/public-relations/

13 http://en.wikipedia.org/wiki/Marketing

14 http://www.huffingtonpost.com/jeremy-harris-lipschultz/realtime-social-media-cre_b_4102446.html

15 http://www.newsrooms365.com/

16 http://www.adweek.com/news/technology/cmos-expect-75-marketing-budgets-be-digital-within-5-years-158481

Marketing Evolution Is Failing In The C-Suite

You can almost picture yourself in the room. It's the time of year again when the marketing team has to put together a strategy, a plan and a budget for the next fiscal year. After carefully considering the seismic shift that is happening across the digital web, the team has come back and determined that it is time to eradicate the marketing of old. Doing things differently is the only way.

Our brand doesn't need another year of stagnation pouring money into old media. Paid media has its place, but the time has come where people are building relationships with brands due to reasons greater than clever commercials and savvy product placement. Owned media, earned media and shared media have become "where it's at."

However, too often these days, the C-suite is not open to these new ideas. They poke holes in the "new way" as it is unproven, or lacks reach; but maybe it isn't lack of proof or reach at all that is to blame, but rather the lack of vision from the C-suite as it turns its back on the evolution of marketing?

Today, we have entered an economy where sharing is a defacto sign of endorsement, and brand ambassadors are no longer celebrities, but rather they are now Joe Average; the every day social media user that has a small yet defined audience of people who genuinely influence those in their circles.

This isn't some kind of far out belief or ideology. It's emphatically true. Study after study, from Google Zero Moment of Truth to the analysts at Forrester and Nielsen

– they all tell us that these trends are here and the buyer's journey is changing. What is your brand doing and more importantly, is it evolving?

IT'S THE WAY WE'VE ALWAYS DONE IT…
BECAUSE IT FEELS GOOD

Consultants rejoice because yes, these are some of the most dangerous words in business. Too often we keep doing it the way we have always done it because it is comfortable. There is a feeling of security that comes with doing what has always worked. Since the past is a tremendous indicator of future behavior, we have long found ourselves looking to the past for validation. As you know, you can seek out data to prove your method should work, whether or not it truly represents the right decision.

In marketing this window into the past is often misused; most notably when it comes to marketing strategy. Before big data, 1:1, Omni-Channel and the modern web, brands found their best means for gathering visibility was through media buys. This was reflected in newspaper, radio, television and then later came online advertisements in the form of banners, pop ups and other on page ads. Why did the first iteration of digital marketing evolve to be merely a recreation of old media online? We could suggest it was because of product evolution, but it is clear that there was certain comfort in the traditional metrics.

When we did media buys before digital we bought reach. Essentially, we had rough ideas of reach and audience demographics so we knew how many people would see our ad. This followed suit on digital as we bought media there as well; spurring an onslaught of discussion about Impressions and whether the words had any meaning. What is clear is that people don't click banner ads, so unless your ad is prevalent, targeted and memorable, your money is being wasted. Have you ever seen these data points on banner ads?

Remember this reference we made earlier from Business Insider?

"You are 31.25 times more likely to win a prize in the Mega Millions than you are to click on a banner ad." Not only that, "you are 87.8 times more likely to apply to Harvard and get in...112.50 times more likely to sign up for and complete NAVY SEAL training...279.64 times more likely to climb Mount Everest... and 475.28 times more likely to survive a plane crash than you are to click on a banner ad."

However, we don't stop because of our lust for numbers. Even though no one is clicking we keep paying. And when it comes to social media, our behavior followed suit.

- Invest time and money to grow our followers on Twitter or Instagram.
- Sponsored posts on Facebook or LinkedIn to increase our number of Likes.
- Using 3rd Party Sponsored links to send traffic (unknowingly) back to your page.
- The purchase of email lists to spam with unwanted content and emails.

The list goes on, but in short, we aren't evolving, only taking our short sighted media approach from the old days and plugging it into our go forward strategy because it feels good, because it is how it has always been done, because it is safe...but is it really?

Marketing is getting more complex. The principles still exists but things have shifted: media consumption, relationship dynamics, heightened privacy concerns, access proliferation, and an always-on economy.

Safety Will Arrive When Your Marketing Evolves

While the safety net that comes with "How it's always been done" may provide a comfort, it is nothing more than an illusion; we have reached a point where marketing must evolve.

Brands need to be thinking about the way they do digital, social and even traditional marketing in new ways. Because the old way has evolved and the new way looks more like this:

OLD WAY		NEW WAY
Old Way: Focus on reach and impressions	⟶	New Way: Focus on meaningful connections through 1:1 engagement.
Old Way: Blast everyone in hopes of any sort of response	⟶	New Way: Targeted content sent to people who ask for it (Opt-In)
Old Way: Paid traffic, sponsored ads and Sneaky Link Bait	⟶	New Way: Building loyal communities of brand ambassadors who become your word of mouth.
Old Way: High volume Cold Calling	⟶	New Way: Targeted social selling through careful social listening and strategic engagement
Old Way: Gut decisions on Marketing Strategy	⟶	New Way: Data driven decisions through the use of widely available and affordable data assets.

Of course there is a place for everything and before everyone starts throwing tomatoes just know that I recognize that Coca-Cola , Doritos and Citibank can benefit from widespread media reach. That is a default benefit for a globally recognized brand.

However, the biggest brands with the most resources aren't entirely dependent on the old way of doing media. If you have any doubts just visit Coke Journey, American Express Open or IBM's SMB community to see how marketing investment is being poured into more personalized, more Direct Marketing that connects brands to buyers with the intent to create a relationship, not a sale. The sale becomes a by-product of everything else they do.

So when that next board meeting happens and the powers that be say no to marketing evolution and yes to more media buys and vanity metrics, stand up and share with them the risk of doing the same thing again, and why the things that have worked in the past will no longer work today.

Marketing must evolve – comfort be damned! The way things have always been done isn't the way they should be done going forward. Unless you believe the consumer landscape hasn't changed in the past 5-10 years.

AFTERWARD

We never set out to write a book about transformation.

When we started this project last spring we were already practicing much of what has been written in this book. We had many frank conversations about why companies weren't doing these things already. It seemed so intuitive.

In the last few years, we've spent time educating clients and speaking about how technology is transforming marketing. We've been met with a lot of skepticism. There seemed to be this resistance to address the change that was happening before our eyes.

Many of our peers in marketing and the agency world have not evolved with the needs of business today. They have felt the rug being pulled out from beneath them and are, only now, trying to hang on, to keep up and stay relevant.

This book for you, the Marketer.

ACKNOWLEDGEMENTS

The ideas, case examples and approaches shared in this book came out of years of dialogue with practitioners, successes from own practices, and professional work from those in our community. Those who have contributed directly or indirectly to this endeavor deserve acknowledgement.

For *Amy Tobin*, friend, editor and late night motivator: Thank you for your patience, your friendship and your incessant pursuit of writing excellence. We are both better writers because of you.

To *Paul Ting*, awesome designer: This book captures the essence of our message. You nailed it. Thank you for your dedication in helping pump this out especially during the holidays.

To our esteemed Contributors: *Gini Dietrich, Shelly Kramer, Olivier Blanchard, Tim MacDonald, Michael Brenner, Amy Vernon, Denise Lee Yohn, Sam Fiorella, Jure Klepic, Michael Brito, and Sean McGinnis:* Being surrounded by thought leaders who advocate for these practices we write about validates everything we're doing. We are privileged to be in your company.

Many companies and colleagues who work in this industry gave their time and insights through interviews, articles and case studies. Thank you to each of you for your contribution: *Daniel Hebert* - Cofounder of Steamfeed, *Andrew Jenkins* - Volterra Consulting, *Yasmin Ranade* - Founder of WhatsYourTech, *Laurie Dillon Schalk* - Director of Digital Strategy at DraftFCB, *Dan Sullivan* - Founder of Crowdly, *Daniel Robinson* - Founder of Antelope, *Matt Hixson* and *Nitin Mayande* - Co-founders of Tellagence, *Mark Zohar* - Founder of Trendspottr, *Kerry Morrison* - Founder of Norm, *Kim Phillips* and *Deb Von Sychowski* – Co-founders of Patch Design, *Tosca Reno, Rachel Corradetti, Kiersten Corradetti* – of TRIM Inc., *Philip Ladovsky* - Owner United Bakery, *Jayson Elliott* and *Gary Gygax* - Gygax Magazine.

From Hessie:

To my husband, Shawn and my kids, Nate and Madelyn: You guys are my life. You keep me honest. Thanks for putting up with my deer-in-headlight moments, my crazy moods, and intermittent forgetfulness. I will make it up to you. Love you guys.

To *Bob Jones*, *Joe Cardillo* and *Susan Silver* of ArCompany for sticking with me all this time; I love being around smart, passionate people; you guys are the epitome of this. Susan, you definitely rock when it comes to truly understanding community.

To *Hugh Oddie*, my advisor and dear friend: Thank you for pushing me and encouraging me. I promise you, your efforts are not futile.

To *Dan Newman*, my co-author: It's been a whirlwind. If I haven't said it already, thank you for your steadfastness and encouragement throughout this process. I can't think of anyone else with whom I could write this book. You are the Yin to my Yang. Together we've done something pretty amazing. I am proud to call you my friend.

From Dan:

To my wife, Lisa and my children, Hailey and Avery: You are my pillar of stability. As an author, it is ironic that sometimes I can't find the right words to show my appreciation, but I know that you guys know how much I care and your support means the world to me. It is your inspiration that has made so many of my accomplishments possible. I cannot thank you all enough for your support.

To the human network, online and off, thanks for your honesty, support and consistent feedback that has helped me shape the ideas that became this book.

To *Hessie Jones*, esteemed co-author: I'm so glad you chose to do this project with me. You always had terrific insights on not only the theory of marketing, but also the science behind it. I admire that and I look forward to seeing what you do next.

BIOGRAPHIES

Daniel Newman

After 12 years of running technology companies including a CEO appointment at the age of 28, Daniel Newman traded the corner office for a chance to drive the discussion on how the digital economy is going to forever change how business is done. Daniel is an MBA, adjunct business professor, a Forbes, Entrepreneur and Huffington Post contributor and a 2x author of best-selling business books including "The Millennial CEO" and "The New Rules of Customer Engagement." With exposure to leading-edge collaboration and analytics solutions, Newman continues to evangelize and educate about the changes in the future of business and what business needs to do to adapt. Currently, Daniel is the Founder of Broadsuite, a specialty marketing firm that helps companies be found, seen and heard in a cluttered digital world. He's also a pianist, soccer fan, husband and father, not in that order.

Hessie Jones

As a seasoned digital strategist, Hessie Jones continues to challenge the notion of complacency. With extensive experience in technology including start-ups, banking, advertising and social media, Hessie has held management positions at Yahoo!, Citi, ONE Advertising and Aegis Media. Launch successes like Yahoo! Answers propelled Hessie into the world of social media. As an active blogger for Huffington Post, Steamfeed, Digital Journal and WhatsYourTech, Hessie is a purveyor for understanding and adapting to change: in marketing practices, in communication, in understanding the evolving consumer mindset and behavior. Currently, Hessie is the Founder of ArCompany, helping companies realize the value of social intelligence and its impact on the inevitable next level of social business. She's also a cellist, MBA guest lecturer, wife and hockey mom.

CPSIA information can be obtained at www.ICGtesting.com
Printed in the USA
LVOW04s1053090315

429641LV00002BA/2/P